Felecia Wrigh

TO OUR BODIES TURN WE THEN

Body as word and sacrament in the works of John Donne

continuum

NEW YORK • LONDON

Copyright © 2005 by Felecia Wright McDuffie

The Continuum International Publishing Group,
15 East 26th Street, New York, NY 10010

The Continuum International Publishing Group Ltd,
The Tower Building, 11 York Road, London SE1 7NX

All rights reserved. No part of this book may be reproduced, stored in a retrieval system, or transmitted in any form or by any means, electronic, mechanical, including photocopying, recording, or otherwise, without the written permission of the publishers.

Scripture quotations are taken from the King James Version of the Bible.

Cover art: La Tour, Georges de (1593–1652). The Penitent Magdelen. Photo: Gerard Blot. Copyright Réunion des Musées Nationaux / Art Resource, NY

Cover design: Corey Kent

Library of Congress Cataloging-in-Publication Data

McDuffie, Felecia Wright, 1951–
  "To our bodies turn we then" : body as word and sacrament in the works of John Donne / Felecia Wright McDuffie.
    p. cm.
  Includes bibliographical references (p.   ) and index.
  ISBN 0-8264-1677-2 (pbk.) — ISBN 0-8264-1676-4 (hardcover)
  1. Donne, John, 1572–1631—Criticism and interpretation. 2. Christianity and literature—England—History—17th century. 3. Christian literature, English—History and criticism. 4. Body, Human, in literature. 5. Sacraments in literature. 6. Symbolism in literature. I. Title.
PR2248.M33   2005
821'.3—dc22
                                                                    2004027184

Printed in the United States of America
05 06 07 08 09 10   10 9 8 7 6 5 4 3 2 1

To my parents,
Mary and Harold Wright

CONTENTS

Acknowledgments		vii
Introduction		ix
1	THE CREATED BODY	1
2	THE FALLEN BODY	27
3	BODIES REDEEMED AND REDEMPTIVE	57
4	THE ESCHATOLOGICAL BODY	83
5	READING THE TRAJECTORY OF SALVATION IN THE BOOK OF THE BODY	105
	Appendix A: Literature Review: The Body in the Context of Donne Scholarship	127
	Appendix B: Donne's Representations of the Body in the Their Historical Context	133
	Works Cited	161
	Index	169

ACKNOWLEDGMENTS

*The memory is so familiar, and so present,
and so ready a faculty, as will always answer,
if we will but speak to it, and ask it,
what God hath done for us, or for others.*

DONNE, *Sermons*

When I speak to my memory, as Donne suggests, it answers with the names of the many friends and colleagues who, from the beginning, made the process of researching and writing this book a rewarding and joyful one. My professors at Emory University's Graduate Division of Religion and Candler School of Theology, where this book was written, welcomed me into a warm and inspiring community of scholars. It was a great pleasure to work with Ted Hackett, Manfred Hoffmann, and Brooks Holifield. I would like to thank Philip Reynolds and Don Saliers, who served on my dissertation committee and gave unstintingly of their time, their knowledge, and their enthusiasm. I am especially grateful to my adviser, David Pacini. Neither my graduate education nor this book would have been possible without his help and encouragement at every step along the way. It has been a privilege to work with him, and I am truly blessed to have him as a teacher, mentor, and friend. Any felicities in the book bear the stamp of my teachers at Emory; any flaws are my own.

My family and friends have surrounded me with love, support, encouragement, and practical help. I can offer only inadequate, but heartfelt, thanks to some of them: my parents, Harold and Mary Wright; my friend Annette Davis and my godson, Whit Davis; my friends Patti Morrow, Ann George, and Susan Tungate; and my colleagues and friends at Young Harris College, especially Lynne Grady. They have been my cheerleaders, sympathetic ears in times of joy and trouble, and companions along the way. They have given me (variously) good conversation, good food and wine, good cheer, editorial feedback, and a roof over my head while I worked. Finally, I would like to thank my husband, Pat Gibbs, for his unfailing love and encouragement and his belief in the project. I could not have done it without him.

INTRODUCTION

To our bodies turn we then, that so
Weak men on love revealed may look;
Love's mysteries in souls do grow,
But yet the body is his book.

JOHN DONNE, "THE ECSTASY"

From his early love poetry to his late religious writing, John Donne speaks of the human body as a book to be read and interpreted. Unlike modern thinkers who understand the body as a purely material phenomenon or postmodern critics who see in it a text produced by culture, Donne understands the body as a sacred text written by God. In this study, I offer a comprehensive interpretation of Donne's reading of the body. Despite acknowledging his preoccupation with the body, the critical literature still lacks an inclusive and coherent interpretation of the subject. It has seemed plausible to many critics that one could construe Donne's theology without significant reference to his representations of the body. Conversely, scholars who are mainly concerned with Donne's literary legacy have tended to interpret his images of the body without grounding them in his theological thinking. The interrelationship between Donne's representations of the human body and his theological imagination is an intimate one that has yet to be fully explored. Addressing this lacuna is the task I undertake.

In Donne's imaginative universe, the human person lies at the center of the great interconnected web of God's signs and acts that is the created order. Donne's God is an artist, a maker and signifier, whose speech forms the material world. The human body is the visible manifestation and sign in which all God's lines of meaning cross. As such, Donne makes it the center and touchstone of his own theology. It is the book he turns to time and again to read of God, cosmos, and the human condition. In one of his sermons, Donne says, "The world is a great volume, and man the index of that book; even in the body of man you may turn to the whole world; this body is an illustration of all nature; God's recapitulation of all he had said before."[1] Donne believes in a radically communicative God, the "metaphor-

ix

ical" God who continually speaks to humankind through signs, symbols, and types. Refusing to restrict God's speaking to the written words of Scripture, contrary to the practices of many Protestants of his time, Donne persists in reading God's messages in a plethora of "books." God continually writes on the pages of nature, history, the human community, and each individual life to point the willing reader toward spiritual truth. In his attempt to discern God's nature and will, Donne turns habitually to the book of the human body as a collection of signs of special significance. He also, at times, represents the human body not as a "mere" sign, to use the language of the eucharistic controversies of his day, but as sacrament: a sign that conveys that to which it refers. In this sense, the human body becomes a vehicle of God's presence and grace.

In his reading of the book of the body, Donne discerns the narrative of salvation history: the trajectory proceeding from creation, through fall, to redemption and resurrection. In a wonderfully metaphysical image from a 1627 wedding sermon, Donne blithely ignores the biblical accounts of Genesis and Revelation, contracting God's dealings on the great stage of universal salvation history instead into a single point: the human body. He says,

> The body of man was the first point that the foot of God's compass was upon: First, he created the body of Adam: and then he carries his compass round, and shuts up where he began, he ends with the body of man again in the glorification thereof in the Resurrection. God is *Alpha* and *Omega*, first, and last: And his *Alpha* and *Omega*, his first, and last work is the body of man too.[2]

While the biblical accounts of creation and renewal begin with the creation of the heavens and the earth (Gen 1:1ff.) and end with John's vision of a new heaven and a new earth (Rev 21:1ff.), in Donne's conceit God *really* begins and ends the mighty acts of creation and redemption by concentrating his attention on the human body. This image of the encapsulation of salvation history in the body is a synecdoche for Donne's theology as a whole. It holds within its compass both the most characteristic content and the most characteristic method of his theology. An examination of that content and method reveals the distinctive nature of his religious imagination.

Donne sets the body and salvation history into a dialogical relationship, always reading one in terms of the other. He grounds his theology, and his representations of the human body, in the doctrine of creation. Donne adheres to the orthodox Christian doctrine that the body, and the entire material world, is the good creation of a loving God. Donne goes further than most theologians, however, in stressing God's great zest for all things material, and for the human body in particular. Donne sees that body as the nexus of the whole creation, an "index" to the book of creatures. Donne's orthodox theology, as well as his own experience, lead him to understand the human body as fallen. Humanity's disobedience and turning away from God have a profound impact on the body. The misery, illness, and death that plague it are signs of a world that is out of joint, with all the hierarchies God set in place disrupted. All the marks of sin in the human body, however, are parts of an ongoing narrative. For those who can correctly read those signs, realizing their human limitations and their radical dependence on God, the story of the body turns toward redemption. Through the body of Christ, the human body can become a redemptive sign, pointing toward a transformed and glorified body that will find its fulfillment in the eschatological kingdom.

Method

I have interpreted Donne's representations of the body using a combination of literary-critical and historical methods. For a figure such as Donne, who combines poetic and theological genius, both are necessary for a full understanding of his work. Many attempts to interpret Donne's work have wrecked on the Scylla of a purely literary reading or the Charybdis of a purely theological one. Some critics have attempted to interpret Donne's work through a particular literary-critical lens without fully appreciating the historical and theological context in which he wrote. Others have tended to interpret his theology in orthodox terms without a full regard for the ways in which his imagery and uses of language transform his religious writing into something distinctive.

My study attempts to steer a course through these hazards. I have combined close literary-critical readings of Donne's work with a larger historical analysis of the cultural and theological context in which those works were written. The result of this method is an interpretation of Donne's representations of the body through categories intrinsic to the material itself: books, sacred texts, sacraments, and the teleological process that moves through the stages of creation, fall, redemption, and eschatological fulfillment. To interpret Donne's various "bodies" in this way is to win several advantages. These categories formed the background against which Donne and most of his theological contemporaries and progenitors lived and wrote. These terms are also specifically intrinsic to the material I am interpreting. Although Donne was not a systematic theologian, his tendency to think in and through these terms informs his writing as a whole. They make visible a coherence behind what can seem to be inconsistent, even contradictory, views of the human body. While some of these inconsistencies indicate truly differing models, others merely reflect the diverse positions of the body at differing stages of salvation history.

Works Considered

In my exploration of Donne's representation of the human body, I have considered all of his extant writings. Although he gains in power, maturity, and theological insight after his ordination, he uses many of the same themes and images when he speaks of the human body throughout his career. By looking at his earlier readings of the body along with the later ones, the themes that preoccupied him from the beginning come more clearly into view, as do suggestive reasons behind their development. Donne's preoccupation with the body, with the sensual, and with religion—as well as his exploitation and exploration of the links among them—form unbroken threads that the reader can follow through all his work, whether "religious" or "secular," poetry or prose, before or after his ordination.

Although the critical literature has lacked such a comprehensive study of Donne's representations of the body, this approach is in harmony with more recent criticism that has attempted to correct the earlier tendency to compartmentalize Donne's work. Such compartmentalization has its roots, in part, in the persistent myth that there were two Donnes: one the young rake and adventurer who wrote love poems and biting satires and the other the solemn and ascetic Dean of Saint Paul's. Donne himself bears at least partial responsibility for initiating the myth.[3] In one incident of such myth-making, Donne sent the only copy of his controversial defense of suicide, written some ten years earlier, to Sir Robert Karre for safekeeping. In the accompanying letter to Karre, Donne asks that he "let any that your discretion admits to the sight of it, know the date of it; and that it is a Book written by Jack Donne, and not by Dr. Donne."[4] He apparently spread a similar story in regard to his love poetry, which, though not published until after his death, was circulated among his friends. In the tricky atmosphere of politics and patronage in which he lived, Donne the priest found it useful to assign his love poetry and certain controversial prose to "Jack," his former self. Upon his death, the friends who eulogized him, his earliest biographer, and his own son perpetuated the distinction. They presented a picture of Donne as a sort of Anglican saint, cut off from the world and his earlier life, preaching "like an angel from a cloud."[5] Their Donne had turned wholly away from his youthful follies and all worldly concerns and thought only of heavenly things.

This way of looking at Donne persisted through the years. In his preface to an 1896 edition of Donne's poems, George Saintsbury called attention to the

> strange . . . division between the two periods of his life and the two classes of his work. Roughly speaking, almost the whole of the secular verse belongs to the first division of his life, almost the whole of the prose to the second. Again,

by far the greater part of the verse is animated by what may be called a spiritualized worldliness and sensuality, and the whole of the prose by a spiritualism which has left worldliness far behind.[6]

Even among those critics and biographers who saw some connection between Donne's earlier and later lives, many tended to understand him as a seventeenth-century Augustine, transformed from sensuality to saintliness by a conversion experience. Donne's early twentieth-century biographer, Hugh Fausset, exemplified this critical slant when he said that Donne's "carnality blossomed into spirituality as a flower that springs from the dung" and that it "was through the agonized errors of sex that Donne rose to the sublimities of religion."[7] Contrary to Fausset, a careful reading of Donne's work reveals that the dung and the flowers, the sensuality and the spirituality, are inextricably intermingled throughout his writing, early and late.[8]

The reader does well to approach Donne's early work with some caution, however. Identifying "Donne as author," much less "Donne the man," with the speaker of any particular piece of writing has even more than the usual pitfalls. It also has been more than usually tempting for critics and biographers down through the years. Scholars have read Donne's love poetry for evidence of his own love life, his satires as biographical evidence, and his sermons for clues to his own spirituality and religious development. This sort of reading is fraught with problems. There are several reasons to proceed with care in using statements from Donne's early writings as proof that he held any particular philosophical opinion or religious doctrine. Donne as author speaks in many voices and proffers many opinions, some of them contradictory.

These multiple voices are a result of a several factors. First, Donne wrote most of his preordination material in genres that do not lend themselves to straightforward interpretations of authorial intent: poetry, satire, and polemic. Second, in common with many Renaissance wits, Donne seemed to love the play of argument for its own sake and was perfectly capable of taking up and arguing a position just to see if he could defend it or of taking up a persona and speaking through it just to see what "it" would say.[9] He was, after all, trained as a lawyer. Third, Donne lived in a complicated arena of shifting political and religious loyalties and contending philosophical and scientific systems. One of the best-read and best-connected men in England at the time, Donne knew the arguments, values, and metaphorical systems of Catholics and Protestants, Platonists and Aristotelians, courtiers and prelates, alchemists and atomists. His representations of the body reflect these multifaceted ways of thinking. Last, and perhaps most significant, Donne wrote many of his early works, both poetry and prose, as part of a campaign for patronage at a time when he was desperate for money to provide for his family and for a secure position in the world. To some extent, Donne's early religious works, both poetry and prose, were addressed to and crafted to please wealthy patrons who could help him obtain a place at court, or at least temporary employment.[10] For all these reasons, it may be unwise to take any statement about the body in Donne's early work as proof of any particular philosophical or theological position on the nature of the human body.

With this caution in mind, however, study of this early material yields some useful insights that contribute to a complete picture of Donne's representations of the body. Although they cannot be read for a consistent theory of the nature of the body, much less for a theological anthropology, Donne's representations of the body in his early writings do contain certain recurring themes and images. When the early material and the later writings are read against each other, I believe that a relatively coherent and significant picture emerges. Thus, when I speak of "Donne's" views of the human body, I have in mind that system of representations that emerges from a consideration of all the writings attributed to him.

Notes

1. Evelyn M. Simpson and George R. Potter, eds., *The Sermons of John Donne,* 10 vols. (Berkeley and Los Angeles: University of California Press, 1953–1962), 7:272. See also 8:177. All quotations from Donne's sermons are from this edition, with references to volume and page numbers. I have chosen to modernize the spelling in all quotations taken from this source for ease of transcription and reading. Winfried Schleiner has pointed out in her book on the imagery in Donne's sermons that he was "unusual in so stressing the topos of the book of creatures as continually to imply that man is a book within a book" and suggests that he may have been influenced by Paracelsus, for whom man as a book also was an important image (*The Imagery in John Donne's Sermons* [Providence: Brown University Press, 1970], 99–100).

2. John Donne, *The Sermons of John Donne,* 10 vols., ed. Evelyn M. Simpson and George R. Potter (Berkeley and Los Angeles: University of California Press, 1953–1962), 8:97.

3. As P. M. Oliver points out in *Donne's Religious Writing: A Discourse of Feigned Devotion* (London and New York: Longman, 1997), 1.

4. Sir Geoffrey Keynes quotes this remark in *A Bibliography of Dr. John Donne, Dean of Saint Paul's,* 4th ed. (Oxford: Clarendon Press, 1973), 113.

5. Izaak Walton, *The Lives of Dr. John Donne, Sir Henry Wotton, Mr. Richard Hooker, Mr. George Herbert and Dr. Robert Sanderson* (London: John Major, 1825), 35. Walton wrote his life of Donne in 1639, not many years after Donne's death, and first published it in 1640 in the first edition of Donne's *LXXX Sermons, Preached by that Learned and Reverend Divine, John Donne* (London: Richard Royston and Richard

Marriott, 1640). In it he paints a picture of Donne as a "second St. Austin" and says that "none was so like him before his conversion, none so like St. Ambrose after it: and if his youth had the infirmities of the one, his age had the excellencies of the other; the learning and holiness of both" (34). Walton says specifically that Donne, both privately and publicly in his sermons, "often . . . mentioned the many changes both of his body and mind, especially his mind from a vertiginous giddiness" of youth, and that he expressed his happiness "that he accounted the former part of his life to be lost; and the beginning of it to be, from his first entering into Sacred Orders" (74). Walton, friends of Donne's and Walton's such as John Cotton and Henry King, and Donne's son (also called John) took care to support the division of his life and of his written work into two distinct periods. See, for instance, the elegies, letters, and accounts of Donne's life appended to the 1840 edition of *Devotions by John Donne DD with Two Sermons (*London: William Pickering, 1840) and the 1650 edition of Donne's poems which his son prepared, reprinted as *Poems on Several Occasions, Written by the Reverend John Donne, D.D., Late Dean of St. Paul's, with Elegies on the Author's Death* (London: printed for J. Tonson, 1719).

6. George Saintsbury, *Prefaces and Essays,* Essay Index Reprint Series (Freeport, N.Y.: Books for Libraries Press, 1933; repr., 1969), 277.

7. Hugh I'Anson Fausset, *John Donne: A Study in Discord* (New York: Russell & Russell, 1924; repr. 1967), 20, 82.

8. The argument over whether there is more continuity or discontinuity between "Jack" and "John" Donne has a large literature of its own. Some of Donne's critics and biographers have followed Walton's lead in separating Donne's two lives. These include Fausset, *John Donne: A Study in Discord* (1924; New York: Russell & Russell, 1967); Edward Le Comte, *Grace to a Witty Sinner: A Life of Donne* (New York: Walker, 1965); and Mary Clive, *Jack and the Doctor* (London, Melbourne, and Toronto: MacMillan; New York: St. Martin's Press, 1966). As an example of a more nuanced account, James S. Baumlin notes that the "two Donnes" are "two versions of personality" that "constitute a large pair, an oppositional pair as it were, of versions of the self. Both are present throughout Donne's career" (*John Donne and the Rhetorics of Renaissance Discourse* [Columbia and London: University of Missouri Press, 1991], 35). Yet even Baumlin, writing of the multiplicity of discourses that inform Donne's writing, says, "With some reason . . . readers may associate Jack Donne with a rhetoric of skepticism, Dr. Donne with a rhetoric of dogmatic assertion" (34). Other critics have seen more continuity in Donne's work. John Carey claims that Jack and the Doctor "weren't two people. The more we read the poems and sermons, the more we can see them as fabrics of the same mind, controlled by similar imaginative needs" (*John Donne: Life, Mind, and Art* [New York: Oxford University Press, 1981], 11). Frank Warnke in his 1987 biography of Donne refers to the "mythical" dichotomy of the two Donnes and says, "The life and personality of the real Donne were less neat and more complicated as well as being, despite their complexity, more unified" (*John Donne* [Boston: Twayne Publishers, 1987], 3). The myth of the two Donnes has been replaced in the critical literature in more recent years by this sort of recognition of unity or by poststructuralist readings that deny any unity at all to Donne's work, understanding it instead as an arena of competing discourses. The latter sort of reading is exemplified by Baumlin's *Renaissance Discourse* and Thomas Docherty's *John Donne, Undone* (London and New York: Methuen, 1986).

9. A perfect example of this is Donne's *Paradoxes*. According to Helen Peters in the general introduction to her edition of *Paradoxes and Problems* (Oxford: Clarendon Press, 1980), they were written while Donne was studying law in the early 1590s (v). Paradoxes, a popular intellectual entertainment in Donne's time and social milieu, consisted of defending a belief or opinion not commonly held. In his paradoxes, Donne defends such contrarian beliefs as "that it is possible to find some virtue in some women" or "that all things kill themselves." The tone is lighthearted, and it is impossible to determine to what extent Donne may have convinced himself by his own argumentative skill. Thus, when Donne argues in another paradox "that the gifts of the body are better than those of the mind or of fortune," one should take what he says about the primacy of the body with more than a grain of salt. This also serves as an illustration of the problem of genre. Peters goes on in her introduction to explain that the genre of the paradox in England in Donne's time derived from several sources. The first was the literary mock encomium, which began in the classical period, persisted through the Middle Ages, and found its most popular expression in Erasmus's *Moriae encomium* (xvi–xviii). The second was another literary form, attributed to Cicero and reintroduced to England in the sixteenth century. The practitioner of this form argued views contrary to those held by contemporary society (xviii–xix). The third source was the paradoxes, which served as popular entertainment at the Inns of Court where Donne received his legal training. These were verbal contests held during the Inns of Court revels each year in which the revelers defended "strange opinions" (xx). The first and third genres tended toward frivolity; the second had a more serious moral intent. It is uncertain what model Donne follows in his paradoxes, so the "intent" of the speaker of any particular paradox is an even more clouded issue.

10. P. M. Oliver argues in his book on Donne's explicitly religious writings that the influence of patronage extends to the substance of his mature religious work and that even his sermons were the expressions of a persona that Donne assumed to express the doctrine and opinions expected from the court preacher and Dean of St. Paul's. While this argument may hold true for some areas of Donne's writings, it does not apply to most of his representations of the body. Donne's emphasis on the body and the way he deployed it in his discourse were unusual for his time and do not seem crafted for any polemical payoff. The only aspect of Donne's presentation of the human body that seems to relate to his search for patronage is his imagery of holy women. For a further discussion of this imagery, see chapters 3, 4, and 5.

THE CREATED BODY

The body of man was the first point that the foot of God's compass was upon: First, he created the body of Adam.
DONNE, *Sermons*

Donne's trajectory of salvation history begins at the point he believes God begins: the created body. Donne ascribes to God an extraordinary love and care for the human body. It forms the "foot of the compass" with which he draws the grand sweep of salvation history. Donne places the foot of his own theological compass on the same point. Creation lies at the heart of his explicit anthropology and of his deployment of the body as an image. According to orthodox tradition, God crafts the human person as a union of soul and material body and declares his creation good.[1] Even after the fall of humanity, which defaces this "original" human body, some of the gifts of its creation remain. One is simple bodily existence. Another is the ability to know the world through the senses. Through these gifts, humanity begins to know God. Donne's God is an artist who loves matter and whose character and intent mark all that he has made. God forms the human person, body and soul, as the epitome of the larger material and spiritual creation. Donne believes, therefore, that he can read it is as a particularly apt summary of the "book of creatures." In addition to understanding the body as the material gift of a loving creator, the seat of the experience and desire that lead to God, Donne peruses it as a collection of signs that points to its divine Author.

I will first turn to an exploration of the created body in Donne's preordination writings through two interrelated themes: the human being as microcosm and the Edenic body. Then I will discuss his exploration of the idea of the body as the book of creatures in a transitional work, *Essays in Divinity*. Finally, I will take up the created body as Donne represents it in his ser-

1

mons. As will become evident, Donne's basic theology of the created body remains constant throughout his career. While he continues to use many of the same concepts and images to present that theology, he does shift his emphasis to some different aspects and images of it after his ordination.

The Created Body in the Preordination Writings

In Donne's writing before his ordination, two principal themes emerge in relation to the created body. The first is the idea of the human being as a microcosm of the universe; the second is the idea that remnants of the Edenic, created body persist in humanity after the fall. One image that pervades Donne's work is that of the human person as microcosm, a little world that mirrors the greater worlds of society or cosmos. He employs the idea of the human soul and body as the epitome of the spiritual and material realms of creation as a key component in his representations of the human body. Donne explicitly links this concept to the Christian doctrine of creation. He believes that both the created body and the created world that corresponds to it have been corrupted by human sin. The original body of God's creation, the Edenic body, is "present" in Donne's work only in fragments. One such fragment is the continuing connection between the microcosm and the macrocosm. As Donne sees it, the ontological connections between the human person and the creation are real, albeit diminished by the fall. A fragment of the innocent, created body persists in the ability of the senses, though fallen, to form a bridge from the soul to human love, to the world, and ultimately to God.

The Human Being as Microcosm

The idea that the human being is a small, self-contained system recapitulating larger, ever-expanding systems of society, world, and cosmos has a long history.[2] Although the idea appears in fragmentary form in Greek thought prior to Plato, and implicitly in some of Plato's dialogues, it becomes explicit in the writings of Philo of Alexandria. Some Christian theologians adapted the concept to Christian ends. These include Gregory Nazianzen, Gregory the Great, Maximus the Confessor, and Thomas Aquinas.[3] Bernard of Clairvaux, whom Donne quotes extensively in his sermons, was one among the medieval theologians in the West who developed this image of the microcosm.[4] Among late medieval and early modern thinkers, Bruno, Nicholas of Cusa, Campanella, Boehme, and Paracelsus all developed the notion of man as a microcosm along their own lines. The philosophical concept of the human being as microcosm survived into the seventeenth century. Even in its demise, the concept enjoyed further intellectual currency as a figure in the literature of the day.

While Donne was familiar with most, if not all, of the authors mentioned above, it is difficult to determine where he derived his ideas of the human person as microcosm. In his sermons, he often quotes the Gregories, Aquinas, Maximus, and Cusanus. Although any of them may have influenced Donne's use of the concept, Paracelsus was his most direct source. A 1573 copy of Paracelsus's *Chirurgia Magna* was in Donne's library at the time of his death.[5] Donne first refers to Paracelsus in *Conclave Ignati (Ignatius His Conclave)*, written in 1610. Allusions to Paracelsus's ideas about the body run through the poems and the sermons. Donne draws most heavily on Paracelsus's ideas and images of the body in his later work *Devotions upon Emergent Occasions*, to which I will return in chapter 5. Whatever his sources, the idea formed a key component of Donne's way of thinking and speaking, not just about people but about the universe, politics, society, and religion.[6]

On a simply aesthetic level, Donne finds the idea of the human being as a little world to be a useful device for word-spinning. Some of Donne's most delightful love poetry and his most trenchant satires depend on witty turns on the image. In some, like "The Good Morrow," two lovers together make up the world.

> And now good morrow to our waking souls,
> Which watch not one another out of fear;
> For love, all love of other sights controls,
> And makes one little room, an every where.
> Let sea-discoverers to new worlds have gone,
> Let maps to others, worlds on worlds have shown,
> Let us possess one world, each hath one, and is one.[7]

"The Sun Rising" depends on the same image of the lovers as the world. The speaker identifies the woman with the earth (the "states"), and thus with the body, while he links the man as prince with the "head" or reason, which should rule the body of the state. Turning from political to cosmological imagery, the lovers' bodies in bed become the earth, the center of the cosmos.

> She is all states, and all princes, I,
> Nothing else is.
> Princes do but play us; compared to this,
> All honour's mimic; all wealth alchemy.
> To warm the world, that's done in warming us.
> Shine here to us, and thou art everywhere;
> This bed thy centre is, these walls, thy sphere.[8]

In "Satire 5" he puts the image to work as political and social commentary. He says there,

> If all things be in all,
> As I think, since all, which were, are, and shall
> Be, be made of the same elements:
> Each thing, each thing implies or represents.
> Then man is a world; in which, officers
> Are the vast ravishing seas; and suitors,
> Springs . . . these self reasons do
> Prove the world a man, in which, officers
> Are the devouring stomach, and suitors
> The excrements, which they void.[9]

The idea Donne expresses here that all things are "made of the same elements" was a common one. The notion that shared substance led to real correspondences between seemingly disparate things plays a significant part in Donne's use of the image of the microcosm. He expresses the same idea in a letter to a friend, saying, "Nature hath made all bodies alike, by mingling and kneading up the same elements in every one."[10]

In his more explicitly religious writing from this period, Donne clearly associates the idea of the human person as a microcosm with God's act of creation, extending the image to the individual and social bodies. Donne's more consciously theological representations of the human being as a microcosm illustrate his understanding of the human person as the deliberate union of two disparate natures. As Donne succinctly says in a verse letter to the Countess of Huntingdon, probably written about 1603, "The soul with body, is a heaven combined / With earth, and for man's ease, but nearer joined."[11] Donne views the human being as a combination of the spiritual and the material realms that epitomizes the whole universe. In a letter to a friend from about 1609, he employs this idea of humanity's dual nature and the notion that the elements or humors make up the human person. To Sir Henry Goodyer, who was concerned about his changing fortunes, Donne points out:

> Wheresoever we are, if we can but tell our selves truly what and where we would be, we may make any state and place such; for we are so composed, that if abundance, or glory scorch and melt us, we have an earthly care, our bodies, to go into by consideration, and cool our selves: and if we be frozen, and contracted with lower and dark fortunes, we have within us a torch, a soul, lighter and warmer than any without: we are therefore our own umbrellas, and our own suns.[12]

In another letter to Sir Henry written about 1611, Donne uses the same image of the human being partaking in both heaven and earth to argue for the basic goodness of bodily life based on God's intent in creation. He says,

> Our nature is meteoric, we respect (because we partake so) both earth and heaven, for as our bodies glorified shall be capable of spiritual joy, so our souls demerged into those bodies, are allowed to partake earthly pleasure. Our soul is not sent hither, only to go back again: we have some errand to do here: nor is it sent into prison, because it comes innocent: and he which sent it, is just.[13]

In Donne's early religious writing, as in the early satirical work, he extends the image of man as a microcosm beyond the individual to the social body. For instance, in "Elegy on the Lady Markham," he says,

> Man is the world, and death the ocean,
> To which God gives the lower parts of man.
> This sea environs all, and though as yet
> God hath set marks, and bounds, 'twixt us and it,
> Yet doth it roar, and gnaw, and still pretend,
> And breaks our banks, when e'er it takes a friend.
> Then our land waters (tears of passion) vent;
> . . . .
> We after God's 'No', drown our world again.[14]

Here Donne identifies the individual human body and the "social body" with the earth, over which God gives the watery chaos of death and human passion a temporary dominion. He employs the same images of earth and water in an earlier love poem, "A Nocturnal upon St. Lucy's Day," in which the mourning speaker drowns the world (himself) with his tears.

To sum up, the idea of the human person as a microcosm plays a significant role in Donne's representations of the human body. He explicitly links the concept to the Christian doctrine of creation. In Donne's view, God deliberately forms the human person as the recapitulation of his whole creation. Since he creates human beings and the rest of the cosmos from the same physical elements (earth, air, fire, and water), the direct correspondences between the microcosm and the macrocosm form a fertile field of images for poetic or theological speculation.

The Edenic Body in Donne's Preordination Writings

Although forming the foundation of his thinking, the original body rarely appears in Donne's writing. Donne believes that sin corrupts both the human body and the world to which it is related. Although Donne looks back to its creation and (as will soon become evident) looks forward to its eschatological renewal, his "present" body is fallen. The body he represents is, therefore, seldom an unfallen world or a natural paradise.[15] The beauty and seemingly unfallen body of much Renaissance art and pastoral poetry appear fleetingly in Donne's work. His portrayal of the body, even in his love poetry, tends to be "warts and all." Donne represents a fallen body, fragmented and mutilated.

A few delightful exceptions do exist. Perhaps the closest Donne comes to portraying the body as the microcosm of an unfallen world is in "To His Mistress Going to Bed." The speaker of the poem orders his lover,

> Off with that girdle, like heaven's zone glistering,
> But a far fairer world encompassing.
> Unpin that spangled breastplate which you wear,
> That the eyes of busy fools may be stopped there.
> Unlace yourself, for that harmonious chime
> Tells me from you, that now 'tis your bed time.[16]

Here Donne represents the woman as a glorious and unfallen cosmos: her clothes are the starry heavens, her clock (indicating bedtime) striking with the music of the celestial spheres. In a reversal of the conventional valuations, her body is the lovely earth, fairer than the heavens surrounding it. Donne then changes the imagery from the astronomical to the Edenic. The speaker asks leave of the lady to be an explorer in the "new-found" America of her body.[17]

Yet even in this poem, which contains rare images of the lover's body as a new or unfallen world, Donne interweaves another set of images entirely: of his beloved's body not as Eden but as eschatological paradise. Donne refers to the bed, toward which he is trying to move his beloved, as "love's hallowed temple," and to the underdress remaining when she has taken off her outer clothing as the "white robes" in which

> . . . heaven's angels used to be
> Received by men; thou angel bring'st with thee
> A heaven like Mahomet's paradise; and though
> Ill spirits walk in white, we easily know
> By this these angels from an evil sprite,
> Those set our hairs, but these our flesh upright.[18]

When the speaker's lover is finally naked, Donne turns to eschatalogical images rather than those suggesting natural or Edenic innocence. Such a turn is typical for Donne, although wildly untypical of love poetry in general. He likens the unclothed bodies of the lovers to the unbodied souls of the resurrection. Women's bodies are "mystic books," covered with clothing to protect them from ignorant eyes. The laity must be dignified by "imputed grace" before they can look on the revealed vision of the unclothed body.[19] The speaker improbably associates the woman's body he hopes to enjoy not with the innocent body of Eden but with the mystic books and naked souls of the resurrection.

In addition to Donne's infrequent references to the Edenic body of the beloved in his erotic poetry, another surviving remnant of this body appears in his early works. For Donne, Eden remains with humanity in the gift of the bodily senses. Even though human faculties are clouded by sin, humanity can know something of God through a combination of the bodily senses and the intellectual faculties. This knowledge can lead, through grace, to a higher and saving knowledge of God. In taking this position, Donne aligns himself with the more Aristotelian position of Thomas Aquinas and the Catholic Church of his day against the prevailing tendencies in English Calvinism. This Calvinism tended to portray the senses and intellectual faculties as hopelessly degraded by sin and incapable, absent intervening grace, of assisting the human person toward knowledge of God. In his view of the role of the senses, he also goes counter to two popular currents in English philosophical thought, which, early in his career, had to a certain extent influenced his thinking: skepticism and Neoplatonism. Both question the reliability of sense experience as a path to true knowledge. Donne, to the contrary, portrays the body as the necessary instrument of the soul. Without the body's ability to perceive the outer world through the senses, the soul would be blind and helpless.

In *Paradoxes and Problems,* Donne argues against the traditional view that the body is "enlivened" by the soul. Because of the nature of the genre in which he writes here, one cannot accept Donne's arguments entirely at face value.[20] Since the views he expresses here are consistent with the importance he gives to sense experience in other less ambiguous works, however, they are worthy of attention. In Paradox XI ("That the gifts of the Body are better than those of the Mind"), he claims that the soul "is enabled by our body, not this by that," and goes on to say that "my body licenseth my soul to see the world's beauties."[21] The fall does not destroy the ability of the body to perceive or to act. Thus, even before a religious conversion, the body can play a redemptive role. Even the fallen senses can "read" God's work in the "book of creatures" (the world), thus providing the mind with material to deduce God's existence and something of his attributes. That, in turn, serves as a step toward true knowledge of God and, eventually, to a restoration of lost union with him.

In some of Donne's secular poetry, the soul's ability to perceive and act through the body facilitates the course of true love. In a letter to Sir Henry

Wotton, written in about 1612, Donne states his thought that love, "though it be directed upon the mind, doth inhere in the body, and find piety entertainment there."[22] In "Air and Angels," Donne's speaker refuses the "lovely glorious nothing" of the Neoplatonist soul as an object of love.[23] Just as the soul "whose child love is, / Takes limbs of flesh, and else could nothing do," love also must become incarnate in the body of the beloved to find realization and fulfillment.[24] Donne likewise rejects the Neoplatonic ideal of disembodied love in "The Ecstasy." Here he pictures two lovers resting on a bank, their hands clasped, each gazing into the other's eyes. At first the poem suggests a turn to Platonic love. The lovers' souls negotiate, while their bodies lie like "sepulchral statues."[25] They are in an "ecstasy," their souls meeting in pure and unmixed communion. The speaker asks,

> . . . alas, so long, so far
> Our bodies why do we forbear?
> They are ours, though they are not we, we are
> The intelligences, they the sphere.
>
> We owe them thanks, because they thus,
> Did us, to us, at first convey,
> Yielded their forces, sense, to us,
> Nor are dross to us, but allay.
> . . . .
>
> So must pure lovers' souls descend
> T'affections, and to faculties,
> Which sense may reach and apprehend,
> Else a great prince in prison lies.[26]

The speaker here asks the same question a Platonist might. Since bodies are inferior to minds, and love is a matter of the mind, why tolerate bodies? He answers the question by insisting that even though the body may be subordinate to the soul, it is not "dross," but an essential component of the human person. In a reversal of the Platonic image of the body as the prison of the soul, the body here is the key that unlocks the prison of isolation that holds captive the "great prince" (the soul). God creates the human person as an embodied, sensate being whose way to both earthly and heavenly love begins in the bodily senses. That being so, Donne's speaker commands, "To our bodies turn we then, that so / Weak mean on love revealed may look; / Love's mysteries in souls do grow, / But yet the body is his book."[27] Just as he does in "To His Mistress Going to Bed," examined above, Donne links the created body with the eschatalogical mysteries and with the book of

Scripture in the image of the body as a revelatory book. Donne often has this image in mind when he speaks of the body, and I turn to a more explicitly theological instance in the next section.

The Body as the Book of Creatures: Essays in Divinity

One way Donne expresses the significance of the created body in his religious work is to represent it as a synecdoche of the "book of creatures," the created world that reveals God to humanity.[28] While this image finds full expression only in *The Anniversaries* and *Devotions upon Emergent Occasions,* Donne makes the theological roots of the motif explicit in his early *Essays in Divinity.* Although the exact date of its composition is uncertain, the *Essays* probably belong to the period immediately prior to his ordination in 1615.[29] They consist of two "books," the first an extended exegesis of Genesis 1:1, followed by a prayer, and the second an extended exegesis of Exodus 1:1, followed by several prayers.

Poised on the threshold of his entry into the priesthood, he presents these as "essays" or trials of his abilities as an exegete written as he struggled with the decision to enter Holy Orders.[30] Neither poetical, satirical, nor polemical, they are the first of his writings to articulate straightforward "divinity." Beginning the *Essays* by quoting Genesis 1:1, "In the Beginning God created Heaven and Earth," Donne goes on to say:

> I do not therefore sit at the door, and meditate upon the threshold, because I may not enter further; for he which is *holy and true, and hath the key of David* . . . hath said to all the humble in one person, *I have set before thee an open door.* . . . The holy Scriptures . . . have these properties of a well provided Castle, that they are easily defensible, and safely defend others. So they have also this, that to strangers they open but a little wicket, and he that will enter, must stoop and humble himself. To reverend Divines, who by an ordinary calling are Officers and Commissioners from God, the great Doors are open. Let me with Lazarus lie at the threshold, and beg their crumbs.[31]

Donne positions himself at two entryways, at the literal entrance to the Scriptures with its first verse and as one who, while "essaying" into divinity, is not yet one of the "Officers and Commissioners" of God. He places himself with the humble and unlearned who sometimes find the Scriptures difficult to enter. Indeed, Donne suggests in this work a sort of hermeneutic of humility through which the unlearned can enter into an understanding of the book of Scripture by first considering the book of creatures, which includes the book of the human microcosm.

Before beginning the actual exegesis of his "threshold" verse, Donne turns to an examination of the Bible as a whole. Opening this section by stating that God has two books of life (the eternal register of the elect and the Bible), he goes on to say that there is another book, subordinate to these, the *liber creaturarum* or "book of creatures." Regarding the first two books, Donne says that "the first book is impossible . . . the second difficult."[32] The book of election is sealed and not available to human knowledge until the day of judgment. The book of Scripture is often obscure and requires interpretation, which many people do not have the learning to undertake. However, the third book, the book of creatures, is available to all. Donne quotes Raymond Sebonde to the effect that the book of creatures "teaches all things, presupposes no other, is soon learned, cannot be forgotten, requires no books, needs no witnesses, and in this, is safer than the Bible it self, that it cannot be falsified by Hereticks."[33] While Donne disagrees here with Sebonde's opinions that the book of creatures is sufficient to teach all the particularities of Christianity, he does see it as an entry to knowledge of God and to the understanding of Scripture. Donne thus shifts his identification of the "little" gate he opens for the humble from the actual verse of Genesis to creation itself, the book of creatures that all may read. Donne emphasizes, however, that this is only a beginning. To enter into true knowledge of God, to know who he is and not just what he does, we require the revelation of Scripture.[34]

When he turns to his actual discussion of God's work of creation in Genesis 1:1, Donne faces the question of what it means for God to create. Weighing the controversies between those who believe that God created out of nothing and those who think he created out of preexistent matter, Donne points out that the Scriptures themselves give no indication. Considering the opinions of the philosophers and church fathers, he admits that "all which can be said hereof is cloudy" and "therefore apt to be mis-imagined and ill interpreted."[35] In such instances, he has previously suggested that the reader turn to the book of creatures as a guide. He turns here to that book in an abridged form, saying,

> I will turn to certain and evident things; and tell thee, O man, which art said to be the Epilogue and compendium of all this world, and the hymen and matrimonial knot of eternal and mortal things, whom one says to be all creatures, because the Gospel, of which only man is capable, is sent to be preached to all creatures; and wast made by God's hands, not his commandments; and hast thy head erected to heaven, and all others to the center; that yet only thy heart of all others, points downwards, and only trembles. And, oh ye chief of men, ye Princes of the Earth . . . know ye by how few descents ye are derived from Nothing? you are the Children of the Lust and Excrements of your parents, they and theirs the children of Adam, the child of dirt, the child of Nothing. Yea, our souls which we magnify so much, and by which we consider

this, is a verier upstart than our body, being but of the first head and immediately made of Nothing.[36]

As the "epilogue and compendium" of nature, the human person can be read for evidence of God's existence, attributes, and acts as well as for evidence of the human condition. A consideration of the body and soul demonstrates that human beings are created from nothing. Donne even reverses the usual hierarchy of soul over body. Both are mortal, part of the created order, and the soul lies even closer to nothingness than the body. Such a reading of the human book can lead to the humility that is the true gateway to Scripture.

The Created Body in the Sermons

After his ordination to the Anglican priesthood, Donne continues to ground his understanding of the human person in the doctrine of creation. While consistent in his use of this foundation, his treatment of the created body in the sermons has some intriguing developments and differences of emphasis. Donne hints at a theme in his early work that he develops fully in the sermons: God's love for the material in general and for the body in particular. Taking up the two themes of the human person as a microcosm and the Edenic body again, it becomes possible to see the ways Donne transforms them in his sermons. This exploration brings into view a significant shift in Donne's preferred way of depicting the relationship between soul and body: while Donne uses cosmological metaphors to represent the relationship between the soul and the body in his early work, after his ordination he most often uses images of marriage to depict this relationship. Hence, while Donne's orthodox view of the created body and the significant role he gives it remain constant through all his works, developments in his depictions of the created body indicate an evolution in his religious sensibilities.

God's Love for Matter and the Body

In Donne's sermons, God creates the human body, as he creates all things, out of sheer love for being and matter. Fascinated by God's creation of all things from nothingness, Donne emphasizes desire as God's primary motivation: a desire for other beings, for a plenitude of material and immaterial creatures to share and perfect his kingdom. In one sermon, Donne zestfully expresses God's attitude toward the material world.

> The Kingdom of Heaven hath not all that it must have to a consummate perfection, till it have bodies too. In those infinite millions of millions of generations, in which the holy, blessed and glorious Trinity enjoyed themselves one another,

and no more, they thought not their glory so perfect, but that it might receive an addition from creatures; and therefore they made a world, a material world, a corporeal world, they would have bodies."[37]

In a later sermon, Donne speaks of "our large, our Communicable God," who, not satisfied within himself alone, proceeded to create the world: the light, the sea, the earth, and the creatures that filled the earth. Still not satisfied, he made one more creature.

And yet God had not shed himself far enough; he had the leviathan, the whale in the sea, and behemoth and the elephant upon the land; and all those great heavenly bodies in the way, and angels in their infinite numbers, and manifold offices, in heaven; but, because angels could not propagate, nor make more angels, he enlarged his love, in making man, that so he might enjoy all natures at once, and have the nature of angels, and the nature of earthly creatures, in one person . . . in whom the whole nature of all the world should meet.[38]

In his sermons, as in his early work, Donne portrays God's creation of human beings as the culmination and the synecdoche of creation out of nothing. Using the image of the microcosm, Donne insists that "man is not only a contributary creature, but a total creature. . . . He is not a piece of the world, but the world itself; and next to the glory of God, the reason why there is a world."[39] God's creation and care for the human body epitomize the miracle of his desire for being, his love of the material, and the way he enacts that love throughout salvation history. For Donne, the body encapsulates salvation history. In a significant image that I referred to in the introduction, Donne insists that God makes the human body "the first point that the foot of [His] compass was upon" in creation and the last point it will touch when God glorifies it in the resurrection.[40] Donne expresses a similar sentiment, although he restricts it to God's dealings with the human composite instead of applying it to salvation history as a whole, when he says that "we that are Christians acknowledge that God's first care of man was his body, he made that first; and his last care is reserved for the body too, at the Resurrection, which is principally for the benefit of the body."[41] Upending the usual hierarchies, Donne makes the body primary: first in God's concern and first in his own imaginative universe.

Given the theological significance Donne accords to God's creation of the body, one easily understands why his sermons contain even fewer of the Platonic representations of the body as a foul garment or a prison than does his early work. Donne speaks of the body rather as a loving creation and gift. Using the traditional imagery of God as a potter molding earth, or his own nontraditional images of the body as a map (as in the compass image referred to above) or a watch, Donne depicts the body as the product of God's particular care, industry, and artistry.[42] God could not have intended such a lovingly crafted piece of work as a prison for the human soul. Even the fall does not make the body into such a prison. In a 1625 Easter Day sermon, Donne waxes eloquent about the wonder of God's love even for the fallen body.

> And therefore be content to wonder at this, that God would have such a care to dignify, and to crown; and to associate to his own everlasting presence, the body of man. God himself is a Spirit, and heaven is his place; my soul is a spirit, and so proportioned to that place. . . . But since we wonder . . . that some late Philosophers have removed the whole earth from the Center . . . and placed it in one of the Spheres of heaven, that this clod of earth, this body of ours should be carried up to the highest heaven. . . . That God, all Spirit . . . should have such an affection, and such a love to this body, this deserves the wonder.[43]

As I will explore in the next chapter, Donne is clear-eyed about the present state of the fallen human body. Yet God's love for bodies survives their fall and lends them some of the dignity of their first creation. While recognizing the need for ascetic practices to discipline the fallen body, Donne opposes punitive disciplines, "inhumane flagellations," or "unnatural macerations . . . and such disciplines as God doth not command, nor authorize, to wither, and shrink, and contract the body, as though the soul were sent into it, as into a prison, or into fetters, and manacles, to wring, and pinch, and torture it."[44] Even the fallen body remains a gift, a blessing, and a responsibility; as Donne points out, "He that does not use a benefit reproaches the benefactor."[45] God intends human beings to enjoy their embodied state and to use their bodies as tools to accomplish their own salvation and to contribute to society.

The Human Person as Microcosm in the Sermons

Donne sometimes turns in his sermons to the image of the human person as a microcosm of creation that so pervaded his early writing. The passage from the 1625 Easter Day sermon discussed in the previous section includes three points that play significant parts in his presentation of the created body. First, the human soul and body form a *hierarchy* in which the spirit naturally holds a place of dominion over the flesh. Second, God creates the human person as a union of the spiritual and material realms. Third, God's almost peculiar love for the human body displaces it from its lower position and bestows upon it a significance even greater than the soul's. Donne sometimes leaps from the traditional belief that God created the human body before the soul to a much less traditional insistence that God's care and activity "begins and ends" with the human body, not with the soul. As will become increasingly evident, Donne finds support for the primacy of the body throughout the history of fall, redemption, and resurrection. I will turn first, however, to two themes that relate to the human being as microcosm: hierarchy and union.

Despite the fact that Donne sometimes reverses the traditional valuation of soul over body in the great chain of being, he often adheres to the more conventional Christian anthropology. That understanding of the human composite organizes the person into a hierarchy of spiritual, mental, and physical attributes. That which was closest to pure spirit was highest. Although Platonism and Neoplatonism influenced it, this notion of hierarchy drew most directly on the biblical notion that God created humanity in his own image. Most later commentators insisted that this image is found specifically in the soul. Quoting Tertullian for support, Donne agrees and states specifically that the image of God is not to be found in the created body.[46] He refers in the sermons to the traditional view that a hierarchy exists even within the soul. Summarizing this view succinctly in an early sermon, he says,

> First, in a natural man we conceive there is a soul of vegetation and of growth; and secondly, a soul of motion and of sense; and then thirdly, a soul of reason, and understanding, an immortal soul. And the first two souls of vegetation, and of sense, we conceive to arise out of the temperament, and good disposition of which that man is made, they arise out of man himself. But the last soul, the perfect and immortal soul, that is immediately infused of God.[47]

The first two souls, of growth and sense, relate respectively to bodily existence and bodily sensation. Thus, they are lower in the hierarchy than reason, which rises beyond the material. In the hierarchy of the universe, the spiritual is naturally higher than the material, so the soul is higher than the body. He uses spatial imagery to reinforce this hierarchy in an early sermon.

> Is your soul less than your body, because it is in it? How easily is a letter in a box, which if it were unfolded, would cover that box? Unfold your soul, and you shall see, that it reaches to heaven; from thence it came, and thither it should pretend; whereas the body is but from that earth, and for that earth, upon which it is now; which is but a short, and an inglorious progress. To contract this, the soul is larger than the body, and the glory, and the joys of heaven, larger than the honours, and the pleasures of this world.[48]

In a much later sermon, Donne pictures the body as a watch case, holding the more precious watch within. He goes on to say that the body must be respected in life and in death because it houses (or will house again) the soul.[49] These passages are typical of the anthropology that Donne inherited, which values the soul over the body.

Donne's God is a God of plenitude, creating a great host of disparate beings arranged in the traditional hierarchy from spiritual intelligences (angels) at the top down to insensate dust at the bottom. While this tradition influences Donne, his ordering of creation and of the human person rests more basically on the intimate *union* of the material and the spiritual realms. Their unity is ultimately more important than gradation or difference. Donne's representations of the body operate within the context of unity in plurality. The human person is by creation and definition a union of body and soul. In an early and succinct statement of this traditional idea, Donne says,

> In the constitution and making of a natural man, the body is not the man, nor the soul is not the man, but the union of these two makes up the man; the spirits in a man which are the thin and active part of the blood, and so are of a kind of middle nature, between soul and body . . . they do the office to unite and apply the faculties of the soul to the organs of the body . . . so there is a man.[50]

Opposed to the Neoplatonic tendencies to identify the person with the soul and to urge the religious seeker to turn away from the things of the body, Donne believes that body and soul "must serve God jointly together, because God having joined them, man may not separate them."[51] Attempts to separate the soul and body in life, even through religiously motivated ascetic practice, stand contrary to God's intent. Quoting Tertullian, Donne cautions his congregation, "Never go about to separate the thoughts of the heart from the fellowship of the body."[52] Donne links this belief in humanity's essential nature as body/soul with his conviction that we find and serve God through embodied means: Scripture, sacraments, and the exercise of our worldly vocations. The human soul is "embedded" in the body for a purpose, just as the human person is embedded in the created world. Donne believes that "man is not a soul alone, but a body too . . . man is not placed in this world only for speculation; he is not sent into this world to live out of it but to live in it."[53] Just as denigration of the body in this life is unnatural, so is the separation of soul and body in death. Death does not "free" a pure and immortal soul from an imprisoning body. Since humans are composite creatures, the soul alone is an incomplete fragment of the human person. In death, the soul waits anxiously to be united with its body at the resurrection. In the whole trajectory from creation to resurrection, from birth through active life in the world to death and beyond, the human person remains a union of body and soul.

The Remnants of the Edenic Body in the Sermons

As in Donne's earlier work, the created body appears in his sermons only in fragmented form. Those fragments are the starting point for his developing evocation of the body as a sign and sacrament of God's power, grace, and love. The fallen body is the "given" for Donne and his early readers and auditors, the present reality offered to them by their theology and by their experience mediated through that theology. Donne, in common with many Christians of his day, reads the marks of the fall in human bodies: lust, sloth, illnesses, accidents, and eventual death. Yet the fall cannot erase all traces of the original human body. These traces, actual and metaphorical, are crucial to Donne's theology.

ACTUAL REMNANTS

Donne speaks of two actual remnants of the created body: sheer material existence and the bodily senses. Donne's God simply loves *being* per se. Nothing is "more contrary to God, and his proceedings, then annihilation, to Be nothing, Do nothing, Think nothing."[54] If not for God's love of being and beings, neither the material world nor the human body would exist. Donne is acutely aware that God's desire alone creates the human person, body and soul, and continues actively to sustain its existence. In a passage from one sermon, Donne links created and resurrected being when he says, "As Man had an eternal not being before the Creation; so he would have an eternal not being after his dissolution by death, in soul, as well as in body, if God did not preserve that being, which he hath imprinted in both."[55]

The other significant material fragment of the Edenic body is bodily sensation, which Donne stresses before and after his ordination. Donne represents the senses, even though fallen, as necessary pathways to God. As he puts it concisely in an early sermon, "The organ that God hath given the natural man is the eye; he sees God in the creature. The organ that God hath given the Christian is the ear; he hears God in his Word."[56] He extends this ability to know God to all the human senses, referring in another sermon to St. Augustine's compendium of all the places in Scripture "where every one of our senses is called a seeing. . . . In all our senses, in our faculties, we may see God if we will."[57]

Donne does not think it possible to know God solely through the mind or the soul. Neither reason nor mystical intuition can lead to knowledge of God without information supplied by the bodily senses. In Donne's anthropology, the human person is above all a composite of spirit and matter. As he says, "A natural man is not made of reason alone, but of reason and sense."[58] Each part of the composite contributes to knowledge of God, and any attempt to circumvent the role of nature or the body is inhuman and futile. In another sermon, Donne speaks of the necessity of balance when viewing the role of nature and the body in the religious life.

> He that attributes more to nature, he that allows her any ability of disposing her self before hand, without prevention of grace, or concurrence and cooperation after, without continual assistance of particular graces, he sets up an idol, and magnifies nature beyond that which appertains unto her. But he that goes not so far as this, that the reason of man, and his natural faculties, are the instruments and organs that God works in by his grace . . . he does not so much with her [nature] as he might do: he hath made her a giant; and then, as though he were afraid of her, he runs away from her.[59]

In Donne's view, the fall diminished the gifts of being and of the senses but did not destroy them. Humans actually have less "being" because of the fall. Donne uses the metaphor of a "damped" fire to express this concept: because of the fall, the fires of being are not as bright as they might be. The senses have suffered the same "damping." Although people can still learn and function through smelling, tasting, touching, seeing, and hearing, all their senses are "clogged" by their separation from God. Donne believes the literal decay of the human race in body, mind, and soul started with the fall of Adam and continued through the generations to produce the diminished humanity of his own day.

Despite such decay, Donne represents the material remnants of the Edenic body as the fertile and necessary ground for God's redeeming grace. In a late sermon, he says, "God proceeds in our conversion, and regeneration, as he did in our first Creation. There man was nothing; but God breathed not a soul into that nothing; but of a clod of earth he made a body, and into that body infused a soul."[60] In this sermon, Donne speaks of the fact that God works by grace through the natural human faculty of reason, which, in Donne's view, is always grounded in the bodily senses. God's work always starts with the natural and the material. The foundations for grace are embodied: the body of the world, the body of the believer, the body of Christ, the material sacraments.

METAPHORICAL REMNANTS

In addition to the actual remnants of the Edenic body that form such a significant part of Donne's theology, the innocent body appears throughout the sermons in metaphorical remnants. As many scholars have pointed out, Donne's sermons abound in "embodied" images.[61] Donne often uses the body, body parts, the bodily senses, sexual love, and sensual pleasure to speak of God, human knowledge of God, and of the religious life.[62] Two tropes that Donne uses often and with great relish in his sermons relate directly to the Edenic body: images of eating and images of erotic love and marriage. These images mark an intriguing difference from his treatment of the Edenic body in his earlier work. There the unfallen body as a beloved and erotic object appears only fleetingly in some of his secular love poetry. Ironically, the unfallen body of sensual enjoyment plays a greater role, metaphorically at least, in the sermons than it ever does in Donne's love poetry. The images of eating and erotic love relate to two of the elements Donne believes are necessary for the human being to know God: desire and sensual knowledge. Both these elements are present in unfallen humanity, are specifically grounded in the body, and remain even after the fall.

Deeply influenced by Augustine, Donne understands desire as a defining element of the human person, body and soul. The attracting power of God, working on the human person in creation, forms the will, and indeed the soul itself, as it turns to God in desire and love.[63] Even natural, fallen man experiences desire for God as the longing for natural satisfaction, happiness, and blessedness on a worldly, or bodily, level.[64] Donne makes no radical distinction between carnal and spiritual desire, seeing them as connected in the very roots of human existence.[65] Far from thinking that desire for the joys of this world separate human beings from God, Donne says that "by the beams of comfort in this life, we come to the body of the Sun, by the Rivers, to the Ocean, by the cheerfulness of heart here, to the brightness, to the fullness of joy hereafter."[66] Donne often tells his congregations to be as amorous, as ambitious, as voluptuous and covetous as they wish, as long as they eventually turn those desires on God, their proper object. Donne agrees with Augustine that only God is large enough to finally satisfy human desire.[67] While Donne identifies human desire and identity closely with the will, he also recognizes that desire has its roots in the body. Bodily desires can *metaphorically* point toward, and lead to, spiritual desire and joy. Images of eating and sexual pleasure evoke the paradise of union with God before the fall, the original union of immediate knowledge and of gratified desire, and at the same time refer to the eschatological union of the marriage supper of the Lamb.

Sensual knowledge also is necessary for knowledge of God. As I discussed in the earlier section on actual remnants of the Edenic body, all human knowledge of God begins with the capacities of the bodily senses. Donne assigns different significance to different senses in his sermons. Donne exploits the sense of sight most often as an *actual* remnant of the Edenic body. He insists that even fallen humanity has basic knowledge of God because it can see the wonders of creation. While the sense of sight holds an important place in Donne's theology, other senses have greater figurative significance. The sense of smell does not play a large role in Donne's representations, except as it catches the whiff of decay and morbidity that marks the fall. He likewise downplays the sense of touch. The senses of hearing and taste, however, carry great metaphorical weight in Donne's religious universe. Hearing is a "redeemed" sense that Donne associates with the hearing of the Word of God. Taste is the sense that transports the Edenic body metaphorically into the present of Donne's sermons.

Donne spices his sermons with lyrical passages that evoke a sensual autumnal ripeness waiting to be plucked and savored: biblical texts are fruits, the church is a walled garden, and he invites his congregations to the marriage feast. Honey is a particularly resonant image for Donne of spiritual joy and of humanity's desire for the sweetness of God's presence. He often speaks of spiritual appetite and fullness, and the satisfaction of that appetite, with all the rich Old Testament imagery of the gifts of God as manna and quails, marrow and fatness, milk and honey, oil and wine.[68] The Scriptures are honey and the psalms are the manna of the church.[69] The gospel is milk, while controversy is like gnawing on bones.[70] Preaching is bread, knowledge of God is meat, and good doctrines are fruits.[71] Donne's emphasis on eating and digestion seems to grow out of several related points: eating is pleasurable, it is the means by which human beings "take in" and apply to themselves that which they need to live, and eating the body of Christ in the Eucharist is the means whereby his spiritual gifts are applied to the individual. Many of Donne's images of eating relate to the ways in which people can become "partakers of the Divine Nature" and satisfy their "holy hunger and thirst" for God.[72] All temporal blessings, the joys and pleasures of the material world that Donne epitomizes in his images of food, are a foretaste of the joy of heaven.

Donne also uses sexual imagery (of erotic love, of marriage, of masculine and feminine attributes) to express humanity's relationship with God. Although he relates these images to a "redeemed" spiritual life, they are rooted in the erotic possibilities of the Edenic body. Donne pictures the preacher (and especially himself as preacher) not as teacher but as lover. He says true instruction "is a making love to the Congregation and to every soul in it; but it is but to the soul . . . we have no way into your hearts, but by sending our hearts."[73] True knowledge of God for Donne has affinities with the biblical sense of "knowing" a woman: it means not knowledge *about* God, but intimate, desirous, and procreative contact with him. The role of preacher-as-lover is not to tell his congregation about God, but to awaken their *desire* for him, to seduce them for God with all the arts at his command. In a sermon preached before King James at Whitehall in 1625, Donne points to God himself as the source of sexual metaphors for the religious life. He says, "God is Love, and the Holy Ghost is amorous in his Metaphors; every where his Scriptures abound with the notion of Love, of Spouse, and Husband, and Marriage Songs, and Marriage Supper, and Marriage-Bed."[74] If the source of these metaphors is scriptural, the poet and the lover in Donne willingly picked them up and made them central to his theology. In a sermon preached before Queen Anne early in his career, Donne states that people have a tendency to retain "some air of their former professions" as well as a tendency toward whatever worldly pleasure "exercised" them before, even when they turn to God and religion. He notes as an example of this rule King Solomon,

> whose disposition was amorous, and excessive in the love of women, when he turned to God, he departed not utterly from his old phrase and language, but having put a new, and a spiritual tincture, and form and habit into all his thoughts, and words, he conveys all his loving approaches and applications to God, and all God's gracious answers to his amorous soul, into songs, and Epithalamions, and meditations upon contracts, and marriages between God and his Church, and between God and his soul.[75]

Donne might well be speaking of himself. Turning from secular love poetry to praise of God, many of his metaphors remain "amorous." While much of his secular love poetry is ironic or bitter in its treatment of relationships between actual men and women, his religious use of sexual metaphors turns lyrical and joyful. The Edenic promise of sexual bliss, often a cheat and a whore in Donne's love poetry, finds fulfillment and future promise in the faithful, "married" love of God for the soul.

Donne's most common metaphor for the relationship between God and the individual is the marriage of Christ to the faithful, feminine soul. He evokes through this image the indissolubility of that relationship and its productive nature.

> Christ loves not but in the way of marriage; if he begin to love thee, he tells thee, *Sponsabo te mihi, I will marry thee unto me,* and *Sponsabo in aeternum, I will marry thee for ever.* For it is a marriage that prevents all mistakings, and excludes all impediments . . . when I have taken thee into my husbandry, thou shalt increase, and multiply, *Seminabo te,* and all that thou doest produce shall be directed upon me.[76]

In this brief passage, Donne encapsulates the whole story of creation ("increase and multiply"), redemption, and eschatological union through images of marriage. He portrays union with God as stable, interactive, mutual, and fruitful.

These tropes of eating and sexual love permeate Donne's sermons and reflect a religious imagination preoccupied with desire and satisfaction, with intimate and visceral knowledge of God. Through the use of these images, he works against the assumption that knowledge of God relies solely on the capacities of the soul, especially on the capacity of human reason alone. Donne grounds the saving experience of God in the capacities and desires of the Edenic body: desire, sensual engagement with the world, and willingness to seek union and satisfaction. Although they refer back to Eden, his representations of eating and erotic love look forward to the eschatalogical marriage supper of the Lamb, where "our way of knowing God . . . cannot be expressed."[77]

THE MARRIAGE OF BODY AND SOUL

Donne also uses the metaphor of marriage to speak of created human nature, specifically the relationship of the body and soul. This marks a departure from his early work, where he most commonly speaks of the created body through the cosmological imagery of the human person as a microcosm of the created universe. Donne almost always links his references to body and soul to the parallel relationship of the earth and the heavens in his earlier work. While he makes use of the concept of the microcosm in his sermons, he shifts his emphasis toward images of marriage to express the character of the relationship between body and soul. In one characteristic passage, Donne says,

> God made the first Marriage, and man made the first divorce; God married the body and soul in the creation, and man divorced the body and soul by death through sin, in his fall. But because God hath made the band of Marriage indissoluble but by death, farther than man can die, this divorce cannot fall upon man; As far as man is immortal, man is a married man still, still in possession of a soul, and a body too; And man is for ever immortal in both; immortal in his soul by preservation, and immortal in his body by reparation in the resurrection. For, though they be separated . . . from bed and board, they are not divorced.[78]

In another sermon, he echoes the familiar language of the marriage service to refer to human nature, saying that body and soul "must serve God jointly together, because God having joined them, man may not separate them."[79] For Donne, as for most theologians of his day, soul and body, as well as husband and wife, are parts of a natural hierarchy in which the higher not only has proper dominion over the lower, but also has duties toward it.[80] In the fallen world, the marriage of soul and body may be a troubled one. Donne points out that the flesh is the weaker marriage partner, and that in this life the soul and body are often contentious spouses.[81] The true and untroubled marriage of body and soul will not take place until the resurrection.[82] By changing his dominant metaphor for the relationship between soul and body from the cosmological one of the heavens and the earth to the more intimate one of husband and wife, Donne chooses to speak in his sermons in terms of a more intimate, personal, and loving relationship. This may reveal an evolution of his own religious sensibilities as well as a recognition of the rhetorical strategies most likely to "woo" his congregations to Christ.

Conclusion

All of Donne's representations of the fallen, the redeemed, and the eschatalogical bodies rest on the foundation of his beliefs about the created body. The human body is the "foot of the compass," the point of origin for the grand sweep of salvation history God is drawing. While the fall defaces this "original" human body, it does not destroy all the gifts with which God endowed it. Existence, senses, and desire—all rooted in the body—are the necessary grounds for the workings of grace and the accomplishment of the work God began in creation. The human person, body and soul, also retains its status as the microcosm of the larger material and spiritual work of the divine Author. The ontological correspondences between body and world, fallen or unfallen, remain. As parts of this web of actual correspondences, body and world retain their significance and their signifying power. Both body and world can be read as the "book of creatures" that reveals something of the nature of God and humanity. In the sermons in particular, Donne exploits metaphorical remnants of the Edenic body based on this ontological reality: images of sensual desire, sensual pleasure, and marriage. Donne uses these metaphors to aid his congregations in understanding the nature and rewards of knowing God and to seduce them into desiring that intimate knowledge. By such holy seduction, Donne hopes to awaken in his congregations their own desires. He sets them on the way of salvation: a path that will restore for them the Edenic links between carnal and spiritual pleasure at the eschatalogical supper of the Lamb.

Notes

1. In some of his preordination writings, Donne occasionally uses Platonic or Pythagorean anthropological models that differ from the Christian idea of the body as part of God's good creation. These depict the relationship of soul and body not as a blessed and natural union, but as an accidental, unfortunate, and somehow unnatural coupling. As I will argue in the next chapter, Donne uses these other models within a larger world of Christian imagery, not to describe the original human composite, but

rather to refer to the fallen state of humanity. Even in Donne's early work, he most often adheres to traditional Christian anthropology. This adherence is, not surprisingly, even more marked in his sermons.

2. George Conger has traced that history in his comprehensive study, *Theories of Macrocosms and Microcosms in the History of Philosophy* (1922; repr., New York: Russell & Russell, 1967). My references to the history of the image are drawn largely from his work, in particular pages 27–32.

3. Gregory Nazianzen, for instance, held that the union of the soul and body of the human person was the mingling of two worlds, and that this made the human being "a kind of second world, great in littleness" (quoted in Conger, *Theories*, 31).

4. Benedict Ashley, *Theologies of the Body: Humanist and Christian* (St. Louis, Mo.: Pope John Center, 1985), 134.

5. Sir Geoffrey Keynes, "Books from Donne's Library," in *A Bibliography of Dr. John Donne, Dean of Saint Paul's,* 4th ed. (Oxford: Clarendon Press, 1973), 273.

6. Many commentators have noted the importance of the ideas of creation and microcosm in Donne's work. Two of the notable examples are Terry Sherwood, *Fulfilling the Circle: A Study of John Donne's Thought* (Toronto: University of Toronto Press, 1984) and Charles Monroe Coffin, *John Donne and the New Philosophy* (Morningside Heights, N.Y.: Columbia University Press, 1937). Sherwood notes that "Donne was preoccupied with Creation" (5). He gives an excellent account of Donne's doctrine of creation, the idea of the body as a microcosm, and the influence of these ideas on some of Donne's representations of the body. Sherwood, in my view, tends to overemphasize the doctrines of creation and incarnation at the expense of those themes of fall, redemption, and resurrection.

7. John Donne, *John Donne: The Complete English Poems,* ed. A. J. Smith (London: Penguin Books, 1971; London: Penguin Classics, 1986), 60, lines 8–14. All quotations from Donne's poetry are to this edition, cited by page and line number. References in endnotes to *Poems* refer to this edition. Unless otherwise noted, I have followed the dating for Donne's poetry from Smith's edition. I have adopted the title conventions for all Donne's poetry from the title list in *The Variorum Edition of the Poetry of John Donne,* ed. Gary Stringer et al. (Bloomington: Indiana University Press, 2000).

8. Ibid., 80–81, lines 21–30.

9. Ibid., 170–71, lines 9–19.

10. John Donne, *Letters to Severall Persons of Honour,* ed. Charles Edmund Merrill Jr. (New York: Sturgis & Walton, 1910), 83. All references to and dating of Donne's prose letters refer to this edition.

11. Donne, *Poems,* "To the Countess of Huntingdon ('That unripe side of earth')," 241, lines 97–98.

12. Donne, *Letters,* 55.

13. Ibid., 40.

14. Donne, *Poems,* 247–48, lines 1–7, 12.

15. The only literal reference to the body as a natural paradise sometimes attributed to Donne is in "Sappho to Philaenis," a poem about lesbian love. The speaker of the poem addresses her lover thus: "Thy body is a natural paradise, / In whose self, unmanured, all pleasure lies, / Nor needs perfection" (ibid., 128, lines 35–37). There has been some question as to whether the poem should be attributed to Donne at all. *The*

Variorium Edition of the elegies includes the poem but notes in the commentary that Helen Gardner, K.W. Gransden, and Arthur Mariotti all questioned its authorship (Gary Stringer et al., eds, *The Elegies*, vol. 2 of *The Variorum Edition of the Poetry of John Donne* [Bloomington: Indiana University Press, 2000], 967–68).

16. Ibid., 124–25, lines 5–10.

17. Ibid., 125, lines 25–30.

18. Ibid., lines 19–24.

19. Ibid., lines 33–43.

20. The paradox was a popular genre among the young lawyers and scholars of Donne's time. In it, one could argue an unpopular or even ridiculous position just for the love of argument.

21. John Donne, *Paradoxes and Problems*, ed. Helen Peters (Oxford: Clarendon Press, 1980), 11.

22. Donne, *Letters*, 103.

23. Donne, *Poems*, 42, line 6.

24. Ibid, lines 7–8.

25. Ibid., line 18.

26. Ibid., 55, lines 49–56, 65–68.

27. Ibid., lines 69–72.

28. Winfried Schleiner in *The Imagery in John Donne's Sermons* (Providence: Brown University Press, 1970), discusses the image of world as text in Donne's work (97–100). For a comprehensive discussion of the history of the idea of nature as a book, see Clarence J. Glacken, *Traces on the Rhodian Shore: Nature and Culture in Western Thought from Ancient Times to the End of the Eighteenth Century* (Berkeley, Los Angeles, and London: University of California Press, 1967).

29. Evelyn Simpson, in the introduction to her edition of the *Essays*, places them at the end of 1614 or the beginning of 1615. John Donne, *Essays in Divinity*, ed. Evelyn M. Simpson (Oxford: Clarendon Press, 1967), ix.

30. Donne's son says, in an introductory address to the reader that prefaces his 1651 edition of the *Essays*, "It is thought fit to let thee know, that these *Essays* were . . . the voluntary sacrifices of several hours, when [the author] had many debates betwixt God and himself, whether he were worthy, and competently learned to enter into Holy Order" (ibid., 4).

31. Ibid., 5.

32. Ibid., 6.

33. Ibid., 7. Sebonde, also known as Raimond Sebond or Raymond of Sabunde was a doctor of medicine and served as a professor of theology at the University of Toulouse in the 1420s and 1430s. He wrote a long treatise entitled *Theologia naturalis seu liber creaturarum*.

34. Donne says, "Men which seek God by reason, and natural strength, (though we do not deny common notions and general impressions of a sovereign power) are like Mariners which voyaged before the invention of the Compass, which were by Coasters, and unwillingly left the sight of the land. Such are they which would arrive at God by this world, and contemplate him only in his Creatures, and seeming Demonstrations. Certainly, every Creature shows God as a glass, but glimmeringly and transitorily, by the

frailty both of the receiver, and beholder" (ibid., 20).
35. Ibid., 29–30.
36. Ibid., 30.
37. Donne, *Sermons*, 4:47.
38. Ibid., 6:154.
39. Ibid., 6:297.
40. Ibid., 8:97.
41. Ibid., 3:83.
42. Ibid., 4:126; 8:97; 9:62, 79.
43. Ibid., 6:265.
44. Ibid., 8:106.
45. Ibid., 7:106. Donne is quoting Tertullian in this passage.
46. Ibid., 9:76.
47. Ibid., 3:85.
48. Ibid., 2:338. See 4:126 for similar use of spatial imagery in service of this idea.
49. Ibid., 9:79.
50. Ibid., 2:261. Other similar statements about the human being as a union of body and soul can be found at 1:207; 4:226; 7:104, 107, 448.
51. Ibid., 7:107.
52. Ibid.
53. Ibid., 7:104.
54. Ibid., 4:85.
55. Ibid., 8:144.
56. Ibid 2:114; see also 6:217.
57. Ibid., 6:236.
58. Ibid., 6:175.
59. Ibid., 6:120.
60. Ibid., 9:354.
61. John Carey points out that one of the remarkable things about Donne's sermons "given Donne's spiritual drift" is the dense presence of the human body in them, sometimes in quite unlikely contexts. *John Donne: Life, Mind, and Art* (New York: Oxford University Press, 1981), 135. While Carey is correct in pointing out the enormous presence of the body in Donne's sermons, I disagree with his conclusion that this presence is surprising. In my reading, Donne's "spiritual drift" is quite consistent with his use of the body in the sermons.
62. Many of these embodied images relate not to the Edenic body, but to other "bodies" that we will examine in later chapters: sinful, redeemed, or resurrected. For instance, Donne imagines sins and doubts as wounds (*Sermons*, 8:345) and God's graces and corrections as medicines (6:237; 8:74, 216). He represents for his congregations the spiritual realities of the soul, Christ, and the Church through the more concrete realities of the body or parts of the body (4:106, 124; 7:302; 8:345).The bodily trope that most pervades Donne's work and fires his religious imagination is the fragmented and resurrected human body that points to the whole story of fall and eschatological renewal.
63. Ibid., 4:310; 6:361; 9:251.
64. Ibid., 8:303; 9:251.

65. Ibid., 1:312–13; 10:110.
66. Ibid., 3:270.
67. Ibid., 3:87; 4:363; 7:390.
68. Ibid., 2:49, 276–77; 3:53, 339, 353, 383; 5:274–75; 7:51, 302.
69. Ibid., 7:51.
70. Ibid., 4:205.
71. Ibid., 2:245, 276; 7:303.
72. Ibid., 8:250.
73. Ibid., 9:350. See also 3:347.
74. Ibid., 7:87.
75. Ibid., 1:237.
76. Ibid., 6:51. See also 3:250–51, 367.
77. Ibid., 7:303.
78. Ibid., 7:257.
79. Ibid., 7:107.
80. For instance, 4:226 and 7:104.
81. Ibid., 3:208.
82. Ibid., 3:112.

THE FALLEN BODY

*I am a little world made cunningly
Of elements, and an angelic sprite,
But black sin hath betrayed to endless night
My world's both parts, and, oh, both
parts must die.*

DONNE, "Divine Meditations"

While the doctrine of creation forms the foundation of his representations of the human person, Donne rarely depicts an innocent or Edenic body directly. The "present" body most often appears in Donne's work as weak, confining, fragmented, earthy, slimy, diseased, or corrupt. This body reflects a pervasive sense of the disruption of soul, body, and cosmos by the fall of humankind and the ravages of sin. Many factors may have influenced Donne's preoccupation with the fall. Among these may simply be the large place that it occupies in traditional Christian thinking. Donne grew up in that tradition and read widely in both the ancient and contemporary documents that informed it. Donne also shared with many of his contemporaries a strong sense of generalized disillusionment with the state of humanity and society that was commonly associated with the mutability and decay of the world and the body. Donne connects such notions with the biblical account of the fall. Further, Donne's own early experiences with love, religious conflict, court life, and political intrigue seem to have demonstrated to him the fallen nature of the world. He often expresses this disillusionment through references to a fallen human body and world. He depicts both with images of ugliness, illness, death, decay, dissolution, fragmentation, and dissection.

In his representations of the fallen body, Donne takes ideas and images from two traditions: the ancient Greek philosophies that speak of a fall *into* the body and the Christian doctrine that depicts a fall *of* the body from an original innocent state. Even before his ordination, many of his writings depict a fallen body that owes much more to biblical material and Christian tradition than to Platonic or Neoplatonic models. In the Judeo-Christian tradition, the fall of humankind from a right relationship with God had consequences for both body and soul. In its original creation, the entire human person was in harmony with God and subject to him. The body was also naturally subject to the control of the innocent soul and pure mind of the individual. With the fall, these natural hierarchies were disrupted. Corrupted by sin, the human person was no longer obedient to God and the body was no longer naturally subject to the human soul. The results for the body were disastrous: disease, pain, death, and dissolution. Body and soul, the integral parts of the human person, were at war with one another. St. Paul and Augustine, whom Donne read assiduously, focused on the image of the loss of control over the body by the soul as a real consequence of sin and an experiential fact of human existence. They also used images of the loss of control over the body as a way of representing the disruption of sin in the human person as well as in the cosmos as a whole.

Donne's preoccupation with the fallen body and many of the images he uses to depict it remain constant throughout his career, but with some differences in emphasis. The shift from secular or philosophical images of the fallen body to a more Christian vocabulary happens very early in his work, before his ordination. He places more emphasis on metaphors of sexuality and ugliness in the more secular works and more emphasis on illness in the more religious ones. The most significant difference in emphasis between his early and his late work is simply a growing emphasis on the eschatological foreshadowing of the resurrected body in and through the fallen body.

The Fallen Body in Donne's Early Work

In examining Donne's early writing, I will first look at the few early works in which imagery from Greek philosophical traditions predominates. Turning to a consideration of more typical early works, I will examine Donne's habit of weaving together images and concepts from Hellenistic and Christian traditions to speak about the human person. Finally, I will take up some of the images that are integral to Donne's depiction of the fallen body in his preordination writings: images of death, decay, fragmentation, and dissection.

The Fall into the Body

At times, Donne draws on Greek philosophical traditions that tend toward a dualistic concept of the human soul and body. These traditions, growing from Hellenistic mystery cults as well as from the writings of such philosophers as Plato and Pythagoras, identify the human person with the soul or mind and represent the soul's entry into the body as a sort of "fall" into a lower realm. Writers who draw on this heritage often depict the body as the "grave" of the soul, or as its prison, house, or garment. Donne bases an early and unfinished poetic satire on the Pythagorean doctrine of the transmigration of souls, and he often uses Platonic imagery in many of his other preordination poems. In some, the speaker seems to espouse the ideals of Platonic love and the view of the body that goes along with it.[1] In others, the speaker undermines these Platonic ideals and revalues the body accordingly. In still other works, Donne, in common with many Christian writers through the centuries, incorporates Platonic dualism into more orthodox Christian views of the body.

When examining these early works, the reader might well hesitate before assuming that Donne actually shares the dualistic view of human nature that underlies the Greek philosophical traditions from which he borrowed some concepts and images. Except for the explicitly religious verse of this period, Donne does not employ these images to put forward a serious or coherent doctrine of the body. The body simply serves for Donne as a fruitful symbolic site for speculation on whatever is his subject at hand: society, love, grief, or fortune. Further, while some poems may sound purely Platonic, others from the same period undermine Platonic representations of the body. It is instructive, however, to observe how often Donne turns to the human body as a source of meaning and a mine of poetic imagery, as well as to observe the images he chooses from among many possible ways of representing the body.

Some of Donne's early love poems, such as "Negative Love," "Air and Angels," and "The Undertaking," speak in Platonic terms of a superior love that simply "overlooks" the body. For instance, "Negative Love" begins, "I never stooped so low, as they / Which on an eye, cheek, lip, can prey."[2] In only two of Donne's poems does his speaker takes a purely Platonic view of human nature and human love. In "The Undertaking," which in some manuscripts is entitled "Platonic Love," Donne refers to women's bodies as garments, extraneous to the true object of love. Real love is directed to the soul alone, separate from both outward appearance and gender.

> But he who loveliness within
> Hath found, all outward loathes,
> For he who colour loves, and skin,
> Loves but their oldest clothes.
> If, as I have, you also do
> Virtue attired in women see,
> And dare love that, and say so too,
> And forget the He and She.[3]

The speaker goes on to say that he has kept his love hidden from "profane eyes" because he has given it no outward expression (including, one assumes, no sexual expression).

Another poem that seems to lean toward this view of love and the body is "A Valediction Forbidding Mourning." Here the speaker removes love as far as possible from earthly and fleshly concerns. He likens the parting of the lovers to the death of virtuous men, whose souls pass quietly and without protest from their bodies.[4] Their love is "refined," not like that of "Dull sublunary lovers' love / (Whose soul is sense)."[5] Such sublunary lovers rely on the sensual since it is that which "elemented," or made up, their love. By calling their love "sublunary," Donne identifies it with the earth and with the body. In the cosmological model he uses here, the earth lies below the moon. Since the "souls" of these lovers consist only in sensation, they do not dwell in the spiritual realm above the moon, but are conflated with the earthly and the bodily. In contrast to these earthly/earthy lovers, the speaker and his mistress are "by a love, so much refined, / That our selves know not what it is, / Inter-assured of the mind, / Care less, eyes, lips, and hands to miss."[6] The speaker identifies these two lovers not with their bodies, but with their minds. Since their minds are connected, they cannot be parted.[7]

Poems like these, which take the purely Platonic view of love and of the body, are the exceptions in Donne's work. His speakers usually present the body as more integral to love and the human person. Even when Donne deploys Platonic imagery in a poem, the substance of the argument often undermines any subordination of the body to the soul. Although I will explore instances of this in a later section, one example here will serve to illustrate the point. In "The Anniversary" Donne refers to the body as the grave of the soul, a typical Platonic image: "When bodies to their graves, souls from their graves remove."[8] Yet the poem rejects the identification of the person exclusively with the soul. Playing with familiar images of the soul as the "prince" over the kingdom of the body and of death as the divorce of body and soul, Donne says,

> Two graves must hide thine and my corse,
> If one might, death were no divorce,
> Alas, as well as other princes, we,
> (Who prince enough in one another be,)
> Must leave at last in death, these eyes, and ears,
> Oft fed with true oaths, and with sweet salt tears.[9]

The two entities divorced by death here are not the soul and the body, but the bodies of the two lovers. The speaker laments that they, as other princes, must finally leave at death the kingdoms they have enjoyed in one another's bodies. Faced with the prospect of a pure and increased love between them when their souls have been removed from the "graves" of their bodies, or even with the prospect that their love will have a greater object in heaven (the beatific vision of God himself), Donne's lover does not react with Platonic joy. He prefers the life and loves of the body to the touted joys of heaven. He cries, "Here upon earth, we are kings, and none but we / Can be such kings. . . . Let us love nobly, and live, and add again / Years and years unto years."[10]

The Transmigration of Souls and the Fall into the Body

In one long, unfinished poem dating from 1601 called *Metempsychosis* or *The Progress of the Soul,* Donne uses a somewhat bizarre mixture of Platonic, Pythagorean, and Christian concepts and images to describe the relationship between souls and bodies. Employing the Pythagorean doctrine of the transmigration of souls as his basic conceit, he proposes to follow the journey of a "deathless soul" through the vagaries of its history in various bodies.[11] Although the poem is unfinished, it is clear that Donne employs the idea of the transmigration of souls both to satirize the human condition and to transfer the lesson of nature's inherent violence to (supposedly) human society.

Even though the nature and interrelationship of the body and soul are not the "point" of the piece, the images Donne chooses in this poem reveal his tendency to think of the human body in the framework of Christian salvation history. Donne forces the Pythagorean doctrine of transmigration of souls and the Christian doctrine of the fall together in the poem, even though the systems are contradictory and their juxtaposition offends both philosophical and poetic logic. Although the doctrine of transmigration of souls is clearly incompatible with Christian orthodoxy, Donne frames the portion of the poem he completed with references to the biblical story of humanity's fall from innocence. The soul's first body in the poem is that of an apple, the fateful apple in the garden of Eden. Its body thus participates in the first sin of humankind. After hundreds of lines in which the narrative follows the soul's adventures through various bodies with no reference to biblical ideas or imagery, Donne returns to the framework of salvation history at the end. He associates the last bodies that the soul inhabits (a wolf's whelp, an ape, and finally, a woman) with various significant figures: Abel, Cain, Seth, Adam, and Eve.

Throughout the poem, whether the wandering soul occupies the body of plant, bird, fish, or land animal, Donne associates all these bodies with *human* sin: lust, violence, greed, deceit, or envy. Although he does not explicitly argue for a link between the fall of humankind and the fall of nature, Donne places his narrative in the *context* of the biblical fall, and the natural world he depicts is certainly fallen.[12] Donne describes the soul's second experience in the body, after the fall of humankind, in decidedly negative terms. It descends into the earth, a "dark and foggy plot," where it takes on the "body" of a mandrake root. Significantly, according to legend, the mandrake is shaped like the body of a man and its fruit can serve as both an aphrodisiac and a contraceptive.[13] Even though the second body the soul inhabits is a plant, Donne associates it directly with the human body (because of its shape) and with human sin (lust and murder). After the soul is "unfettered" by the death of the mandrake, it is swiftly "confined," "enjailed," and "enclosed" in the small blue shell of a bird's egg. Donne depicts the resulting cocksparrow, the new and "moving inn" of the soul, as the epitome of animal lust. The sparrow, forgetting self-preservation, quickly "spends" himself in copulation, freeing the soul once again.[14] From there, the soul passes into and "informs" the body of a fish and is promptly swallowed by a swan, thus finding itself in the double prison of the fish's body and the swan's stomach.[15] The soul passes on to the bodies of other fish, a whale, a mouse, a wolf, an ape, and finally, to the body of a woman. None of these bodies are "innocent." Ironically, they are "bestial" in a specifically human sense and reflect the characteristics of fallen humanity.

This poem and the representations of the body within it are uneasy mixtures of Greek and Christian concepts and images. On one level, Donne's point seems to be that humanity, and human society, are ruled by the "animal" instincts that he associates with the bodies through which the soul passes. As is typical in the Hellenistic traditions from which Donne draws, the soul is essentially innocent. It is the passions of the body that finally degrade it. The poem is full of Platonic references to the body as a prison or temporary dwelling place. On another level, one can read the poem in the Greek tradition of the fable, in which animals serve as cover for a critique of human nature and society. The combination of this tradition with the references to the biblical story of the fall suggests that the bodies here are merely images for human sin, and that the "fallen" bodies Donne portrays are the result, rather than the cause, of humanity's predicament.

Donne often uses ideas and images from Greek philosophical traditions that suggest the "real" person consists of a soul trapped, or temporarily housed, in a human body. He uses these conventions in their "pure" form only in a few instances, in poems that draw on the tradition of Platonic love for their ideas of love and the human person. More frequently, Donne juxtaposes these "Greek" representations with images of the body taken from Judeo-Christian traditions.

The Fall from an Innocent Body

In much of Donne's preordination writing, he clearly subordinates Platonic elements in his representations of the fallen body to those which are clearly biblical. In biblical anthropology, both the human body and soul are originally innocent. Through deliberate sin, humankind ruins the original goodness of both. In one of the "Divine Meditations" written before his ordination, Donne beautifully presents the biblical view of the human person, created and fallen, using the familiar image of the person as a microcosm of the world.[16] He writes,

> I am a little world made cunningly
> Of elements, and an angelic sprite,
> But black sin hath betrayed to endless night
> My world's both parts, and, oh, both
> parts must die.[17]

Donne here refers to the creation of the human person as a little world and to the fact that sin has condemned both parts of that person (body and soul) to darkness and death. He goes on in the poem to connect the body to the rest of the trajectory of salvation history and to imply that both parts participate in redemption. The speaker's tears of repentance suggest the flood with which God cleansed the sinful world in Noah's time as well as the waters of baptism. After his world is "drowned" by tears of repentance, he realizes that this is not sufficient to cleanse it and says, "But oh it must be burnt."[18] He subtly connects the fiery zeal that he asks to eat up his sin with the fires of the apocalypse that will cleanse the world at the last day. Throughout, Donne links God's dealings with the speaker of the poem, body and soul, to God's dealings with the material and spiritual worlds of salvation history.

Even within the Christian narrative of sin and redemption, Donne sometimes uses Neoplatonic language to talk about the soul's "descent" into the body or the world. While at times maintaining the original goodness of the material creation and the body, at others he seems to shift the weight of blame for sin to the body itself. In the 1610 prose work *Pseudo-Martyr*, he says,

> ... so, till it please the Lord, and owner of our life to take home into his treasury, this rich carbuncle our soul, which gives us light in our night of ignorance, and our dark body of earth, we are still anguished and travailed, as well with a continual defensive war to preserve our life from sicknesses, and other offensive violences; as with a diverse and contrary covetousness.[19]

While the jewel of the soul and the dark earth of the body are both part of the human person and both intended for heaven, Donne identifies the soul with light even in this life, while he associates the body with darkness and with the evils of disease, violence, and greed that plague human life. In the same work, he discusses the corruption of popes through their involvement with worldly power by using an analogy of the soul and body. He says that even if popes at first were "mere souls" (i.e., wholly concerned with things of the spirit), "yet as the purest souls become stained and corrupt with sin, as soon as it touches the body," so the popes, by entering into secular concerns, have contracted all the "diseases" of the worldly condition.[20]

Even poems that at first glance seem to condemn the body invite other readings. One example is a verse letter Donne wrote to the Countess of Bedford sometime between 1607 and 1609. Using a popular tradition that linked the human mind, soul, and body to, respectively, the sun, moon, and earth, Donne at first seems to blame the body for its bad influence on the soul.

> As new philosophy arrests the sun,
> And bids the passive earth about it run,
> So we have dulled our mind, it hath no ends;
> Only the body's busy, and pretends;
> As dead low earth eclipses and controls
> The quick high moon: so doth the body, souls.
> . . . .
> Good seed degenerates, and oft obeys
> The soil's disease, and into cockle strays.
> Let the mind's thought be but transplanted so,
> Into the body, and bastardly they grow.[21]

A careful reading reveals that it is "we" who have interfered with the proper hierarchy and allowed the body to exert an improper control over the soul and the mind. The "passive" body has no business controlling those faculties that should be active for good. As the rest of the poem makes clear, the sinful soul first removed its own "inborn dignities" along with those of the body.[22] Bodies were originally "caskets of souls; temples, and palaces," and will one day be redeemed from death even as sinful souls must be. God created neither the soul nor the body "naturally" immortal, contrary to Platonic doctrine.[23] Donne goes on to say,

> As men to our prisons, new souls to us are sent,
> Which learn vice there, and come in innocent.
> First seeds of every creature are in us,
> Whate'er the world hath bad, or precious,
> Man's body can produce, hence hath it been
> That stones, worms, frogs, and snakes in man are seen:
> But who e'er saw, though nature can work so,
> That pearl, or gold, or corn in man did grow?[24]

Again, a typical Platonic interpretation of this passage would read the "prison" as the corrupt human body. The reference to stones, worm, frogs, and snakes certainly suggests that the body itself is degenerate and might corrupt anything that touches it. This metaphor relies on the folk belief that the diseased or dead human body could actually produce worms, snakes, and other evil or painful things. However, a careful reading reveals that Donne uses the traditional doctrine of man as a microcosm of the world to point out that all creatures find their referents in the human body: good and bad, gold and corn as well as frogs and snakes. It is the human will that originally corrupted the human body, although that degenerate body can in turn work deleterious effects on the soul.

In two letters to Sir Henry Goodyer, Donne expresses the idea, compatible with Platonic thought, that the soul actually gains something from its journey into the corruption of the world. In a verse letter, he says,

> [o]ur soul, whose country's heaven, and God her father,
> Into this world, corruption's sink, is sent,
> Yet, so much in her travail she doth gather,
> That she returns home, wiser than she went.[25]

In another letter to Sir Henry, Donne expresses a similar idea when he says that human nature is "meteoric," partaking of both earth and heaven, "for as our bodies glorified shall be capable of spiritual joy, so our souls demerged into those bodies, are allowed to partake earthly pleasure. Our soul is not sent hither, only to go back again: we have some errand to do here: nor is it sent into prison, because it comes innocent: and he which sent it, is just."[26]

While Donne employs the language of a "descent" into a lower world, he expresses it within the Christian framework of a good creation and heavenly fulfillment.

Donne's mixture of Platonic and Christian representations of body and soul continues in the overtly religious poems written before his ordination. In the sonnet sequence *La Corona,* Donne speaks of the incarnation as Christ's assumption of a body in order to make himself weak enough to enter our world and to die.[27] Donne associates Jesus' body and the means by which he assumes it (Mary's womb) with Platonic imagery. The womb is a "prison" and a "little room." Christ "wears" the flesh he takes from Mary, invoking the Platonic idea of the body as a garment for the soul. Yet Donne moves beyond a simply Platonic use of the images. Because both Mary and Jesus are without sin, their bodies are not evil but simply weak. Paradoxically, it is this weakness that allows Christ to assume the sins of the world and die. Donne describes the "imprisonment" of Mary's womb in a positive way. He wonders at the paradox that Mary is "Thy maker's maker, and thy father's mother, / Thou hast light in dark; and shutt'st in little room, / Immensity cloistered in thy dear womb."[28] The body is Christ's means of fulfilling his intent and calling.[29] One of the "Divine Meditations" contains another instance of this theme. Building on images of the crucifixion of Christ, the speaker cries,

> O let me then, his strange love still admire:
> Kings pardon, but he bore our punishment.
> And Jacob come clothed in vile harsh attire
> But to supplant, and with gainful intent:
> God clothed himself in vile man's flesh, that so
> He might be weak enough to suffer woe.[30]

Here the body has a double meaning. Donne describes it as a mere garment, vile and harsh, but it also becomes the means of humanity's salvation when Christ takes it upon himself.

The same ambiguity about the body applies to the speaker's own body in "A Litany." The speaker prays to the Holy Ghost,

> ... whose temple I
> Am, but of mud walls, and condensed dust,
> And being sacrilegiously
> Half wasted with youth's fires, of pride and lust,
> Must with new storms be weatherbeat;
> Double in my heart thy flame,
> Which let devout sad tears intend; and let
> (Though this glass lanthorn, flesh, do suffer maim)
> Fire, sacrifice, priest, altar be the same.[31]

Here there is only a faint echo of Platonic ideas in the dualism of the soul and body. Donne identifies the unchanging soul with the Holy Ghost and holy things, while he depicts the body as external, changing, and identified with sin. Still, the imagery is mostly Christian. Although Donne refers to the body at first as made of "mud walls and condensed dust," he associates it with God's creation through the implied reference to the story of Adam's creation out of clay. He then transforms the body into the glass of a lantern through which the reader glimpses the fire of the indwelling Holy Spirit.

In much of his preordination work, Donne uses a clearly biblical model of the human person. Even though he often incorporates Platonic attitudes and depictions into that model, he tends to subordinate any true Platonic dualism to his belief that the human person was created by God as a union of body and soul, but that both have fallen through sin. In this, he simply reflects much of the history of Christian anthropology, which has been influenced by Greek philosophy from its earliest days and yet in most cases has tried to maintain the original goodness of both the material creation and the body. Donne is particularly fascinated by the connection between the microcosm of the body and the macrocosm of the world in their fallen states and gives hints of the coming redemption of both even in his depictions of the fallen body.

Images of the Fallen Body

Although Donne's early work shifts between Platonic and Christian, secular and sacred, satirical and serious, several significant image complexes relating to the fallen body remain constant: images of ugliness, decay, fragmentation, and dissection. It is now time to take up these images and to explore their significance. With few exceptions, Donne praises neither the beauty of the human body nor the human capacity for unsullied pleasure.

In two of Donne's elegies, probably written in the 1590s, he follows a sixteenth-century fashion for poems that made fun of the Petrarchan convention of hyperbolic praise of women by celebrating instead women who were ugly or grotesque.[32] In "The Anagram," the speaker addresses a friend who is about to marry an ugly woman. He urges him to go ahead with the marriage, since "she / Hath all things, whereby others beauteous be, / For, though her eyes be small, her mouth is great, / Though they be ivory, yet her teeth are jet."[33] The speaker goes on to say that love built on beauty dies as soon as the beauty that inspires it dies, but this woman is so ugly now, she will not change for the worse in old age. In "The Comparison," the speaker compares the sweat of his mistress with that of a friend's mistress.[34] Although the speaker ostensibly praises his own beloved, the very few words he accords her body are ambiguous at best. The very fact that the speaker chooses sweat as the basis for comparison and that he represents his lover's sweat not only as pearls and sweet perfume, but as "that which from chafed musk cat's pores doth trill," places her body as a vehicle for base lust. His description of his friend's mistress is not at all ambiguous. He likens her sweat, and the lust associated with it, to the issue of menstruous boils, scum, and warts. He then moves on to describe the bodies of both his "friend" and his friend's mistress in grotesque terms: unfinished statues, graves, carrots, envenomed sores.

Most of Donne's poems in which the speaker describes his own mistress represent the female body in some state of decay, through age, illness, or death. In "The Autumnal," Donne's speaker is fascinated with aging beauty and with decay. In a poem filled with references that associate the aging body with graves, tombs, and the resurrection, he says that he would "rather stay / With tombs, than cradles, to wear out a day / . . . Not panting after growing beauties, so, / I shall ebb out with them, who homeward go."[35] He writes some poems about the literal death, or impending death, of the beloved, and he writes many using death as a metaphor for a parting that is as bitter as death. The death of the body and the "divorce" of body and soul disrupt the proper union of the lovers. "The Dissolution" deals with the literal death of the speaker's beloved. He notes that all the dead dissolve into their "first elements": earth, air, fire, water.[36] Since they were united and were "elements of each other," their bodies were one. When the dead woman's body begins to dissolve into its elements, her lover's body receives them. This overabundance of bodily "elements" results in the growth of passion, grief, and despair. Another of Donne's poems that deals with the death of a lover is the chilling "A Nocturnal upon St. Lucy's Day." The speaker describes how his love for his now dead mistress actually created him, alchemically making something of his previous nothingness.[37] When they were absent from each other, their souls withdrew and made them both carcasses.[38] The dead body, the carcass resulting from the soul's departure, is an image Donne often uses to express the disruption of the union of lovers through absence or death.[39] With her literal death, he is worse than a carcass. He has reverted to the state in which love found him: he is nothing.

When one of Donne's poetic personae refers to his own body, he most frequently uses images of a bodily fragmentation through separation, torture, or dissection. Such images of bodily fragmentation not only express the pain of love, but evoke a larger, fallen world of pain, deceit, lust, and false passion in which Donne's small dramas play themselves out. For instance, in "The Blossom," a man is about to leave a cold and unresponsive woman whom he loves, but his unruly heart wants to stay with her. The heart addresses its owner thus:

> Alas, if you must go, what's that to me?
> Here lies my business, and here I will stay:
> You go to friends, whose love and means present
> Various content
> To your eyes, ears, and tongue, and every part.
> If then your body go, what need you a heart?[40]

The man tells the heart that it is making a sad mistake, since "a naked thinking heart, that makes no show, / Is to a woman, but a kind of ghost."[41] Since she does not have a heart herself, she would not recognize his heart for what it is. The speaker implies that she has use for only one part of a man (the penis), and doesn't have the capacity for recognizing any other. He ends with a plea to his heart to go with him, since he would like to give it "to another friend, whom we shall find / As glad to have my body, as my mind."[42] In this poem, Donne expresses the "fallen" state of love in the world of the courtier through his images of a fragmented body. In that world, love and lust have come uncoupled. Hearts, minds, and bodies (and thus love, intellect, and desire) do not live in a natural unity, although the speaker ends the poem with a hope of unity through a redemptive love.

Two other poems that express the pain and violence of love through images of the fragmentation of the suitor's body are "The Legacy" and "The Message." In "The Legacy," the speaker "dies" when he leaves his love.[43] He attempts to send her his heart as a "legacy," but when he rips himself open to reach it, he finds it gone. He has already exchanged hearts with his beloved, and what he finds inside himself are some cold and artificial fragments of "something like a heart." She has betrayed him and divided her heart with others. In "The Message," the straying body parts (his eyes and his heart) are corrupted by their contact with his false love, and he refuses to take them back again. The eyes learn "forced fashions and false passion" by looking on her, and her faithless heart has taught his to be just as flippant and deceitful.[44] Donne exploits these images of disparate pieces of bodies to satirize conventional love poetry, which praised the isolated body parts of the poet's mistress: lips like cherries, eyes like stars, and so forth. But Donne's twisting of this convention has both a bitter edge and a more developed point. Donne uses images of fragmented bodies to condemn the kind of love that will not accept the whole person, body and soul, in a faithful relationship.

In three other poems, Donne employs as a central image a specific form of bodily fragmentation that fascinated him throughout his life: medical dissection. In "The Damp," the speaker suffers death because of the rejection of his cruel lover. He pictures his body being "anatomized" by his doctors at the request of his friends, curious to know the cause of death.[45] When the anatomists reach his heart, they find a picture of his cruel beloved engraved there. This reference to the anatomists finding a picture engraved on the heart is a backhanded reference to the practice of cutting up saintly or royal personages to find signs and omens in their internal organs. These holy signs (things like crosses made of ligaments found in the heart) gave evidence of sanctity and inspired and blessed the observers. In this case, all of the onlookers, seeing the false beloved's image graven on the dead man's heart, are struck by the same plague that killed him, "a sudden damp of love" that kills them all. The cruel mistress becomes responsible not just for the speaker's murder, but for the "massacre" of all his friends. The theme is the same here as the preceding poem, but Donne expresses it in even more violent images. By refusing to take his body in sexual love, his lover not only kills him, but is responsible for the fragmentation of his body through dissection and, further, for the deaths of all his friends through a plague of desire. The same image of violent dissection appears in the poem "Love's Exchange." Here the speaker has resisted love's first attempt on him.

> For this Love is enraged with me,
> Yet kills not. If I must example be
> To future rebels; if th'unborn
> Must learn, by my being cut up, and torn:
> Kill, and dissect me, Love; for this
> Torture against thine own end is,
> Racked carcasses make ill anatomies.[46]

Here Donne plays with the conventions of the practice of anatomy, for which criminals were favorite subjects. Doctors and observers alike believed that the "sacrifice" of the bodies of wrongdoers to the cause of science in part expiated their sins. Tortured criminals were not favored subjects for anatomy demonstrations, however, since too much damage had already been done to their bodies. The speaker in this poem is willing to atone for his transgression by being anatomized, but suggests that love quit torturing him and go ahead and kill him before he is too damaged to be of any use as an instructional tool.

In the third poem that uses the image of medical anatomy, "A Valediction of My Name in the Window," the speaker carves his name in the glass of his beloved's window so that she will remember him while he is gone from her. The "ragged, bony name" that he scratches in the glass becomes his "ruinous anatomy," the demonstration of his fragmentation caused by being removed from his love.[47] He is "torn apart" by the parting from her. His soul is "emparadised" in her and no longer travels with his body. His skeleton—the name carved in the window—also remains with her. His other parts (muscles, sinews, and veins) travel with him. His "scattered body" will be recompacted only with his return to her, an image that obliquely reflects Donne's fascination with the recompaction of the scattered bodies of the redeemed at the final resurrection of the dead. If she is unfaithful to him, he will not be able to reunite the parts, and he will die.[48]

Images of the fragmentation, death, and dissolution of the body also play a large part in the early poetry Donne wrote on more explicitly religious themes. In these poems, Donne uses images of the death and fragmentation of the body to refer to the results of sin in the world and in the (still living) individual person.[49] On the most fundamental level, Donne sees the literal death of the body as a consequence of sin. In one of the "Divine Meditations," he explicitly says that "black sin" has betrayed both parts of his little world, body and soul, to death.[50] In other poems in the "Divine Meditations," Donne portrays the consequences of sin for both body and soul through images in which sin occasions the illness, decay, and even rape of the body.[51] In "A Litany," Donne employs images of the created, ruined, and resurrected body to represent his fallen soul and to plead for its rehabilitation short of the grave. He calls on the Father who made him to come "and re-create me, now grown ruinous: / My heart is by dejection, clay, / And by self-murder, red."[52] The speaker places his plea to God to redeem him from sin in the context of God's original re-creation of the world. As is almost habitual with Donne, the background for this poem is the connection between the world and the human person. God created both, but the speaker is now ruined by sin and needs re-creation. His reference to his heart as red earth is double-edged. It acknowledges his sinfulness (dejection and self-murder) while subtly reminding God that he originally created humankind from just such red clay.[53] Thus evoking God's creation of the world and of humankind, the speaker pleads for his own remaking. In this poem, as in several others, Donne presents not just the fallen body but the whole trajectory of the body in salvation history. Living in a fallen state (expressed through images of a fallen body), the speaker looks back to God's creation of humanity and forward to redemption and (bodily) resurrection ("that new fashioned / I may rise up from death, before I am dead").[54] This is typical of Donne's early work. Although his "present" body is fallen, he tends to evokes its creation and redemption within his representations of its fragmented reality.

The Fallen Body in the Sermons

Essentially the same fallen body permeates Donne's sermons. I will bring many of the same ideas and images from Donne's early work into the context of the sermons: microcosm, hierarchy, disease, decay, death, and fragmentation. The significant difference between his earlier and later work is not in his theology of the fallen body or in the images he uses to depict it. Rather, it lies in a shift in emphasis that will become apparent only in the context of the next two chapters. Paradoxically, although his depictions of the sinful, dying, putrefying, and fragmented body grow more powerful in the sermons and the "present" body remains fallen, Donne's evocation of the eschatological promise of a redeemed and glorious body in and through the fallen body also grows more powerful. Donne hints at this theme in his early work, but it is only later that he rhetorically resurrects the fallen, dying body in the present moment of his preaching.

Doctrines of the Fallen Body

Donne owes much of his theology of the fallen body to Augustine and often quotes him directly on this subject. Even when he does not give Augustine credit, most of Donne's ideas about original sin, the role of the body in the fall, and the consequences of the fall for the human person echo *The City of God* (books 13 and 14) and *The Grace of Christ and Original Sin*. Like Augustine, Donne insists that the human body was originally innocent and did not carry the seeds of damnation in itself. Humanity's willful turn away from God corrupted the body. Donne believes that the human body is God's good creation. God crafts the human body out of the substances he used to make the cosmos: earth, air, fire, and water. In a reference to these elements, which are identified in human beings as the humors, Donne points out that the devil had no hand in making up the body.

> The Devil did not create me, nor bring materials to my creation; the Devil did not infuse into me, that choler, that makes me ignorantly and indiscreetly zealous, nor that phlegm that chokes me with a stupid indevotion; he did not infuse into me that blood, that inflames me in licentiousness, nor that melancholy that damps me in a jealousy and suspicion, a diffidence and distrust in God. The Devil had no hand in composing me in my constitution. But the Devil knows, which of these govern, and prevail in me, and ministers such temptations, as are most acceptable to me.[55]

Donne also follows Augustine in his belief that the root of the fall of humankind was not in the body but the will, which turned away from God to self.[56] He echoes Augustine in his insistence that this "original" sin infected all of humankind.

> For though original sin seems to be contracted without our will, yet *Sicut omnium natura, ita omnium voluntates fuere originaliter in Adam*, says S. Augustine, As the whole nature of mankind, and so of every particular man, was in Adam, so also were the faculties, and so the will of every particular man in him[,] so this death hath invaded every particular man.[57]

Like Augustine, Donne says that human beings are conceived in sin, since the act through which they are generated is sinful. Further, they come under the taint of original sin in the very instant of becoming human, when body and soul are joined in the moment of generation, since it was human nature itself that was corrupted by Adam and Eve.[58]

While Donne again agrees with Augustine that the fall corrupts the human body, subjecting it to sin and death, he departs from his mentor in one significant respect. While Augustine seems concerned only with making clear that all of human nature was altered for the worse by the fall, Donne takes care to maintain that the *separate* substances of both body and soul are still innocent after the fall. Since they take on the burden of original sin the moment they are joined in the generation of an actual human being, this might seem a distinction without a difference. For example, Augustine says,

> God created man aright, for God is the author of nature.... But man was willingly perverted and justly condemned, and so begot perverted and condemned offspring. For we were all in that one man, seeing that we all *were* that one man.... We did not yet possess forms individually created and assigned to us for us to live in them as individuals; but there already existed the seminal nature from which we were to be begotten. And of course, when this was vitiated through sin, and bound with death's fetters in its just condemnation, man could not be born of man in any other condition.[59]

In another passage, Augustine maintains that although the first humans were made from the (innocent) dust of the earth, later offspring were "made" by their parents out of already corrupted flesh.[60] Donne, on the other hand, wants to maintain the innocence of *each* individual body, indeed, of human flesh as a whole.[61] He agrees with Augustine that human beings are conceived in sin but insists that "there was no sin in that substance of which we were made; for if there had been . . . that substance might be damn'd, though God should never infuse a soul into it; and that cannot be well said."[62] He maintains here, and in other places in the sermons, that the soul and the body are both innocent yet come under the taint of original sin at the moment of their union into a human person.[63] However innocent the material and spiritual substances that originally made up the human person, however, Donne agrees with Augustine that original sin had the inevitable effect of corrupting both body and soul.

The Fallen Body and the Macrocosm

Just as Donne represents the created human person, body and soul, as the microcosm of the created order, so also does he relate the fall of that human person to a fall of the macrocosm. Humanity through its sin disrupted the whole ordering of creation precisely because that ordering is centered on the human person. While Donne often exploits the popular seventeenth-century doctrine of the decay of nature as a *metaphor* for human sin, he does not argue that the macrocosm simply partook in and reflected the fall of the microcosm. The closest he comes to claiming a direct causal link between the sin of humanity and nature's decline is in an early sermon preached at Lincoln's Inn. There he says, "Sin hath cast a curse upon all the creatures of the world, they are all worse than they were at first."[64] In a later sermon he explains the decay of nature through the Genesis account of God's curse of the earth as a direct punishment for human sin, while using the metaphorical parallel between the human body and the earth.

> Our bodies, of themselves, if they had no souls, have no disposition to any evil; yet, these bodies which are but instruments, must burn in hell. The earth was accursed for man's sin, though the earth had not been so much as an instrument of his sin; only, because it was, after, to conduce to the punishment of his children, it was accursed, God withdrew his love from it.[65]

Yet in other places in the sermons he implies that only humanity is fallen and that the other creatures are still innocent. In one such sermon, he says,

> There is no creature but man that degenerates willingly from his natural Dignity: Those degrees of goodness, which God imprinted in them at first, they preserve still, As God saw they were good then, so he may see they are good still; They have kept their Talent, They have not bought nor sold; They have not gained nor lost; they are not departed from their native and natural dignity, by any thing that they have done.[66]

The crux of Donne's views about the relationship between human sin and the disruption of the natural order may lie in the meeting of his Renaissance concentration on man as the measure of all things with his deep Augustinianism. In a sermon preached early in his career at Lincoln's Inn on the text from Psalm 38, "There is no soundness in my flesh because of thine anger" (v. 3), he interprets flesh in many ways, from the microcosm of the individual body to the macrocosm of the universe. In this sermon, Donne makes a subtle point about the "fall" of nature.

> Take flesh in the largest extent and signification, that may be, as Moses calls God, *The God of the spirits of all flesh,* that is, of the being of all Creatures, and take all the Creatures to be ours in that Donation *Subjicite & dominamini, Subdue, and rule all Creatures,* yet there is not soundness in our flesh, for, all these Creatures are corrupted, and become worse than they were, (to us) by the sin of Adam.[67]

The crucial words here are the parenthesized "to us." Donne does not claim here that the sin of humanity corrupted the substance and being of nature in itself. Rather, because humanity through its sin has lost its rightful dominion over nature, nature in relationship to humanity loses its proper place and character. Shadowing this passage are Augustine's ideas about the right use of creatures. In Augustine's thought, humanity lost dominion over both the body and "creatures." Since sinful humanity can neither perceive nor use nature as God originally intended, it is effectively corrupted and corrupting. Quoting Pope Leo, Donne says,

> *Mentis principatus in peccato obliviscimur;* we resign, we disavow that sovereignty, which God hath given us, when we sin. God spake not only of the beasts of the forest, but of those beasts, that is, those brutish affections, that are in us, when he said, *Subjicite & dominamini,* subdue, and govern the world; and in sinning we lose this dominion over our selves, and forfeit our dominion over the creature too.[68]

By "displacing" itself, humanity has taken away from nature "that which is the Jewel at the chain, that which is the burden of the Song, Man himself."[69]

Sin overthrows all the proper hierarchies: God over the human person, soul over body, humanity over nature. Before the fall, God is sovereign over humanity; after the fall, humanity is under the dominion of Satan.[70] Donne particularly represents the body as the property of Satan in this life, subject to the pain, sickness, death, and corruption that are the wages of sin. In one sermon he says, "The Kingdom of Christ, which must be perfected . . . is not yet perfected, not accomplished yet. Why? What lacks it? It lacks the bodies of men, which yet lie under the dominion of another."[71] Where once the body obeyed the dictates of the individual soul, it is now in rebellion.

Through its sin, humankind loses its proper place in the middle of the hierarchy of being. Since the soul no longer controls the body, human beings descend to the level of animals. In a sermon on Psalm 32:9 ("Be ye not as the horse, or as the mule, which have no understanding"), Donne argues that human beings should keep their proper place in the ontological order. That place is one of dignity, since God "imprinted" humankind with his image at creation and put on that nature in his own incarnation.[72] Humanity has turned from its own nature, descending down the great chain of being and grovelling in the dirt with beasts.

The Effects of Sin on the Body

Humanity's willful abnegation of spiritual sovereignty has direct and devastating consequences for the body. In a Whitsunday sermon, Donne describes these effects.

> As original sin hath relation to our souls, It is called that indelible foulness, and uncleanness which God discovers in us all. . . . As it hath relation to our bodies, so it is not only called *Lex carnis,* A law which the flesh cannot disobey, and *Lex in membris,* A law written and imprinted naturally in our bodies, and inseparably inherent there, but it is a law that hath got *Posse comitatus,* All our strength, and munition into her own hands, all our powers, and faculties to execute her purposes against us, and (As the Apostle expresses it fully) *hath force in our members, to bring forth fruits unto death.*[73]

No longer under the control of the law of God, the body wars with the soul, attempting to tyrannize over it and lead it astray.[74] Donne agrees with Augustine that the penis is the most rebellious part of man and that humanity's lack of control over it is a mark of the fall. In one sermon he quotes Augustine, "*Ad hominis inobedientiam redarguendam, sua inobedientia quodammodo caro testimonium perhibit,* to reproach Man's rebellion to God, God hath left one part of Man's body, to rebel against him."[75] He also quotes St. Bernard, saying that "though the seeds of this rebellion be dispersed through the body, yet, *In illa parte magis regnat additamentum Leviathan* . . . the spawn of Leviathan, the seed of sin . . . abounds and reigns most in that part of the body."[76] That reign of sin has particular consequences for the body. First, the fallen body has a propensity to commit actual sins. Second, the body suffers the "manifold encumbrances of these mortal bodies" that result from original and actual sin.[77] Third, and most significant for Donne, the body is subject to death and dissolution.

The fallen body, cut off from the control of a righteous soul, becomes corrupt and gives rise to actual sins such as lust, gluttony, and sloth. As he said in one sermon, "Man carries the spawn and seed and eggs of affliction in his own flesh, and his own thoughts make haste to hatch them, and bring them up."[78] Donne here invokes the belief, common in his time, that a dead body generated the maggots and serpents that in turn devoured it. He uses the image to vividly portray the body that is dead in sin. He speaks elsewhere of the "artificial flesh" people add to their frames through gluttony as the "daughter of sins . . . punishment of former sins and the occasion of future."[79] Although Donne believes that the *substance* of the body is innocent, he represents the *actual* human body as corrupt. He is careful to lay equal blame on the soul and often depicts it leading the body into sin, while also acknowledging that the body can drag down the soul and tempt it to sin.

Both actual and original sin are responsible for the many "encumbrances" the body suffers in this life: labor, pain, deformity, injury, and illness. Although Donne discusses all these results of the fall in his sermons, it is illness that most captures his imagination as a way to talk about the wages of sin.[80] Donne speaks of the relationship between sin and illness in three ways. First, illness is the direct result of the loss of immortality in the garden of Eden. Donne agrees with Augustine that even before the fall, human beings were "passible," not static in perfection, but needing to sleep and eat to sustain life. However, human beings were made to be immortal. Sickness, with its pain and possibility of death, was punishment for the fall. Donne often dramatically focuses on illness as a sign of humanity's state after the fall. Donne says that "God created man in health, but health continued but a few hours, and sickness hath had the Dominion 6000 years," continuing with a long discussion of the miseries of illness and its power over humanity.[81] "In every part of the body death can find a door, or make a breach," says Donne, "mortal diseases breed in every part."[82] In a later sermon, Donne described himself, a fallen person, as "a volume of diseases bound up together."[83]

Second, individuals bring specific illnesses on themselves through the practice of actual sins, such as lust and gluttony.[84] In a 1625 Easter sermon, Donne says,

> No man ever hated his own body; and yet, no outward enemy is able so to macerate our body as our own licentiousness. Christ, who took all our bodily infirmities upon him, hunger, and thirst, and sweat, and cold, took no bodily deformities upon him, he took not a lame, a blind, a crooked body; and we, by our intemperance, and licentiousness, deform that body which is his, all these ways.[85]

Donne often says that many illnesses and diseases can be traced, if the sufferers were honest with themselves, to specific sins that directly brought on the trouble.

Third, God sends illnesses directly as punishments for sin or as "chastisements" for the good of the sufferer.[86] God punishes humanity not only for original sin, but for particular sins.[87] In one sermon, Donne uses the story of the healing of the paralytic to assert that Christ taught "that sins were the true causes of all bodily diseases."[88] He then lays out several reasons God may send an illness to a particular person: purging, punishment, humiliation, trial, and for his own glory in their removal.

Donne fixes on death as the most devastating and most resonant result of the fall. It encapsulates the consequences of the fall and serves as the ultimate metaphor for expressing all the losses that the fall entails. Donne implies that in his use of metaphor he is following the example of the "metaphorical God," the God who loves to use metaphors in his actions and his Word. Preaching at the royal residence of Whitehall in 1621, Donne says that God metaphorically hammers home the fact that death permeates humanity's fallen state through some typological symbols.

> As soon as we were clothed by God, our very apparel was an emblem of death. In the skins of dead beasts, he covered the skins of dying men. As soon as God set us on work, our very occupation was an emblem of death; it was to dig the earth ... graves for our selves.... We die every day, and we die all the day long; and because we are not absolutely dead, we call that an eternity, an eternity of dying: And is there comfort in that state? Why, that is the state of hell itself, eternal dying, and not dead.[89]

In his last sermon, Donne quotes from 2 Corinthians 5:6, "Whilst we are in the body, we are but in a pilgrimage, and we are absent from the Lord." He glosses Paul's words by saying, "He [the Apostle] might have said dead, for this whole world is but an universal church-yard, but our common grave."[90] Although death is but the final consequence of humanity's fall, it serves Donne as a synecdoche of all of humanity's fallen life.

Donne sees death first in the traditional juridical sense as direct punishment from God for humanity's disobedience. However, he is more interested in its ontological effects: the overturning of hierarchies and the loss of identity. He adheres to the traditional view that God created human beings to be immortal. Death is a punishment for, or at least a direct consequence of, Adam and Eve's original disobedience. Donne often quotes Romans 6:23, where Paul says that death is the "reward" of sin.[91] He says that if humanity had not sinned in Adam, we would have "had our transmigration from this to the other world, without any mortality, and corruption at all."[92] Although death is the punishment for sin and evidence of God's wrath, humanity "created" it. "Death then is from our selves, it is our own," Donne says, "but the executioner is from God."[93] He quotes Tertullian to the effect that everyone who dies "kills himself, and sin is his sword."[94] In another sermon, he refers to Augustine's statement, "*Ne permittas Domine quod non fecisti, dominar Creaturae quam fecisti* (suffer not O lord, death, whom thou didst not make, to have dominion over me whom thou didst)," to support the point that God did not "make" death but that he has "taken death into the number of his servants, and made Death his Commissioner to punish sin."[95]

Death is not simply a juridical punishment, however. Rather, it flows from a profound ontological change in the human person. This ontological change and its consequences are not obviated even by the death of Christ and the salvation of the soul. Appropriately using legal language when addressing a congregation of lawyers at Lincoln's Inn, Donne says that even the saints of God are not protected from death, that "upon that part of the sentence . . . 'To dust thou shalt return,' there is no *non obstante*; though thou turn to God, thou must turn into the grave; for, he that redeemed thee from the other death [the eternal death of the soul], redeemed not himself from this."[96] In a later sermon, he makes a similar legal point, saying that "the temporary, the natural death, God never takes away from us, he never pardons that punishment, because he never takes away the sin that occasioned it, which is original sin."[97]

For Donne, death represents the upsetting of created hierarchies on the microcosmic level of the individual human composite and on the macrocosmic levels of society and cosmos. On the microcosmic level, death is the most radical result of the soul's loss of its natural dominion over the body. Not only is death the *result* of the divorce of the body and soul in sin, but it in itself represents the most radical divorce of these two partners that were married by God in creation.[98]

Donne habitually uses a metaphorical continuum in which the insults to the body of violence and illness on the way *toward* death blend symbolically into the coming separation of soul and body and the dissolution of the body *in* death. The whole continuum stands for sin's overturning of created hierarchies. Because of sin, neither the "husband" soul nor the Father God can protect the vulnerable body. Instead, in this fallen world, "a bullet will ask a man, where's your arm; and a wolf will ask a woman, where's your breast? A sentence in the Star Chamber will ask him, where's your ear, and a months close prison will ask him, where's your flesh? A fever will ask him, where's your red, and a morphew will ask him, where's your white?"[99]

This passage holds up for inspection a human body disintegrating even while alive. Donne presents the reality of the human body in the clutches of the destructive forces of evil, the consequences of sin. Using the metaphorical continuum of loss of control, he pictures himself on his deathbed.

> When I lie under the hands of that enemy [Death], that hath reserved himself to the last, to my last bed ... when I shall be able to stir no limb in any other measure than a fever or a palsy shall shake them, when everlasting darkness shall have an inchoation in the present dimness of mine eyes, and the everlasting gnashing in the present chattering of my teeth, and the everlasting worm in the present gnawing of the agonies of my body ... when he hath sported himself with my misery upon that stage, my death-bed, shall shift the scene, and throw me from that bed, into the grave, and there triumph over me, God knows, how many generations, till the Redeemer, my Redeemer, the Redeemer of all me, body, as well as soul, come again.[100]

Here Donne skillfully uses the loss of control over the body in sickness, which he believes is a direct result of sin, to "prophesy" the loss of control of death, where Satan will control the passive body.

This passage suggests the more macrocosmic reversal of hierarchies: the usurpation by Satan of God's proper reign and right over the human body. In an anniversary sermon commemorating the death of a parishioner, Donne uses the text Genesis 3:14, "And dust shalt thou eat all the days of thy life." He interprets the dust here to mean the dead bodies of humankind. Although Satan cannot have the souls of the redeemed, "that body, which for all the precious ransom, and the rich and large mercy of the Messias, must die, that dust is left to the Serpent, to Satan, that is, to that dissolution, and that putrification, which he hath induced upon man in death."[101] In a related image, Donne personifies Death itself as the enemy of God. He preached a sermon before the royal court at Whitehall in March of 1621 on the text from 1 Corinthians 15:26, "The last enemy that shall be destroyed is death." In that sermon, he argues that Christ's kingdom is not perfect because it lacks the bodies of men, which "yet lie under the dominion of another."[102] That enemy is death,

> an enemy that may thus far think himself equal to God, that as no man ever saw God, and lived; so no man ever saw this enemy and lived . . . and in this may think himself in number superior to God, that many men live who shall never see God; But . . . [quoting Ps 89:48] "is there any man that lives, and shall not see death?" An enemy that is so well victualled against man, as that he cannot want as long as there are men, for he feeds upon man himself. . . . We have other enemies; Satan about us, sin within us; but the power of both those, this enemy shall destroy; but when they are destroyed he shall retain a hostile, and triumphant dominion over us.[103]

Satan's dominion of the human body is highly unnatural and runs counter to God's design and intent for the body in creation. God's desire to reclaim those bodies will lend impetus to the whole of the trajectory of salvation history as it moves forward toward the climax of bodily resurrection.

The sin of humanity further upsets the cosmic hierarchy by disrupting the great chain of being. God made the human person to be the linchpin of the material and spiritual realms. The body's upright posture signifies that place and God's intention that humanity lift the material realm into the higher ordering of the spirit through proper control. Donne observes that death, in which the body literally falls to the ground, signifies the lack of control and upsetting of the cosmic hierarchy.

> Doth not that body that boasted but yesterday of that privilege above all creatures, that it only could go upright, lie today as flat upon the earth as the body of a horse, or of a dog? And doth it not tomorrow lose his other privilege, of looking up to heaven? Is it not farther removed from the eye of heaven, the sun, than any dog, or horse, by being covered with the earth, which they are not? Painters have presented to us with some horror, the skeleton, the frame of the bonds of a man's body; but the state of a body, in the dissolution of the grave, no pencil can present to us. Between that excremental jelly that thy body is made of at first, and that jelly which thy body dissolves to at last; there is not so noisome, so putrid a thing in nature.[104]

Death upsets not only the cosmic hierarchy, but the social hierarchy ordained by God. Death erases proper differences and distinctions of rank and position. As Donne puts it in an early sermon, "To the destroying of skin and body by worms, all men are equal; thus far all's common law, and no prerogative."[105] Donne, a loyal monarchist and a great striver after social position himself, is fascinated and disturbed by the way death obliterated distinctions of position, wealth, rank, gender, and kinship. He returns frequently in his sermons to variations on this theme. One of the most eloquent is the Lenten sermon he preached before the king in 1630, the last sermon of his life. I quote here a long passage to give the reader the full flavor of Donne's passionate eloquence and of the anxious preoccupation that seems to haunt the theme for him.

> For us that die now and sleep in the state of the dead, we must all pass this posthumous death, this death after death, nay this death after burial, this dissolution after dissolution, this death of corruption and putrification, of vermiculation and incineration, of dissolution and dispersion in and from the grave. When those bodies that have been the children of royal parents, and the parents of royal children, must say with Job, to corruption "thou art my father," and to the worm "thou art my mother and my sister." Miserable riddle, when the same worm must be my mother, and my sister, and my self. Miserable incest, when I must be married to my mother and my sister . . . beget, and bear that worm which is all that miserable penury; when my mouth shall be filled with dust, and the worm shall feed, and feed sweetly upon me, when the ambitious man shall have no satisfaction, if the poorest alive tread upon him, nor the poorest receive any contentment in being made equal to Princes, for they shall be equal but in dust. . . . Even those bodies that were the temples of the holy Ghost, come to this dilapidation, to ruin, to rubbish, to dust. . . . That the Monarch, who spread over many nations alive must in his dust lie in a corner . . . and that private and retired man, that though himself his own for ever, and never came forth, must in his dust of the grave be published, and . . . be mingled in his dust, with the dust of every highway and ever dunghill. . . . This is the most inglorious and contemptible vilification, the most deadly and peremptory nullification of man, that we can consider.[106]

Underlying these themes of the scattering and putrification of the human body in death, the overturning of hierarchies, and the loss of rank and place, is the threat of the loss of personal identity in death. Donne fixes on the metaphor of dust as the end result of all the ravages and insults of sin, illness, and death. In sermon after sermon, Donne presents his congregation with vivid pictures of the putrification and fragmentation of the dead body. It is not enough for Donne to say we die. He follows, fascinated, the gradual atomization of the human body in the grave until all that is left is dust, which is then blown by the winds and mingled with the dirt of the road. Death blows human identity into fragments. It not only separates the human body and soul from each other, rending the composite that makes a person by definition human, but it reduces the body into unidentifiable and unrecognizable dust: all marks of individuality, even of gender and rank, are gone.[107] Donne pursues this theme in an early sermon at Lincoln's Inn on the text from Job 19:26, "And though after my skin worms destroy this body, yet in my flesh shall I see God." He points out that the word "destroy" used here "is a word of as heavy a signification, to express an utter abolition, and annihilation, as perchance can be found in all the Scriptures." He exhorts his congregation with the prediction, "Thy skin and thy body shall be ground away, trod away upon the ground. . . . Dust upon the Kings highway, and dust upon the Kings grave, are both, or neither, Dust Royal, and may change places; who knows the revolutions of dust?"[108] Such exhortations served to remind his congregations that not only their lives but their very identity and integrity as persons lie not in their own will, but wholly in the mind and will of God.

Of course, Donne does not leave himself or his listeners in the humiliation of that dust. The text from Job continues, as does Donne's whole theology, "Yet in my flesh shall I see God." It is important to Donne to be able to say, "I, as I am the same man, made up of the same body, and the same soul" shall rise, that "Ego, I, I the same body, and the same soul, shall be recompact again, and be identically, numerically, individually the same man. . . . I shall be all there, my body, and my soul, and all my body and all my soul."[109] Donne finally sees the "utter annihilation" of death as the necessary gateway to the resurrection.[110] The fragmentation of the human body into dust is simply the lowest point in the circle God is drawing with his great compass. He will complete that circle. Donne always reminds his congregations that death is "a descent with an ascension: Our grave is upward."[111] It is to that upward trajectory of the body that I turn in the next two chapters.

Conclusion

Donne's work, early and late, reflects a pervasive sense of the disruption of soul, body, and cosmos that flowed from the fall of humanity and the ravages of sin. The fall overturns the natural, created order in which the body was subject to the control and the life-giving sustenance of God and soul. The results for the body are disorder, disease, pain, death, and dissolution. Although these marks of the fall are devastating, they are not the terminus of human life. The fallen body places a natural limit on human pride and pretension, but not on God's power and love. The body's frailties and dissolution are powerful signs, if they are read correctly, of the perils of the soul and the need for God. It is at this nadir that the trajectory of salvation history turns upward.

Notes

1. What I refer to here as "Platonic" notions of love and the body were well-established conventions that had come to be identified with Plato and his followers. These "disembodied" notions do not necessarily reflect Plato's own writings on *eros* and the body.
2. John Donne, *John Donne: The Complete English Poems,* ed. A. J. Smith (London: Penguin Books, 1971), 71, lines 1–2.
3. Ibid., 83, lines 13–20.
4. Ibid., 83, lines 1–4.
5. Ibid., lines 13–14.
6. Ibid., lines 17–20.
7. Ibid., lines 21–36.
8. Ibid., 42, line 20.
9. Ibid., lines 11–16.
10. Ibid., lines 23–29.
11. In the epistle to the reader with which he prefaces the poem, Donne notes that "the Pythagorean doctrine doth not only carry one soul from man to man, nor man to beast, but indifferently to plants also: and therefore you must not grudge to find the same soul in an emperor, in a post-horse, and in a mushroom" (ibid., 176).
12. Whether drawing on Greek or Christian traditions, Donne never represents nature as innocent, or as itself a proper guide for human behavior. In *Paradoxes and Problems,* Paradox IV, he argues, "Nature is our worst guide." Contrary to received opinion, he maintains that nature should not be the guide of human conduct since she is a creature like us. What is "natural" for the human being he either connects with sin (saying that lust and anger are "natural" to humans) or with the degradations of the body (6). The reader can interpret his statements about the body in this argument through either a Christian or a Platonic lens. He says that our inclinations cannot guide us, since "alas, how unable a guide is that which follows the temperature of our slimy bodies?" (6). He goes on to say that "our complexions and whole bodies we inherit from parents, our inclinations and minds follow that. For our mind is heavy with our bodies afflictions, and rejoiceth in the bodies pleasure: How then shall this nature govern us, which is governed by the worst part of us? Nature though we chase it away will return. 'Tis true: but those good motions and inspirations which be our guides, must be wooed and courted, and welcomed or else they abandon us" (7). This same argument, that human beings must overcome both the body and nature, appears in the long tract Donne wrote on suicide, *Biathanatos*.
13. Donne, *Poems,* 182–83, lines 120–50.
14. Ibid., 183–84, lines 181–209.
15. Ibid., 184–85, lines 231–42.
16. In her edition of *Divine Poems,* Helen Gardner makes a convincing case that the poem, although not published until 1635, was written before Donne's ordination, and suggests a date between 1609 and the first half of 1611. (*John Donne: The Divine Poems,* 2nd ed. (Oxford: Clarendon Press, 1978), xxxvii–lv, 74–75.
17. Ibid., 310, lines 1–4.
18. Ibid., 311, lines 10–15.

19. John Donne, *Pseudo-Martyr*, ed. Anthony Raspa (Montreal: McGill-Queens University Press, 1993), 2.
20. Ibid., 25.
21. Donne, *Poems*, "To the Countess of Bedford ('To have written then')," 228, lines 37–40, 49–52. The dating for the poem is suggested by Smith, 549.
22. Ibid., lines 53–55.
23. Ibid., lines 56–58.
24. Ibid., lines 59–66.
25. Donne, *Poems*, "To Sir Henry Goodyer," 211, lines 29–32.
26. John Donne, *Letters to Severall Persons of Honour*, ed. Charles Edmund Merrill Jr. (New York: Sturgis & Walton, 1910), 40.
27. Donne, *Poems*, "Annunciation," 306, lines 7–8, and "Nativity," 307, lines 3–4.
28. Ibid., "Annunciation," 306, lines 12–14.
29. Ibid., "Nativity," 307, lines 3–4.
30. Ibid., "Spit in my face," 313, lines 9–14.
31. Ibid., "A Litany," 318, lines 19–27.
32. Smith argues that most of the *Elegies* date from the 1590s (Donne, *Poems*, 415). John Carey dates "The Anagram" in the 1590s (*John Donne: Life, Mind, and Art* [New York: Oxford University Press, 1981], 104). See also the commentary on the dates of the poems in the *Variorium Edition* (Gary Stringer et al., eds., *The Elegies*, vol. 2 of *The Variorium Edition of the Poetry of John Donne* [Bloomington: Indiana University Press, 2000], 434, 757).
33. Donne, *Poems*, 96, lines 1–4.
34. Ibid., 103.
35. Ibid., 106, lines 45–50.
36. Ibid., 52, line 2.
37. Ibid., 72, lines 1–22.
38. Ibid., lines 26–27.
39. In "The Fever," Donne exploits the image of the human being as a microcosm of the world to claim that the death of his beloved, the soul of the world, would leave that world a dead carcass (58, lines 9–12), an image he will exploit at length in *The Anniversaries*. He also uses this image in a letter to Bridget White, written during the same time period as *The Anniversaries*. In that letter he writes, "Your going away hath made London a dead carcass. . . . I think the only reason why the plague is somewhat slackened is because the place is dead already, and no body left worth the killing" (Donne, *Letters*, 1).
40. Donne, *Poems*, 44, lines 19–24.
41. Ibid., lines 27–28.
42. Ibid., 45, lines 38–40.
43. Ibid., 63.
44. Ibid., 70.
45. Ibid., 51, lines 1–3.
46. Ibid., 68, lines 36–42.
47. Ibid., 87, lines 2–24. In the conventions of Donne's time, an "anatomy" could refer to the act of dissection or the "ruined" (cut-up) body that was the subject of the demonstration. One particularly striking method of representation that was popular in anatomical texts at the time was the depiction of dissected bodies standing alone, appar-

ently under their own power, pointing to the relevant part of their anatomies. This sort of illustration may have been in Donne's mind when he pictures his name as a "bony anatomy" that demonstrates his fragmentation. My understanding of these conventions of anatomy current during Donne's career draws on Jonathan Sawday's *The Body Emblazoned: Dissection and the Human Body in Renaissance Culture* (London and New York: Routledge, 1995).

48. Ibid., lines 25–32.

49. In a revealing exception, his many elegies on the actual deaths of friends, patrons, and well-known personages give images of the fragmentation of the body a decidedly different turn. As we will examine in the following two sections, Donne tends to portray the bodies of the righteous dead in terms of their redemption or eschatological promise. Their fragmentation becomes a sign not of the fall, but of God's power and love.

50. Ibid., "I am a little world," 311, lines 2–4.

51. Ibid., "As due by many titles," 309, line 10.

52. Ibid., "A Litany," 317, 4–6.

53. Donne loved biblical words and was familiar with the wordplay in the Genesis story whereby humankind *('adham)* was created out of the earth itself *('adhamah)*. According to the commentary in the *Oxford Annotated Bible,* this was part of an Old Testament tradition that associated humankind with the ground from which God formed him, like a potter forms clay (see Jer 18:6). *The New Oxford Annotated Bible with the Apocrypha, Expanded Edition, Revised Standard Version,* ed. Herbert G. May and Bruce M. Metzger (New York: Oxford University Press, 1977), 3.

54. Donne, *Poems,* "A Litany," lines 8–9.

55. John Donne, *The Sermons of John Donne,* 10 vols., ed. Evelyn M. Simpson and George R. Potter (Berkeley and Los Angeles: University of California Press, 1953–62), 3:3.

56. Ibid., 7:218.

57. Ibid., 6:117.

58. Ibid., 2:58.

59. Augustine, *Concerning the City of God against the Pagans,* trans. Henry Bettenson (London: Pelican Books, 1972; repr., London: Penguin Classics, 1984), 13:14.

60. Ibid., 13:3.

61. Donne, *Sermons,* 2:123.

62. Ibid., 2:58.

63. Ibid., 5:172; 7:103; 10:182.

64. Ibid., 2:63.

65. Ibid., 10:182.

66. Ibid., 9:372–3.

67. Ibid., 2:82.

68. Ibid., 2:100.

69. Ibid., 9:373.

70. Ibid., 10:187.

71. Ibid., 4:45.

72. Ibid., 9:371.

73. Ibid., 6:117. Donne here quotes Romans 7:5. An astute reader of St. Paul, he is careful not to confuse Paul's "flesh" with the body. For instance, he interprets Paul's reference to the "flesh" which cannot inherit the kingdom and the "carnal mind" by saying

that the "flesh and blood" which are at enmity with God are "all those works which proceed merely out of the nature of man, without the regeneration of the Spirit of God" (3:131). However, it is clear in this passage that he refers to the effects of sin on the human body itself.

74. See 4:48; 6:117; 7:104.
75. Ibid., 6:191.
76. Ibid., 6:191–92.
77. Ibid., 8:62; see also 2:55.
78. Ibid., 10:198.
79. Ibid., 7:105–6; see also 5:287.
80. For general results of the fall, see 1:159; 2:55, 100–101; 5:287.
81. Ibid, 2:79.
82. Ibid., 81.
83. Ibid., 7:390.
84. See, for instance, 1:159; 3:55; 10:79.
85. Ibid., 6:268.
86. Ibid., 3:55.
87. Ibid., 10:206.
88. Ibid., 10:79.
89. Ibid., 4:52.
90. Ibid., 10:234.
91. Ibid., 2:203; 8:310.
92. Ibid., 10:236. See also 6:349; 10:187.
93. Ibid., 6:349.
94. Ibid., 8:107.
95. Ibid., 4:54.
96. Ibid., 3:102.
97. Ibid., 8:210. See also 2:121.
98. Ibid., 7:104, 257.
99. Ibid., 3:113.
100. Ibid., 4:56.
101. Ibid., 10:185.
102. Ibid., 4:45.
103. Ibid., 4:46.
104. Ibid., 3:105. See also 9:371ff.
105. Ibid., 3:107.
106. Ibid., 10:238–39.
107. Ibid., 4:53, for instance.
108. Ibid., 3:105–6.
109. Ibid., 3:109–10.
110. Ibid., 6:272–73.
111. Ibid., 6:51.

BODIES REDEEMED AND REDEMPTIVE

[Christ] hath an Earth of his own in this place. Our flesh is earth, and God hath invested our flesh, and in that flesh of ours, which suffered death for us, he returns to us in this place.
DONNE, *Sermons*

His pervasive sense of the fall and its effects notwithstanding, Donne portrays the human body as both redeemed and redemptive throughout his writings. Using similar themes and representations before and after his ordination, he explores the body's role in the salvation and restoration of the human race to God. First, Donne portrays a body that, despite the fall, retains some of its Edenic gifts. Second, he represents the human body as the necessary instrument of the incarnation and sacrifice of Christ, which then works (at least potentially) to redeem all human bodies. Third, Donne presents a human body that can actively participate in Christ's redeemed body through its own sacrifice and suffering. Fourth, Donne reads the body as a sign and sacrament of redemption, grounding that reading in his own theology of the sacraments.

Edenic Remnants as Redemptive

As I pointed out in the first two chapters, Donne believes that some remnants of the created body survive the fall. Here, I need only recall those created gifts and point to their connection to human redemption. Donne insists in many of his sermons that grace always grows in nature, just as seeds must germinate and grow in the soil.[1] Certain aspects of the created human body provide the necessary ground for the growth of the mustard seeds of faith. First, in spite of the fall, the natural human body still *exists*. When the body fell from its close and proper relationship to soul and God, it did not descend into utter alienation or nothingness. While the human body still exists, grace can work in and through it.

The second ground of grace lies in the fertile soil of the human senses. God created the senses in part to serve as gateways of knowledge to him. Even fallen, they still serve that function and play a part in the process of human restoration to God. In one of his sermons, Donne says, "The ordinary way, even of the Holy Ghost, for the conveying of faith, and supernatural graces, is (as the way of worldly knowledge is) by the senses."[2] He condemns those whom he calls in one sermon "Pharisees," separatists who dream of union and identification with God in this life through "immediate and continual infusions and inspiration."[3] Donne instead points to the senses, imagination, and reason as the pathways to knowledge of God in this life.[4]

The Body of Christ: Incarnation and Sacrifice

Since the poor soil of human nature cannot, of itself, support the workings of grace, human salvation requires something more. God freely chose the way of justice to redeem humanity, and that redemption required a unique being, fully human and fully God. The human body becomes involved in this divine plan as a necessary instrument of grace. Satisfaction of God's justice required a being who was both sinless and subject to suffering and death. Christ's nature as God and his embodiment as a human person made his efficacious sacrifice possible. Transformed in and through him, the human body becomes an instrument of human redemption. Christ's "descent" into the body lifts up the fallen bodies of humanity, restores their dignity, and offers a way to their restoration.

Donne's belief in the necessity of incarnate love appears even in his early poems. Donne uses the language of incarnation even in his love poetry. In "Air and Angels," for example, love must assume a body to do its work. In his early religious works, such bodily salvation requires more than human love. The true restoration of humanity, body and soul, comes only through the embodiment and suffering of Christ. In Donne's early religious poems, love literally assumes a body in the incarnation of Jesus. In this redemptive incarnation, the bodies of both Jesus and Mary serve as instruments for the salvation of humankind. In "A Litany," he speaks of "that fair blessed mother-maid, / Whose flesh redeemed us; that she-cherubin, / Which unlocked Paradise."[5] In "Goodfriday, 1613. Riding Westward," Donne refers to Mary as "God's partner" who "furnished thus / Half of that sacrifice, which ransomed us": Jesus' body.[6] This redemptive flesh is at the same time the body of Mary *and* the body of Jesus, since (according to an old tradition that Donne exploits) a child derives its body from its mother and its soul or intellect from its father.[7] The bodies of Mary and Jesus occupy a border territory between the realms of fallen and unfallen flesh. Their bodies are subject to death and weakness, but not to sin. By Mary's innocence, virtue, and obedience, she has "disseized sin," broken the hold of sin over herself, her son, and (potentially) all of humankind.[8] For Donne, Mary's body is a "middle kind between earth and heaven."[9] He emphasizes the paradox of this liminal position by referring to Mary's womb in one poem as both a prison and a cloister and in another as a "strange heaven."[10]

In his early work, Donne sees Christ's incarnation as a redemptive descent, a "fortunate fall" into the body and thus into human weakness and death. In *La Corona*, "Annunciation," Donne says that Christ "yields himself to lie / In Prison, in thy womb; and though he there / Can take no sin, nor thou give, yet he will wear / Taken from thence, flesh, which death's force may try."[11] It is this descent into the body that makes possible humanity's redemption. In a letter to "Sir H.G.," Donne says that the "advantage of nearer familiarity with God, which the act of incarnation gave us, is grounded upon God's assuming us, not our going to him. And, our accesses to his presence are but his descents unto us."[12]

While Donne carries significant themes from his early work into his sermons (the necessity of incarnate love, the role of the body in satisfying God's justice, and the incarnation as descent and humiliation), he tends to downplay the doctrine of incarnation when he preaches. In that context, he consistently displays more interest and expends more eloquence on salvation than on incarnation, on eschatology than ontology, and on the body as sign rather than the body as object. While he subordinates the doctrine of the incarnation in the sermons, however, he never denies that it is a crucial part of God's chosen plan for the salvation of the human race.[13] A careful reading of his Christmas Day sermons reveals that, while orthodox in his treatment of the incarnation, Donne seldom seizes the obvious opportunity to wax eloquent about it.[14] Rather, he treats the incarnation only glancingly when he speaks of it at all. Certainly he does not celebrate it with the same intensity and lyricism he brings to the doctrine of the resurrection of the body. While orthodox in his insistence that Christ's body is fully real, fully human, and a necessary condition of humanity's salvation, Donne rarely indulges in the evocations of celebratory fullness that other Anglicans, notably his contemporary Lancelot Andrewes, brought to the theme.[15] Donne remains guarded about making any deep exploration or celebration of the incarnation in any of his sermons. He treats it at once as a great mystery about which we cannot speak coherently and as a necessary (and, in many cases, rather dryly contractual) condition of what are his true interests: the redemption of humankind, the re-creation and eventual resurrection of the human body, and the indications and assurances of God by signs of those redemptions.[16]

The main theme Donne sounds in all his Christmas sermons is not the incarnation of Christ but the redemption of humankind. The strongest secondary theme is the manifestation of that redemption or its signs (Scripture, types, promises, and prophecies). In his Christmas sermon for 1625, for instance, Donne takes as his text Isaiah 7:14, "Therefore the Lord himself shall give you a sign."[17] Although he does deal with the doctrine of the incarnation and the mystery of the God/man union, he emphasizes the theme of Christ's birth as sign. While Donne does speak of Christ's birth as the *material* referent and terminus of the types and signs of the Old Testament, he immediately puts the incarnation back into play as yet another sign and type pointing toward a still deferred fulfillment. The *sign* of Christ's birth signifies a further coming in the material church, which in turn becomes a sign and type of the final fulfillment: the New Jerusalem. Notice what he does in this passage from his Christmas Day sermon for 1629:

> Christ comes to us, in this, that he hath constituted, and established a Church. ... From this day, in which, the first stone of that building, was laid. (for, though the foundations of the Church were laid in eternity, yet, that was underground, the first stone above ground, that is, the manifestation of God's purpose to the world was laid this day in Christ's birth).[18]

Christ's birth is simply the "first stone above ground," the revelation of God's eternal purpose from creation and the cornerstone of the eschatological New Jerusalem.

Instead of focusing on the direct subject of embodiment, Donne most often evokes the related themes of epiphany (manifestation) and signs (types or prophecy). In fact, he often literally reaches forward in the church calendar and brings Epiphany back into his Christmas Day sermons. In the 1629 Christmas sermon, he conflates Christmas Day and Epiphany thus:

> The Church celebrates this day, the Birth of our Lord and Savior Christ Jesus.... It is a day that consists of twelve days; a day not measured by the natural and ordinary motion of the sun, but by a supernatural and extraordinary star, which appeared to the wisemen of the East, this day, and brought them to Christ, at Bethlehem, upon Twelfth day. That day, Twelfth day, the Church now calls the Epiphany; The ancient Church called this day (Christmas day) the Epiphany. Both days together, and all the days between, this day, when Christ was manifested to the Jews ... and Twelfth day, when Christ was manifested to the Gentiles ... make up the Epiphany, that is, the manifestation of God to Man.[19]

Donne similarly associates Christmas and Epiphany, incarnation and manifestation, in his Christmas Day sermons for 1621 and 1626. In his 1626 sermon, he tells his congregation that Christ's

> birth and death were but one continual act, and his Christmas-day and his Good Friday, are but the evening and morning of one and the same day. And as even his birth, is his death, so every action and passage that manifests Christ to us, is his birth; for *Epiphany is manifestation*. . . . Every manifestation of Christ to the world, to the Church, to a particular soul, is an Epiphany, a Christmas Day.[20]

In spite of his emphasis on Christ's birth as sign, Donne carefully preserves the connection between Christ's birth and his very physical suffering and death. The means of human salvation are rooted in Christ's body because God willed it so. Since Christ took a body in order to be able to suffer and die, Donne foreshadows that suffering and death in the Christmas sermons. His interest often focuses on the Infant Jesus' suffering, which he believes contributed to humanity's salvation. In his Christmas sermon for 1625, he says that "the work of our redemption was an entire work, and all that Christ said, or did, or suffered, concurred to our salvation . . . as well his cold lying in the manger, as his cold dying upon the Cross."[21] He returns to the same theme in the Christmas sermon for the following year, saying, "The whole life of Christ was a continual Passion; others die martyrs, but Christ was born a Martyr. He found a Golgotha . . . even in Bethlehem, where he was born; for, to his tenderness then, the straws were almost as sharp as the thorns after; and his manger as uneasy at first, as his cross at last."[22]

When Donne considers Christ's actual passion and its salvific power, he most often uses the bodily synecdoche of blood to represent it. He employs this traditional motif many times in his early religious poems.[23] These images usually run along traditional and biblical lines: Christ's blood moistens the stony or dry heart of the sinner, the transgressor bathes in the blood of the Lamb, blood seals the pardon of the unjust or buys a release, or the blood of the lamb marks the households of the chosen people. These images do not function as "mere" metaphors, either for Donne or for the biblical tradition from which he draws. The historical and bodily suffering and death of Christ give them their life and power. For Donne, Christ's blood functions as a synecdoche for all his atoning actions and as a literal fulfillment of the blood sacrifices of the Old Testament.

Donne's fascination with Jesus' blood spans the whole period of his ministry. He often dramatizes its efficacy through the habit of focusing his poetic eyes on one drop of it. He says that such a drop "is of infinite value" and imagines it moistening the dry soul of a sinner or redeeming thousands on thousands of worlds.[24] This motif, which he employs several times in his sermons, appears in his early work in "Resurrection" *(La Corona)* and in "Upon the Annunciation and Passion." In one early sermon, he insists that the salvation of humankind began with the circumcision of Jesus, when he submitted himself to the law for humanity "and began to shed some drops of his blood for us."[25] Preaching several years later, Donne refers to the blood of Christ as "my cordial," the medicine that heals and restores the sinner.[26] Toward the end of his career, he tells his congregation that human sins are "buried in the sea of the blood of Christ Jesus.[27]

For one of his most interesting sermons on the theme of Christ's blood, Donne chooses the "inappropriate" occasion of Christmas 1622 to expound on Colossians 1:19–20: "For it pleased the Father that in him should all fullness dwell; and, having made peace through the blood of his cross, by him to reconcile all things unto himself; by him, I say, whether they be things in earth, or things in heaven." He begins the sermon by saying, "The whole journey of a Christian is in these words."[28] He places the occasion of Christmas Day, the celebration of the incarnation, into the context that interests him and his listeners most: "the great mystery of our reconciliation to God."[29] That reconciliation, he notes, can be accomplished only by blood, "by the blood of his cross, that is, his death; the blood of his circumcision, the blood of his agony, the blood of his scourging was not enough."[30] Referring back to the text, Donne explores the theme of the fullness that was in Christ. He notes that

> this fullness is not fully expressed in the Hypostatical union of the two natures; God and Man in the person of Christ. For, (concerning the divine Nature) here was not a dram of glory in this union. This was a strange fullness, for it was a fullness of emptiness; it was all humiliation, all exinanition, all evacuation of himself, by his obedience to the death of the cross.[31]

The true "fullness" in this sermon proves elusive, for what Donne seems to give with one hand, he removes with the other. Taking as his subject the "fullness" dwelling in Christ at the incarnation, he continually displaces and defers that fullness. Donne makes clear that any incarnational fullness or "merit" in Christ lies not so much in his dual nature as in the free gift of God, a gift to be poured out, first in blood and then in word and sacrament.[32] The will of the Father requires payment of human debt through blood sacrifice. The reader may then think that the fullness lies in Christ's blood, one drop of which, Donne tells his listeners, "had been enough to have redeemed infinite worlds, if it had been so contracted, and so applied, yet he gave us, a morning shower of his blood in his circumcision, and an evening shower at his passion, and a shower after sunset, in the piercing of his side."[33]

But Donne defers fullness yet again. The reader may find a clue to the true locus of fullness in this sermon by paying careful attention to the division Donne marks out at its beginning. He tells his congregation that he will discuss first the qualification of the person (Christ's incarnation), then the pacification and way of reconciliation (the blood of the cross), and finally the reconciliation itself: "That all things, whether they be things in earth, or things in heaven, might be reconciled unto him."[34] He says, "Now let us labor for our Reconciliation; for all things are reconciled to him, in Christ, *that is, offered a way of reconciliation.*"[35] Neither the fulfillment of promise that is the incarnation, nor the sacrifice on the cross that "accomplished" the reconciliation of God and humanity, contains the fullness of salvation. The present "reconciliation" is simply a *way* toward a future reconciliation. Although Donne says, "Then are we reconciled by the blood of his cross, when having crucified our selves by a true repentance, we receive the seal of reconciliation, in his blood in the Sacrament," the seal is only a promise of future redemption.[36] Although Donne speaks eloquently about the riches of the Church (its empowerment by the Holy Spirit, its sacraments, and the communion of saints), a careful reading of the sermon's conclusion reveals that the end of salvation is in the future tense, waiting for the faithful only in heaven when all things are gathered into their fullness in Christ.[37] Although some reconciliation between body and soul (and between human nature and God) can take place in this life, true union and glorification of body and soul wait for the next world.

Donne's references to the suffering and blood of Christ, and indeed the incarnation of Christ, take on a more ambiguous and eschatological tone in his sermons than in his religious poetry. The reason for this difference lies in the difference of genre and in part in Donne's efforts in his sermons not to sound too "Catholic." While always acknowledging that Christ's physical and historical suffering and death (encapsulated in his blood) form the foundation of the Church and the ground of all individual salvation, Donne avoids making that blood too "present" for fear of evoking the heresy of transubstantiation.[38] Donne takes care to link any meditation on the suffering of Christ directly into the trajectory of salvation history, with the "real presence" of the salvation bought by that suffering located in future glory. This reference to the "real presence" is particularly apropos, since the same techniques, tenor, and images that form Donne's thinking on the suffering body of the historical Jesus inform his theology of signs in general, and of the Eucharist in particular. I will return to this conjunction of body theology and eucharistic theology in the last section of this chapter.

The Bodies of the Redeemed: Participation, Sacrifice, and Suffering

Donne believes that Christ transforms the valuation and potential of the fallen human body. By becoming fully human, he lifts up that which the fall had cast down. The actual deliverance of the body from the results of sin and its restoration to glory, however, take place for most of the faithful in the eschatological future, not in the ontological present. The promise that the human body will be restored is just that: a promise realized on this earth only in particular bodies and only in limited ways. In the fallen world, Christians can reach toward the transformed body through suffering, ascetic discipline, and appropriation of the body as a sign of future redemption.

By assuming a human body, Christ gives all bodies a new dignity in spite of the reality of their still fallen nature. Donne believes that just as God's hand gave dignity to the natural body in its creation, so Christ restores that dignity through his birth, suffering, and death. In a late sermon, Donne says that Jesus "took our nature, that he might know our infirmities experimentally; He brought down a better nature that he might recover us, restore us powerfully, effectually. The God-head wrought as much in our Redemption as in our Creation; and the Man-hood more; for it began but then."[39]

By his atonement, Christ *potentially* reverses the fall. This reversal shares the same Augustinian metaphysic that attempts to account for Adam's "poisoning" of the whole of human nature through his own sin. In a late sermon, attributed to 1630, Donne says that "since the devil had so surprised us all, as to take mankind all in one lump, in a corner, in Adam's loins, and poisoned us all then in the fountain, in the root, Christ, to deliver us entirely, took all mankind upon him."[40] Donne often speaks of Christ "investing" and putting on human nature, especially the body, as a descent on his part that in turn lifts up, dignifies, and tempers the fallen body.[41]

Donne relates Christ's descent into the body and the consequent "lifting up" of that body to the cosmological controversies of his time. In one significant passage, he evokes the new astronomy's discovery that the earth is one of a number of spheres orbiting the sun to express his wonder at God's love for the human body.

> And therefore be content to wonder at this, that God would have such a care to dignify, and to crown, and to associate to his own everlasting presence, the body of man. God himself is a Spirit, and heaven is his place, my soul is a spirit, and so proportioned to that place.... But since we wonder, and justly, that some late Philosophers have removed the whole earth from the Center, and carried it up, and placed it in one of the Sphears of heaven, that this clod of earth, this body of ours should be carried up to the highest heaven.... That

God, all Spirit . . . should have such an affection, and such a love to this body, this earthly body, this deserves the wonder.[42]

In a later sermon, he uses the opposite convention of the old astronomy, which understood the earth as the center of the universe, to make essentially the same point. He says that the Church

> which is his Vineyard, is his *ubi*, his place, his Center, to which he is naturally affected. . . . And as he hath a place of his own here, so he hath an Earth of his own in this place. Our flesh is earth, and God hath invested our flesh, and in that flesh of ours, which suffered death for us, he returns to us in this place, as often as he maketh us partakers of his flesh, and in his blood, in the blessed Sacrament. . . . In his entering into me in his flesh and blood, he returns to me as to his Earth, that Earth which he has made his by assuming my nature.[43]

Donne works miracles of symbolic layering in this passage, all aimed at reassuring his listeners that the human body is God's intimate concern and, indeed, his home. He evokes the link of microcosm with macrocosm to suggest that the body be identified with the earth. Just as the planets are attracted through "centric" force to the earth at the center of the universe, so is Christ (although now in the spheres of heaven with his Father) still "drawn" to earth/body. In this short passage, Donne identifies this embodied center, as is his habit, with all of salvation history. He evokes Eden through the well-known convention that the Garden was located at the center of the earth. He recalls the covenant with Israel and its fulfillment in Christ, the Vine, through his reference to the vineyard. He recalls Christ's incarnation, suffering, and death through the complex play on the image of earth-as-flesh. He further evokes, somewhat obliquely, Christ's second coming. Donne conflates Christ's second coming to earth with his return to the "earth" of the individual body of the believer through the Eucharist. Perhaps the most fascinating part of this rich passage is Donne's statement that "Christ returns to me as to his earth," recalling Jesus' poignant statement that even foxes had "earths," while he had no place to lay his head. Donne points out that Christ has finally found his "earth" in the human body. Donne does not seem to care whether tradition finds the earth (and its analog, the body) at the lowly center or science shifts it to the highest heavens. The important points for him are God's continuing focus on the human body and his continuing love and care for it.

Donne brings these cosmic concerns down to the level of individual believers whose own bodies must participate in a real process of sanctification in this life. He believes that the bodily suffering and sacrifice of individual believers play a role in their own redemption and in the salvation of others, although this role is sometimes hard to pin down. Throughout his work, he closely associates all suffering and sacrifice with those of Christ. In his early work, Donne turns this idea to a witty secular use in one of his marriage songs, "Epithalamion made at Lincoln's Inn." Donne pictures the bride rising from the "grave" of her barren single bed and happily sacrificing her solitude and virginity on "love's altar," the marriage bed, which will be a cradle of love and of children.[44] She becomes the lamb that her husband, as priest, will "embowel."[45] With the bodily sacrifice on the altar of sex and motherhood, the bride "put[s] on perfection and a woman's name," the refrain that runs throughout the poem. Although Donne never directly exploits the connection, there are resonances between the description of the bride and his images of the Virgin Mary in his early religious poems. In both cases, the woman's body is an efficacious sacrifice. In the more explicitly religious work from this early period, the bodily sacrifices of the redeemed involve ascetic tribulations that purify body and soul (as in "The Cross," "Ascension," and "A Litany"); images of bodily suffering that describe the tribulations of the soul (as in "Spit in my face," and "Batter my heart); and the actual sacrifices of the martyrs (as in "A Litany" or the many descriptions of martyrdom in *Biathanatos*).

In his sermons, Donne often uses the dual themes of suffering as a way of participating in Christ's atonement and suffering as a way of moving toward sanctification (making the body purer and more obedient to the soul). These themes apply to both voluntary and involuntary asceticism. Involuntary asceticism for Donne includes all those "changes and chances of this transitory life": illness, injury, loss of position, loss of fortune, and the death of loved ones. Donne particularly focuses on illness as a prime example and metaphor for such involuntary austerities. Donne believes all sickness is, to some extent, a punishment for sin. The sinner can embrace God's physical judgment and use it for the good of the soul.[46] Illnesses often plagued Donne and those he loved, and he was fascinated by symptoms and their cures. He tends to speak in medical terms of all such involuntary asceticism, whether physical, spiritual, emotional, or social. In one late sermon, Donne uses a brilliant series of metaphors through which he envisions God's hand intimately involved in human suffering. He says that

> as long as God punishes me, he gives me physic; if he draw his knife, it is but to prune his vine, and if he draw blood, it is but to rectify a distemper: if God break my bones, it is but to set them straighter, and if he bruise me in a mortar, it is but that I might exhale, and breath up a sweet savor, in his nostrils: I am his handiwork, and if one hand be under me, let the other lie as heavy, as he shall be pleased to lay it, upon me, let God handle me how he will, so he cast me not out of his hands.[47]

God hovers over the human body in this passage as apothecary, surgeon (who lurks metaphorically behind the vinedresser), leech, and bonesetter. Donne then ties all these medicinal images into a picture of God as creator, artisan, and lover. He evokes in all this a God intimately, if sometimes painfully, involved in the bodies and fortunes of humankind.

According to Donne, all human suffering can have a salutary effect by enabling people to see more clearly through the haze cast over their vision by the fall. In one sermon he tells his congregation that "God made the Sun, and Moon, and Stars, glorious lights for man to see by; but man's infirmity requires spectacles; and affliction does that office."[48] This statement stands against Calvin's reference in his *Institutes* to the Scriptures as the spectacles through which the fallen and distorted human senses can discern the world correctly.[49] Donne's familiarity with the *Institutes* and his choice of the distinctive word "spectacles" suggest that he may have intended a comparison with Calvin, deliberately elevating personal, bodily experience (specifically the experience of suffering) to the status of Scripture as a way to know God. Donne goes on to say,

> As the body of man is mellowed in the grave, and made fit for glory in the resurrection, so the mind of man by suffering is suppled . . . and he may see. . . . it is a seeing of God, not as before, in his works abroad, but in his working upon himself, at home. Such a man God strikes so, as that when he strikes, he strikes fire, and lights him a candle, to see his presence by . . . Eternal life hereafter is *visio Dei*, the sight of God, and the way to that here, is to see God here: and the eye-salve for that is, to be crossed in our desires in this world, by the hand of God.[50]

Donne uses the sacrament of baptism as another metaphorical and actual link to involuntary asceticism. Through baptism, human beings become members of Christ's body. For Donne, this means not only that with baptism a person becomes a member of the Church (as body), but that the body of the newly baptized person is metaphysically linked to the human body of Jesus. By the sacrament of baptism "we are so incorporated into Christ, that in all our afflictions after we fulfill the sufferings of Christ in our flesh."[51] He quotes Augustine to the effect that in baptism "we are conformed to Christ as he suffered, died, and was buried."[52] He says in the same sermon that

> the whole life of a regenerate man is a baptism. For as in putting on Christ, sanctification doth accompany faith, so in baptism, the imitation of his death (that is, mortification) and the application of his passion, (by fulfilling the sufferings of Christ in our flesh) is that baptism into his death. . . . Not that any

BODIES REDEEMED AND REDEMPTIVE   67

mortification of mine, works any thing, as a cause of my redemption, but as an assurance and testimony of it; *ut sit pignus & sigillum redemptionis;* It is a pledge, and it is a seal, of my redemption.[53]

As sanctification is inextricably joined to faith, so mortification is inextricably joined to baptism: each is the working out of the other. Donne emphasizes the same point concerning the bodily suffering of the redeemed that he makes about Christ's own agony: neither accomplishes redemption ontologically. They rather serve as *signs* and *seals* of redemption.

The believer also can embrace suffering voluntarily. Donne often defends traditional ascetic practices against the charge of "papistry." He shares the traditional view that disciplines of the body such as fasting or other mortifications are means of keeping the rebellious body subdued and in order. In a late sermon, he addresses his congregation thus:

> Beloved, there are some things in which all religions agree; the worship of God, the holiness of life; and therefore, if when I study this holiness of life, and fast and pray, and submit myself to discreet and medicinal mortifications, for the subduing of my body, any man will say, this is Papistical, Papists do this, it is a blessed Protestation, and no man is the less a Protestant, nor the worse a Protestant for making it, men and brethren, I am a Papist, that is, I will fast and pray as much as any Papist, and enable myself for the service of God, as seriously, as sedulously, as laboriously as any Papist.[54]

He advocates moderation and respect for the body in the conduct of such necessary mortifications, warning against "uncommanded and inhuman flagellations" that dishonor or deform the body that has been dignified by Christ's incarnation.[55] He also carefully makes clear to his Protestant congregations that he is not implying that they can merit salvation through asceticism.[56]

Although asceticism is not necessary to salvation, Donne sees it as a necessary part of the process of sanctification. Since corrupt flesh cannot enter the kingdom of heaven, it must be purged and prepared here *in via*.[57] In one sermon he says,

> I must have this body with me to heaven, or else salvation itself is not perfect; and yet I cannot have this body thither, except as St. Paul did his, I beat down this body, attenuate the body by mortification. . . . I have not body enough for my body, and I have too much body for my soul; not body enough, not blood enough, not strength enough, to sustain myself in health, and yet body enough to destroy my soul, and frustrate the grace of God in that miserable, perplexed, riddling condition of man.[58]

According to Donne, the Christian "puts on" Christ in election not only so that God sees Christ's innocence in the one elected, but so that one can put on Christ as a person, can become him, through the process of sanctification.[59] Through discipline and mortification, Donne believes that the body can be imprinted with the "stigmata," the marks of Jesus.[60] Such participation in Christ's suffering goes some way toward restoring the control of the soul over the body, which was destroyed by the fall.[61]

The Redeemed Body as Sign and Sacrament

While Donne grounds redemption in the material bodies of humanity in general and Jesus in particular, he never leaves the redeemed body solely in the material order. Just as he embraces the traditional view of the human person as a unique combination of the material and spiritual that ties together the created order, so also does he present the human person as the linchpin of the redemptive order. He lifts the created body toward the realm of spirit, and he lifts the redeemed body into the realm of signs. For Donne the redeemed body is first and foremost *significative,* a material object that can exhibit or point to spiritual realities. In some instances, Donne presents the body not only as a sign, but as a sacrament that conveys that to which it refers.[62] The redeemed body for Donne lies suspended between earth and heaven, partaking of and linking both realms through sacramentality and signification. Just as the body of Christ was lifted between earth and heaven on the cross, so also are the bodies of the redeemed lifted and given sacramental power to link people to God.

Donne's theology always emphasizes the human need of visible, material signs. As he puts it in one sermon, "A natural man is not made of reason alone, but of reason and sense: a regenerate man is not made of faith alone, but of faith and reason; and signs, external things, assist us all."[63] Human beings require a sensible bridge between spirits and bodies, and between themselves and God. Donne believes that God embodies his Word in many things: Jesus, Scripture, preaching, the Eucharist, miracles, events.[64] Donne's most distinctive focus is the embodiment of the Word in body itself, not only in the incarnation of Christ, but in the bodies of all of humanity. He consistently uses the human body as a sign of redemption throughout his career, but he emphasizes different images before his ordination than he does afterward. In his early work, he emphasizes the bodies of women as signs of redemption, with the body of the human Jesus and the bodies of male believers as secondary signs. In the sermons, he turns primarily to the eucharistic body of Christ as the sign and sacrament of present redemption, with the bodies of the human Jesus and of believers themselves as of secondary significative value.

In Donne's early work, the bodies of the redeemed serve as signs and sacraments of God's grace. In chapter 1, I examined "The Ecstasy" as an instance of Donne's emphasis on the necessity of the senses for the realization of love. As I pointed out in that analysis, the poem goes further. The bodies of the lovers serve not just their own love; rather, their bodies serve as "books" through which others can be redeemed. Donne's speaker ends the poem by saying,

> To our bodies turn we then, that so
> Weak men on love revealed may look;
> Love's mysteries in souls do grow,
> But yet the body is his book.
> And if some lover, such as we,
> Have heard this dialogue of one,
> Let him still mark us, he shall see
> Small change, when we'are to bodies gone.[65]

Donne introduces two images here that are important to his religious rhetoric of the redeemed body. The first image is that of the body as a book. In an allusion to the power of the Scripture, the bodies of the lovers become books wherein love reveals its mysteries to the weak. The second image is the bodies of the lovers reflecting the purity of their loving souls (an observer of their souls would "see / Small change, when we'are to bodies gone"). The bodies of the lovers act as "outward and visible signs of an inward and spiritual grace," as church tradition describes the sacraments.

In his more overtly religious poetry, Donne employs the same idea of the bodies of the redeemed as signs of spiritual love and virtue and as conveyors of grace to "weaker" onlookers. As in "The Ecstasy," bodies reflect the purity of souls. Redemption of the soul through Christ can, at least in part, repair the toll that the fall has taken on the body. In a verse letter written for the Countess of Salisbury, Donne uses the familiar image of the human person as a microcosm of the world. He begins,

> Fair, great and good, since seeing you, we see
> What heaven can do, and what any earth can be:
> Since now your beauty shines, now when the sun
> Grown stale, is to so low a value run . . .
> . . . .
> . . . you come to repair
> God's book of creatures, teaching what is fair.[66]

In the rest of this long poem, Donne laments the state of the world, "withered, shrunk, and dried, / All virtue ebbed out to a dead low tide."[67] The countess dares to practice virtue in a fallen world. Because of her virtue, her body becomes a "book" that teaches true beauty and goodness to a world that has forgotten it.[68] Her virtue, and the beauty which is its bodily concomitant, demonstrates what "any earth" (any human person) can be through grace. She serves as an object of contemplation through which the sinful may, by degrees, reach toward that which is infinite.[69] She also, in a macrocosmic sense, "repairs God's book of creatures."[70] By this, Donne indicates not that her beauty actually restores the fallen world, but that she serves as a new "book" for humankind, supplying the defects of the (now fallen) book of creatures. The "book of creatures," the created world, was supposed to teach God's existence and power by its order and beauty, but the fall defaced it. The countess's beauty, as a reflection of her redeemed soul, "repairs" those defects and gives the onlooker a new book in which to read God.

Similar representations of the body transformed by and reflecting the goodness of the soul frequently figure in Donne's work. In his religious writing, he employs the motif only when writing of women. The only instances in which a male body reflects love or purity of soul occur, and then rarely, in the early love poems. In his early religious work, he either ignores the bodies of virtuous men altogether or portrays them as affected by the fall. For instance, in the verse letter to Sir Henry Goodyer, Donne represents Goodyer's body as changing and eventually declining with age, even as his "noble soul by age grows lustier."[71]

Several plausible reasons may account for Donne's differing treatment of the bodies of virtuous men and women. Donne wrote his poems about virtuous women to patronesses and likely thought that praise of their beauty along with their virtue would please them. He also may have adapted the tradition of courtly love poetry to more serious ends, using the conventional praise of a woman's beauty as a way to speak of her goodness. Doubtless these factors contribute to Donne's depiction of women's bodies, but more than courtly flattery is at work. Donne's association of women with the redeemed body is consistent with a larger tradition, which he often exploits, linking woman with body and man with mind. Donne explicitly uses this association in his portrayals of the redemptive power of the flesh of the Virgin Mary. Within this worldview, a woman's virtue would naturally affect that which is her essence: her body.

In a verse letter to the Countess of Bedford, Donne utilizes similar motifs of the virtuous woman's body as a sign of goodness and as an object of contemplation for the faithful. To her he says,

> But one, 'tis best light to contemplate you.
> You, for whose body God made better clay,
> Or took soul's stuff such as shall late decay,

> Or such as needs small change at the last day.
> This, as an amber drop enwraps a bee,
> Covering discovers your quick soul; that we
> May in your through-shine front your heart's thoughts see.
> You teach (though we learn not) a thing unknown
> To our late times, the use of specular stone,
> Through which all things within without were shown.
> Of such were temples; so and of such you are.[72]

Here Donne pursues the conceit that the countess's body was created out of a finer material, closer in nature to the rarified "matter" of the soul. Tradition held that angels' bodies were made of just such an ethereal, but still material, substance. Such a rarified body reveals spirit instead of concealing it. Therefore, next to the beatific vision of God himself, her body provides the best way of contemplating heavenly things. Worshipers can approach God in the temple of her body and worship him there. Donne uses similar representations of the "soulful" body in "A Letter to the Lady Carey and Mrs. Essex Rich," in verse letters to several other patronesses, and in elegies on the deaths of virtuous women. The long poems that commemorate the death of fourteen-year-old Elizabeth Drury contain Donne's most extensive use of this motif.[73]

Donne lifts the redeemed body into the realm of signs through another striking representational pattern in his early work: poetically "nailing" Christ directly onto the believer's body. This figure appears in four poems: "What if this present," "A Litany," "The Cross," and "Spit in my face." In the first two poems, Donne subtly draws on the tradition in Catholic hagiography in which God directly inscribes some holy scene or significant mark on the bodies of saints. Such markings often were found, to the wonder of onlookers, in holy bodies when they were autopsied and divided into relics.[74] In Donne's religious poetry, it is not the saint but the sinner in the process of redemption who looks for the sign of Christ's sacrifice on or in his body. In one of the "Divine Meditations," the speaker turns to a picture of the crucified Christ metaphorically inscribed on his heart as an object of meditation in preparation for the last judgment, the "world's last night" of the poem.[75] In "A Litany," the repentant sinner pleads with Christ,

> O be thou nailed unto my heart,
> And crucified again,
> Part not from it, though it from thee would part,
> But let it be by applying so thy pain,
> Drowned in thy blood, and in thy passion slain.[76]

In the other two poems, Donne "enacts" the crucifixion directly through the body of the believer. In "The Cross," Donne addresses the controversy over the use of the cross in public worship. He points out that even if crucifixes are banned from churches and the use of the sign of the cross from public worship, the cross still remains with believers. It is a sign that can be found everywhere, even in their own bodies.

> Who can blot out the Cross, which th'instrument
> Of God, dewed on me in the Sacrament?
> Who can deny me power, and liberty
> To stretch mine arms, and mine own cross to be?
> Swim, and at every stroke, thou art thy cross.[77]

In the sonnet "Spit in my face," Donne identifies the body of the contrite sinner with the body of the suffering Christ. In what he realizes is a vain wish to enact a reversal of substitutionary atonement, the speaker of the poem cries out,

> Spit in my face ye Jews, and pierce my side,
> Buffet, and scoff, scourge, and crucify me,
> For I have sinned, and sinned, and only he,
> Who could do no iniquity, hath died:
> But by my death can not be satisfied
> My sins, which pass the Jews' impiety:
> They killed once an inglorious man, but I
> Crucify him daily, being now glorified.[78]

In these examples, Donne uses the bodies of repentant sinners to represent the body of Christ to themselves. Their own bodies serve as signs and reminders of Christ's sacrifice. With that anamnesis, they also act as sacraments, conveying the grace of Christ's atonement through the sign of the sinner's own body.

In the sermons, the bodies of believers and the human body of Jesus have a more limited role as signs of *present* redemption. The weight of representation of the redeemed body falls to the eucharistic body of Christ. In spite of his recognition of certain redemptive aspects of the fallen body, Donne tends to defer the true redemption of the body until the final resurrection. This ambiguity between a redeemed body that is present and one that is deferred reflects a basic ambiguity in Donne's theology. Caught between Catholic and Protestant theologies, and perhaps between his own desires for present bodily fulfillment on the one hand and his ascetic impulses on the other, Donne makes contradictory statements about the extent to which the transformation of bodies can be realized in this life and the extent to which redemption is a promise to be fully realized only in the life to come. This ambivalence relates to two significant aspects of his theology: his views on the sacraments and his views on justification. Salvation is *near* to us but is not accomplished *in us* either by the incarnation or the death of Christ. It will only be accomplished in heaven. In one early sermon, Donne says that

> salvation is salvation perfected, consummated; salvation which was brought near in baptism, and near in outward holiness, must be brought nearer than that. . . . Here then salvation is eternal salvation; not the outward seals of the Church upon the person, not visible Sacraments, nor the outward seal of the Spirit, assurance here, but fruition, possession of glory, in the Kingdom of Heaven, where we shall be infinitely rich.[79]

Unlike Donne's earlier work, the sermons allow the bodies of redeemed believers an extremely limited role as signs and sacraments of redemption. The suffering body can be the epiphany or manifestation of God's presence. This epiphany has two aspects. First, Donne depicts the sufferings of believers, voluntary or involuntary, as a sign of God's grace and presence in the one who suffers. In the 1627 memorial sermon for his patroness Lady Danvers, Donne quotes Origen: "*Indigemus sacramento ignis, baptismo ignis,* that all our fiery tribulations fall under the nature, and definitions of sacraments, that they are so many visible signs of invisible grace, that every correction from God's hand is a Rebaptization to me."[80] In a sermon the next year, he makes a similar point, saying that suffering and calamities are to be interpreted as the sign of the cross on God's saints. The afflicted person should take that sign as a promise that "the Son of Man Christ Jesus is coming towards thee; and as thou hast the sign, thou shalt have the substance, as thou hast his cross, thou shalt have his glory."[81] Donne habitually refers to tribulations directly as sacraments or speaks of them surrounded by indirect sacramental terms or images: seals, cups, blood, water, signs, and substance.[82] Second, when a believer voluntary embraces the pains and sacrifices of ascetic practice, that person can manifest Christ to others in his or her own body. That body fulfills the suffering of Christ in present flesh and becomes part of a continuum of signs, pointing to the suffering of Christ, which in turn points toward God's promise of salvation to all.[83]

Even the suffering body of Jesus, while necessary to God's plan of salvation, functions not so much as present salvation, but as a sign and seal of God's *promise* of salvation to come. Donne most often subscribes to the Protestant viewpoint that salvation is contractual, not (presently) ontological. God seals the contract of redemption he offers the sinner with the suffering body of Jesus. He also accepts that body back again as a kind of token or pledge for all the human bodies still under the rule of Satan. Donne quotes Tertullian when he says, "*Nobis arrhabonem spiritus reliquit & arrhabonem a nobis accepit,* God hath given us his earnest, and a pawn from him upon earth, in giving us the Holy Ghost, and he hath received our earnest, and a pawn from us into heaven, by receiving our nature, in the body of Christ Jesus there."[84] Again, the passage turns on legal terminology and points to the essentially future nature of the redeemed human body. God has taken into heaven the only truly redeemed human body, that of Christ, as a guarantor of that which will be but is not yet for all of human nature. Christ as seal, however, does have an ontological as well as an eschatological status. Donne refers to the first seal God gave humankind, imprinted on the powers of the soul at creation. Then humanity is sealed again,

> sealed in our very flesh, our mortal flesh, when the image of the invisible God, Christ Jesus, the only Son of God, took our nature.... As entirely, as all mankind was in Adam, all mankind was in Christ, and as the seal of the Serpent is in all, by original sin, so the seal of God, Christ Jesus, is on us all, by his assuming our nature. Christ Jesus took our souls, and our bodies, our whole nature.[85]

For Donne, Christ has a special status because he both *had* and *was* the seal of the living God: "It is not only his Commission that is sealed, but his Nature, he himself is sealed."[86] Christ embodied and accomplished, in his human and historical life, all the previous signs from the laws, prophecies, and ceremonies of the Old Testament. He was "not only a verbal but an actual manifestation."[87] He is the Word made flesh, the will of God actualized in material form.[88]

Even so, this Christ becomes the beginning point in yet another chain of signifiers that leads the pilgrims of the earth home to heaven. The very fact that God and man are met in his person, says Donne, "is a sign to me, that God, and I, shall never be parted."[89] Sinners can "read" Christ's human body for knowledge of God's intentions toward them, just as they can read Scripture for the same purpose. In one striking passage, Donne directs his congregation to look at the suffering body of Christ as a book in which they can read their own election.

> Shalt thou not find an eternal decree, and a book of life in thy behalf, if thou look for it by this light, and reach to it with this hand, and acceptation of this reconciliation? They are written in those reverend and sacred records, and rolls, and parchments, even the skin and flesh of our Blessed Savior; written in those his stripes, and those his wounds.[90]

That body presents itself to the Church militant not only as a memory of Jesus' human body, but as the eucharistic body. That eucharistic body provides yet another link in the chain of signifiers that points beyond itself. The bread refers to and embodies the human body that is absent, the body of Christ that is "removed out of our sight."[91] Donne emphatically rejects any notion that Christ's human body is present in the eucharistic elements, understood either in the traditional Catholic doctrine of transubstantiation or the newer Lutheran doctrine of the real presence (ubiquity).[92] His own account of the nature of the Eucharist comes closest to the account of Calvin, whom he often quotes. He attempts, like Calvin, to avoid Catholic or Protestants extremes in his view of the Eucharist, and uses the same language of signs, bonds, and seals with which Calvin tries to steer a middle course in sacramental doctrine.[93] In an early sermon, Donne quotes Calvin to the effect that sacraments are seals of grace, external and visible means by which believers can assure themselves of the mercy of God.[94] In another sermon he says that the sacraments are "glasses" in which believers can see their election: "As we cannot see the essence of God, but must see him in his glasses, in his images, in his creatures, so we cannot see the decrees of God, but must see them in their duplicates, in their exemplification in the sacraments."[95] Donne agrees with Calvin, as well as more radical reformers such as Zwingli, that the physical and historical body of Christ could not be present in the elements of communion since it was "seated at the right hand of the father in heaven."[96] While he often indicates that Christ's "flesh" is on earth in believers who partake of eucharistic bread, he hastens to make clear that this happens only through sacramental communication, so that Christ's presence is not bodily, but "effectual."[97]

One intriguing area marks a difference between Donne and Calvin in their eucharistic theologies. In spite of Donne's repeated references to Christ sitting at the right hand of the Father, his *metaphorical* reaction to this location differs from Calvin's. Calvin logically refers to the act of taking communion as *lifting up* the believer to the body of Christ in heaven. Donne, while theologically agreeing with Calvin about the physical location of Christ's human body, refuses such logical representation when describing the Eucharist. He instead persists in imagining Christ bodily *descending* to the earth, into the very body of believers: in the act of communion, he enters into us, he returns to us, he comes *down* to take us to heaven *with* him, he pours himself out from the hand of the priest to the waiting congregation.[98]

Donne represents the eucharistic bread as sign and sacrament. It points to and manifests, it exhibits and conveys grace, although it does not incarnate Christ's body again on the earth.[99] Donne makes clear that he does not consider this belief inconsistent with the traditions of the Fathers. He says,

> We refuse not the words of the Fathers, in which they have expressed themselves in this Mystery: Not *Irenaeus* his *est corpus*, that the bread is his body now; Not *Tertullians fecit corpus*, that that bread is made his body, which was not so before . . . so the bread hath received a new form, a new essence, a new nature. . . . We say the sacramental bread is the body of Christ, because God hath shed his Ordinance upon it, and made it of another nature in the use, though not in the substance.[100]

The bread is a stand-in, a placeholder, a signifier for the body of Christ, which God ordains to a sacramental and spiritual use.

Conclusion

Redemptive and redeemed bodies have a significant but sometimes elusive role in Donne's trajectory of salvation history. The *redemptive* body plays a clear and unambiguous part in that history in three ways. First, the Edenic remnants of existence and sensation persist in the bodies of fallen humanity as necessary conditions of salvation. Second, the human body of Christ provides another of the necessary components of God's chosen way of saving the human race. Christ had to be fully human, soul and body, to be an adequate representative of humanity in redeeming Adam's sin. He also had to have a human body in order to pay the price for that sin: suffering and death. Third, the human body can serve as a sign or sacrament leading the sinner to salvation. Donne believes that God always uses materials things to express and convey himself to human beings as an accommodation to their own status as material beings. Donne's "communicative" God uses the human body as one of a number of material things through which he expresses himself and embodies his will, his love, and his grace.

The status of the *redeemed* body in Donne's work proves more ambiguous. Donne represents Christ (through his incarnation, suffering, death, resurrection, and ascension) "lifting up" the fallen human body, giving it new dignity and new potential. Donne does not make clear, however, whether or to what extent Christians *in this life* can experience or enact a redeemed body. The only fully redeemed body that appears in Donne's sermons is Christ's, a body "present" on earth only in the memories of his followers or in the highly equivocal form of eucharistic bread. In his preordination writings, Donne shows his readers what seem to be the fully redeemed bodies of women as examples of the potential of all Christian bodies. They function more as poetic signs pointing to an eschatological fulfillment than as practical patterns for the Christian life, however.[101] Donne's redeemed body occupies an ambiguous territory, caught between Catholic and Protestant traditions and between his own pervasive sense of the reality of the fallen body and the hope for the glorified human body in heaven that continually draws his imagination. The redeemed body walks through the sermons *in via,* a pilgrim and a stranger.

Notes

1. John Donne, *The Sermons of John Donne,* 10 vols., ed. Evelyn M. Simpson and George R. Potter, (Berkeley and Los Angeles: University of California Press, 1953–62), 6:120, for instance.

2. Ibid., 4:225.

3. Donne here refers to the small congregations of English separatists that had grown up in England from about the 1570s. Some developed on the left wing of Puritanism, while others were related directly to Anabaptist influence from the Continent. Unlike the main branch of Puritanism, these groups did not attempt to reform the Anglican Church from within, but simply set up covenantal congregations outside the established church. Donne's reference to "Pharisees" refers to what he considered their self-righteous stance as the only pure church of "true" Christians. Donne thought their claims to direct, individual inspiration from God were bad epistemology and bad church polity as well.

4. Ibid., 9:169.

5. John Donne, *John Donne: The Complete English Poems,* ed. A. J. Smith (London: Penguin Books, 1971; repr., London: Penguin Classics, 1986), 318, lines 37–41.

6. Ibid., 329, lines 31–32. My analysis here runs counter to Smith's commentary on the poem. Smith believes that "half of that sacrifice" refers to the fact that in the pain of bearing Jesus and seeing his suffering on the cross, she made her own sacrifice (655). I think my reading accords better with the context, with Donne's other explicit references to Mary providing the "flesh" of Christ, and with Donne's knowledge of the tradition whereby the female provided the "matter" of a child and the father the "form."

7. Donne refers to this tradition in a verse letter "To Mr. B.B." in which he says that his muse has deserted him and therefore "these rhymes which never had / Mother, want matter, and they only have / A little form, the which their father gave" (ibid., 201, lines 23–25).

8. Ibid., 318, line 40.

9. Ibid., 322, lines 155–56.

10. Ibid., *La Corona,* "Annunciation," 306, lines 6, 14; "A Litany," 318, line 41.

11. Ibid., *La Corona,* "Annunciation," 306, lines 5–8. Donne expresses the same idea when he says, "Kings pardon, but he bore our punishment. / And Jacob came clothed in vile harsh attire / But to supplant, and with gainful intent: / God clothed himself in vile man's flesh, that so / He might be weak enough to suffer woe" ("Spit in my face," 313, lines 10–14).

12. John Donne, *Letters to Severall Persons of Honour,* ed. Charles Edmund Merrill Jr. (New York: Sturgis & Walton, 1910), 95–96.

13. In the long argument in the history of theology between those who thought Christ would have been incarnate whether or not human beings had fallen and those who did not think so, Donne sides with those who see the incarnation as a direct response to

human sin, not something God intended from creation. Further, Donne thinks that God could have chosen another way to redeem humanity (see, for instance, *Sermons*, 1:309). However, once God "purposed to himself the way of Justice," as Donne points out in a 1618 sermon preached at the Palace of Whitehall, "then none could be capable of that employment but a mixt person; for God could not die, nor man could not satisfy by death" (ibid). In one of his early Lincoln's Inn sermons, Donne says that Christ "could not have redeemed man, by that way that was contracted between him and his Father, that is, by way of satisfaction, except he had taken the very body, and the very soul of man" (ibid., 2:238; see also 4:284, 288).

14. Particularly notable by her absence from the Christmas sermons is the Virgin Mary. Donne does not carry over into the sermons his earlier emphasis on Mary's role in the incarnation or the secondary theme of Mary's flesh as itself redemptive. Two plausible explanations for this absence are, first, his caution about using any sermonic theme that would raise the hackles of his Protestant congregations or his Protestant mentors at court, and second, the fact that the Marian themes appear in his early work exclusively in poetry where they could evoke powerful imagistic connections without being taken literally as theology.

15. George Potter, one of the twentieth-century editors of Donne's sermons, shows his exasperation with Donne's lack of the proper Yuletide spirit in this critique of an especially unfestive Christmas discourse. He says that "Donne showed some perversity in taking as his text a verse from the book of Exodus, 'O my Lord, send I pray thee, by the hand of him whom thou wilt send.' . . . Still, something suitable might have been made out of it, had Donne been in the right mood. On the contrary, as a Christmas sermon it is a complete disappointment. It contains a great deal about Moses, and very little about Jesus Christ. It lacks the eloquent outbursts of joy at the mercy of God shown in the Incarnation, which had distinguished some of Donne's earlier Christmas sermons" (introduction to *Sermons*, 11–12.) In his frustration at Donne's "perversity," and out of a deeply Anglican desire for some "outbursts of joy" around the doctrine of the incarnation, Potter tends to misread all of Donne's Christmas addresses.

16. As I will discuss in more detail in the later section on the redeemed body as sign and sacrament, there is a basic ambiguity in Donne's theology that is reflected in his representations of the body. Influenced by Protestant eucharistic theology and soteriology, Donne is wary of claiming redeemed "presence" for the earthly body. He instead tends to emphasize its role as a sign of future redemption. I believe that tendency accounts, at least in part, for his lack of emphasis on incarnational presence. This does not represent a slackening of interest in the human body, only a transmutation in the way he chooses to use it theologically.

17. Ibid., 6:8.
18. Ibid., 9:151.
19. Ibid., 9:131.
20. Ibid., 7:279. See also 3:212.
21. Ibid., 6:333.
22. Ibid., 7:279.
23. Notable instances are found in *La Corona* ("Crucifying," "Resurrection," and "Ascension"), "Divine Meditations" ("As due by many titles," "O my black soul," "At

the round earth's imagined corners," "If poisonous minerals," and "What if this present"), "A Litany" (sections II and XXVIII), and "Upon the Annunciation and Passion."

24. Donne, *Sermons*, 1:160, for instance.
25. Ibid., 1:311.
26. Ibid., 6:237.
27. Ibid., 9:306. See also 4:66.
28. Ibid., 4:283.
29. Ibid., 4:284.
30. Ibid., 6:285.
31. Ibid., 4:289.
32. Ibid., 4:289–91.
33. Ibid., 4:296.
34. Ibid., 4:298.
35. Ibid., 4:298, emphasis added.
36. Ibid., 4:300
37. Ibid., 4:299–300.
38. Ibid., 7:231–32, for instance.
39. Ibid., 10:48. See also 9:247.
40. Ibid., 9:247.
41. Ibid., 1:308; 5:351, 368; 6:265; 9:66, 371.
42. Ibid., 6:265.
43. Ibid., 5:368.
44. Donne, *Poems*, 135, lines 73–80.
45. Ibid., lines 89–90.
46. Donne, *Sermons*, 3:55.
47. Ibid., 7:82–83.
48. Ibid., 4:171.
49. John Calvin, *Calvin: Institutes of the Christian Religion*, ed. John T. McNeill, trans. Ford L. Battles, vols. 20 and 21, *The Library of Christian Classics* (Philadelphia: Westminster Press, 1960), bk. 1, chap. 6, sec. 15.
50. Donne, *Sermons*, 4:172–73.
51. Ibid., 5:107.
52. Ibid., 5:165.
53. Ibid., 5:164–65.
54. Ibid., 9:166.
55. Ibid., 4:271. See also 6:203; 7:106–7; 10:223.
56. Ibid., 10:223, 247.
57. Ibid., 3:117.
58. Ibid., 2:63.
59. Ibid., 5:159. See also 3:116.
60. Ibid., 4:48. See also 7:319–20; 8:185–86.
61. Ibid., 4:48, 112; 5:221, 224; 10:56.
62. Donne attempts to make a distinction between signs and sacraments, although in practice his use of the terms lies on a continuum and is sometimes inconsistent. Donne most often uses the word *signs* for objects, acts, or words that simply stand for or point

to other things, ideas, or mysteries. He uses the word *sacraments* to refer to manifestations of the grace and power of God. Sacraments are "sensible" things (objects, acts, or words) that, while remaining themselves, are "consecrated to another use." In one sermon, he criticizes those who confuse ceremonies (like lighting candles) that are simply *significative* with sacraments that are *effective*. Signs simply refer to sacred mysteries, while sacraments *are* mysteries, "powerful and effectual in themselves" (ibid., 10:90–91; see also 2:258).

63. Ibid., 6:175.

64. For instance, he refers to miracles as "transitory and occasional sacraments, as they are visible signs of invisible grace, though not seals thereof" (ibid., 10:69).

65. Donne, *Poems*, 55, lines 69–76.

66. Ibid., "To the Countess of Salisbury," 242, lines 1–4, 7–8.

67. Ibid., line 9–10.

68. Ibid., 243, line 71.

69. Ibid., lines 20–39.

70. Ibid., lines 7–8.

71. Ibid., "To Sir Henry Goodyer," 210, lines 9–13.

72. Ibid., "To the Countess of Bedford ('Honor is so sublime')," 223–24, lines 21–31.

73. I will analyze *The Anniversaries* at length in the final chapter.

74. I previously examined Donne's secular and satirical use of this theme in the poem "The Damp" during the discussion of the fragmented body in chapter 2.

75. Donne, "What if this present," *Poems*, 314.

76. Ibid., "A Litany" (sec. II, "The Son"), 317, lines 14–18.

77. Ibid., "The Cross," 326, lines 15–18.

78. Ibid., "Spit in my face," 313, lines 1–8.

79. Donne, *Sermons*, 2:265–66. See also 7:439–40.

80. Ibid., 8:71.

81. Ibid., 8:319.

82. Ibid., 4:60; 7:319; 8:185; 9:332; 10:227.

83. Ibid., 3:213; 7:319. The dead bodies of the saints also can become, in a limited way, signs pointing toward salvation in that they are *memento mori,* signs of the death that comes to all and toward which all must look and prepare. These relate more to eschatological signs than to signs of present redemption, and I will discuss them in the following chapter.

84. Ibid., 3:116.

85. Ibid., 6:158–59.

86. Ibid., 10:54.

87. Ibid., 3:349. See also 6:152.

88. Ibid., 1:287; 2:250; 3:259; 5:56; 6:216.

89. Ibid., 6:178, emphasis added.

90. Ibid., 10:137.

91. Ibid., 6:271.

92. Ibid., 2:258; 4:68; 6:270–71; 7:294; 9:77, 201–2.

93. Ibid., 1:154; 6:175; 7:267; 10:43. Jarislov Pelikan identifies these words as key to Calvin's efforts to avoid the extreme positions of either side in discussions of the sacra-

ments. *The Christian Tradition: A History of the Development of Doctrine,* vol. 4 of *Reformation of Church and Dogma* (Chicago: University of Chicago Press, 1983; repr., 1985), 191.

94. Donne, *Sermons,* 2:254. See also 5:141.

95. Ibid., 5:161.

96. The latter was a key phrase often used in traditional Protestant arguments against transubstantiation or consubstantiation. Ibid., 4:68; 6:271; 9:77; 10:52.

97. Ibid., 5:149, 368; 6:184; 9:248; 10:190.

98. Ibid., 5:368; 6:184; 9:325.

99. Ibid., 2:254, 258; 6:184.

100. Ibid., 7:295–96.

101. Donne depicts the body of the Virgin Mary as the one example of a "middle" kind of human flesh, positioned between heaven and earth. Donne's treatment of Mary in his early religious poetry implies a historical, ontological reality as well as an eschatological sign. However, Donne does not pursue this depiction of redeemed flesh and its possibilities into the mature theology of his sermons.

THE ESCHATOLOGICAL BODY

Our grave is upward, and our heart is upon Jacob's Ladder. . . .
We rise in the descent to death, and so we do in the descent
to the contemplation of it.

DONNE, *Sermons*

Although the body of Jesus forms the foundation and holds the promise of a restored human body, God will fulfill that promise only through a re-creation and transformation of all human bodies, living and dead, at the time of the "last things": the second coming of Christ, the resurrection of all the dead, the last judgment, and the fulfillment of human and cosmic history in the kingdom of heaven. Donne tends to read all these eschatological events in the book of the body. He seldom preaches on the cosmic apocalypse, the second coming of Christ, or the last judgment directly. The only eschatological event that really captures his imagination is the general, bodily resurrection of the dead. He turns time and again to the themes of the death, fragmentation, bodily resurrection, and glorification of the body as a microcosm of the last things.

Donne focuses his eschatological musings particularly on the dead and rising bodies of the saints. Their death and disintegration represents God's "last judgment" of sin and, at the same time, a gateway into the kingdom of heaven. He uses the reintegration and transformation of their scattered bodies as a master image that points to the attributes of God's nature (love, knowledge, will, and power) that promise the re-creation of the fallen universe. For Donne the whole trajectory of salvation history springs from the divine nature and the divine desire. It is that nature and that desire that encompass our beginning and our end, that will reunite heaven with earth, God with humanity, and soul with body.

Donne, Death, and the Macabre

Donne is famous, or infamous, depending on the critic, for his preoccupation with death and with bodily fragmentation and putrification. Representations of death and related topics—disease, decay, graves, relics, anatomies, skeletons, ghosts, disintegrating dead bodies, and bodily resurrection—permeate his work from the early love poems to his last sermon. Out of the fifty-five poems that make up the *Songs and Sonnets,* many of which date from the 1590s, twenty-five contain imagery having to do with death and the associated topics mentioned above.[1] Such motifs recur frequently throughout his sermons. In the throes of his final illness during the Lenten season of 1630, he stood before the king and court at Whitehall to preach his last sermon. He took as his text Psalm 68:20, "And unto God the Lord belong the issues of death."[2] Marshaling with great relish all his rhetorical flourishes on graves, worms, decay, and dust, he reminds his listeners that they are powerless before death. He informs his distinguished congregation, "In the grave the worms do not kill us, we breed and feed, and then kill those worms which we our selves produced." Pressing home the point that death is not the final humiliation, he asks,

> But then is that [death] the end of all? Is that dissolution of body and soul, the last death that the body shall suffer? . . . It is not. Though this be *exitus a morte,* it is *introitus in mortem;* though it be an issue from the manifold deaths of this world, yet it is an entrance into the death of corruption and putrefaction and vermiculation and incineration, and dispersion in and from the grave, in which every dead man dies over again.[3]

He tells the king and court that even if the dead bodies were children of royal parents or parents of royal children, they must all say with Job, "To corruption thou art my father, and to the worm thou art my mother and my sister," since all people go alike to the grave and become equal in the dust.[4]

Some have called such language about death morbid, unhealthy, macabre, and narcissistic.[5] Such characterizations tend to pass over both the traditional sources of Donne's representations of dead bodies and the subtle uses to which he puts them. Reading Donne's images of death solely as evidence of his own anxiety or narcissism ignores the rich heritage of theological and devotional representations of death and resurrection in which Donne was well versed. It also minimizes the influence of the genre of the works in which these images appear: sermons, eulogies, and anniversaries. Reading Donne's rhetoric of death as part of a theological and devotional tradition and as part of his own well-developed theology of the human body reveals it as consistent, powerfully evocative, and theologically sophisticated.

Donne draws many of his images of death, bodily disintegration, and reunion from arguments by the Church Fathers and their medieval commentators on the subject of bodily resurrection, not from his own "morbid" imagination. Images of bodily fragmentation and material continuity have a long tradition with immediate theological relevance to issues of the nature of body and human identity that preoccupied theologians for decades.[6] These same issues were of immediate concern to Donne, and it is likely that his wide study of the Fathers and the scholastics would have included these very arguments. Donne's musings on how God would gather together the various bits of human beings (whether eaten by wild animals, dissolved in the ocean, blown apart by cannon fire, or nibbled by fish) may strike the modern reader as bizarre, but they were commonplace in patristic and medieval arguments over the resurrection.

Donne's word pictures of death also probably owe something to the medieval devotional traditions that gave rise to the *danse macabre* and the *transi* tomb, a monument that juxtaposed a life-sized image of the deceased as he appeared in life with another life-sized image of a decomposing corpse or skeleton that was meant to reveal his state in death.[7] He made his own original contribution to the tradition of tomb sculpture. More generally, he tends to try to accomplish through rhetoric the same end that these traditions pursued visually: the vivid reminder of human mortality in the service of exhortations to repentance.

Donne was just as concerned as his patristic and medieval predecessors with drawing the attention of the faithful to the transitory nature of their present life and to their coming deaths. While I would not discount elements of anxiety in Donne's fascination with death, I suggest that the voice in the sermons is that of a dramatist using an effective device. He focuses the energy of the natural human horror of death, both his own and his congregation's, for a higher religious purpose. Far from being narcissistic, Donne in his sermons turns outward to address the needs of his listeners. Donne as preacher uses his vivid word pictures of dead and disintegrating bodies to point to the results of sin (present and future) and to powerfully illustrate to his congregations their own powerlessness before their own coming deaths.

The Necessity of Bodily Resurrection

Donne emphasizes the resurrection, in part, simply as a logical extension of his beliefs about creation. Donne puts great emphasis on God's love of the material. This love extends, in particular, to that epitome and microcosm of the material world, the human body. As he makes clear in the following passage, God creates all matter, including bodies, not as a Platonic overflowing of perfection, but out of desire for perfect fullness and loving union. He says,

> The Kingdom of Heaven hath not all that it must have to a consummate perfection, till it have bodies too. In these infinite millions of millions of generations, in which the holy, blessed and glorious Trinity enjoyed themselves one another, and no more, they thought not their glory so perfect, but that it might receive an addition from creatures; and therefore they made a world, a material world, a corporeal world, they would have bodies.[8]

The fall robbed God of this perfection. Salvation history unfolds the story of God's recovery of that which he created out of love and then lost. The body that God made with his own hands and animated with his own breath, the body that Jesus assumed and redeemed at great cost, forms the major focus of that trajectory of salvation history toward the restoration and consummation of all of God's material creation. Until human spirit and human flesh are reconciled, the restoration of all things in heaven and earth through Christ "is not accomplished."[9]

Donne often employs the traditional image of the circle to represent this perfection. In a passage already touched on briefly in the introduction, Donne refers to the "body of man" as the "first point that the foot of God's compas was upon."[10] He argues that the resurrected human body is the "shutting up" of the circle God began with creation, a necessary component of the fulfilled eschatological kingdom. This statement is from the sermon Donne preached at the marriage of Lady Mary, the Earl of Bridgewater's daughter, in 1627. Donne always tends to have the eschatological marriage supper of the Lamb in mind when he speaks of human marriage, both parts of the great circle he rhetorically inscribes here. The resurrection and glorification of the human body encapsulate for Donne the victory of God and the perfect fulfillment of his purposes in creation. The perfected kingdom requires "the bodies of men, which yet lie under the dominion of another."[11] This lack, in part, fuels the dynamism of salvation history toward its consummation.

Just as the larger macrocosmic and universal ordering cannot be perfected without human bodies, so also the fragmented human person on the microcosmic level must have its body restored in order to be perfect. Having a soul in heaven is not enough for human happiness or identity. Donne asks rhetorically in one sermon, "What needs all this heat . . . all this vehemence about the Resurrection? May not man be happy enough in heaven, though his body never come thither. . . . What necessity of bodies in Heaven?[12]

Answering his own question, he insists that the human person is body as well as soul and that the separation of these two in death is contrary to nature.[13] Since Donne defines the human person as a hybrid creature, the perfected eschatological person must have his or her body restored or the person God created is lost.[14] In order to be "Ego-I," as Donne says in one sermon, he must have the same soul and the same body to be "identically, numerically, individually the same man."[15] Not only does human identity depend on the union of soul and body: human happiness does as well. Donne says that the soul, "even in heaven, shall receive an addition, and access of joy, and glory in the resurrection of our bodies in the consummation.[16] Preaching to the royal household at Whitehall in 1621, he insists that a person's own body will be returned to him at the resurrection. He cites Irenaeus's statement that "Christ did not fetch another sheep to the flock, in the place of that which was lost, but the same sheep: God shall not give me another, a better body at the resurrection, but the same body made better."[17]

Although the soul would be "less perfect" without the body, Donne carefully preserves the created hierarchy of soul over body in the next life. He makes it clear, for instance, that only the soul will have the *visio Dei* (the vision of God in his essence, which is the epitome of heaven), while the body will see only the glory shed from God.[18] God does not exclude the body from the joys of heaven, however. Transformed bodily eyes will see the glory of God and the transfigured glory of Christ the Savior in the flesh.[19] God will purify and transform the bodies of the saints into a glorified state like that of the transfigured body of Jesus.[20] Indeed, the bodies of the saints in heaven will be "assimilated to the flesh" of Christ "and made the same flesh" as that of the glorified Christ who sits at the right hand of God.[21] It was for that purpose that the Word was made flesh. Describing the role of the body in heaven in an early sermon preached at Lincoln's Inn, Donne says:

> The bodies of the saints of God, shall receive all impressions of glory in themselves, and they shall do all that is to be done, for the glory of God there. There, they shall stand in his service, and they shall kneel in his worship, and they shall fall in his reverence, and they shall sing in his glory, they shall glorify him in all positions of the body; They shall be glorified in themselves passively, and they shall glorify God actively, *sicut Nix, sicut Lux*, their being, their doing shall be all for him; Thus they shall shine as the sun; Thus their garments shall be white, white as snow, in being glorified in their own bodies, white as light, in glorifying God in all the actions of those bodies.[22]

Donne speaks of a body that has found its proper place as servant to the soul and to the God who made it.

Death as Eschatological Gateway

The death of the body is never God's final word for Donne. He finds the transformations of the human body, living or dead, fascinating. The body in Donne's imaginative universe is never static but always *in via* and in process. In life, it is in flux: growing, changing, aging, dying.[23] Even in death, the body remains active: putrefying, disintegrating, and dispersing into the dust from which God made it. As dust—indeed, even as atoms—it retains its teleological dynamism, pointing toward the general resurrection when God will raise all the dead. As Donne was fond of saying, death touches the resurrection. For the redeemed, the future is glorious. Their bodies and souls will be not only reintegrated, but transformed. The grave resembles an alchemical alembic: it is the site of a necessary and miraculous process of change.

Donne employs images of the divorce of body and soul in death, and consequent bodily disintegration, to indicate the consequences of sin. He understands death and disintegration as direct and literal results of original sin. They also serve as poetic figures for the damage sin does to the soul and to the whole cosmos. Even the redeemed person must suffer these consequences. In one of the "Divine Meditations," Donne's speaker looks toward the ending of his life, his "play's last scene," and realizes that nothing can save him from "gluttonous death," who "will instantly unjoint / My body, and soul, and I shall sleep a space."[24] Once parted from its animating soul, the body putrefies and disintegrates. In this piecemeal condition, the human person awaits the general resurrection and the last judgment. In one of his best-known poems, Donne pictures fragmented humanity arising on that last day.

> At the round earth's imagined corners, blow
> Your trumpets, angels, and arise, arise
> From death, you numberless infinities
> Of souls, and to your scattered bodies go,
> All whom the flood did, and fire shall o'erthrow,
> All whom war, dearth, age, agues, tyrannies,
> Despair, law, chance, hath slain.[25]

Donne uses the figures of scattered and putrefying bodies and the reintegration of those bodies in the last day even more regularly in his sermons than in his early work. He employs them for a distinctly theological and pastoral purpose. In his famous last sermon preached before the king in 1630, Donne considers at length the dissolution of the body, invaded by worms and eventually falling to dust. Underscoring the humiliation and loss of identity that such a dissolution entails, he calls the body's decay

> The most inglorious and contemptible vilification, the most deadly and peremptory nullification of man, that we can consider. God seems to have carried the declaration of his power to a great height, when he sets the Prophet Ezekiel in a valley of dry bones and says, *Son of man can these bones live?* . . . But in that case there were bones to be seen, something visible of which it might be said, can this thing live? But in this death of incineration and dispersion of dust, we see nothing that we can call that man's.[26]

If the "divorce" of body from soul in death represents the wages of sin, the fragmentation and dispersion of the body signify God's judgment on that sin and (to a limited extent) his abandonment of the body, his turning away his face. Although Jesus' body and soul were "divorced" in death, his body never saw corruption because God did not abandon him. Donne tells his congregations, "Even in his death, both parts were still, not only inhabited by but united to the God-head itself."[27] In contrast to the preservation of Jesus' body, the dispersal of the sinner's body into fragments represents the final triumph of Satan and the (seeming) abandonment of the body by God. The disintegration of the human body marks the nadir of loss for Donne: loss of life, loss of human coherence, loss of identity, loss of God.

Donne presents his vivid word pictures of the putrefying human body to his congregations not primarily out of his own morbid interest in death or out of a desire for pulpit dramatics, although these certainly may play some part, but rather for a practical pastoral purpose. Donne in the sermons follows rhetorically the course he believes God pursues actually in the deaths of the redeemed. In a 1624 sermon on the conversion of St. Paul, Donne says that God "brings us to death, that by that gate he might lead us into life everlasting."[28] In this sermon, he takes as his text Acts 9:4, "And he fell to the earth, and heard a voice saying unto him, Saul, Saul, why persecutest thou me?" Donne weaves together Paul's fall to earth with the falling apart of bodies in the earth. He shows how God works on the bodies of his saints in life through affliction to bring them down to a place of humility and teachableness so that he may save them. His "working" on his saints in the grave is simply the physical working out of this same principle. Donne tells his congregation,

> I take no farther occasion from the circumstance [of God casting Paul to the earth], but to arm you with consolation, how low soever God be pleased to cast you, though it be to the earth, yet he does not so much cast you down, in doing that, as bring you home. Death is not a banishing of you out of this world; but it is a visitation of your kindred that lie in the earth; neither are any nearer of kin to you, than the earth it self, and the worms of the earth . . . when thou readest, that God makes thy bed in thy sickness, rejoice in this, not only

that he makes that bed, where thou doest lie, but that bed where thou shalt lie; that God, that made the whole earth, is now making thy bed in the earth, a quiet grave, where thou shalt sleep in peace, till the Angel's trumpet wake thee at the resurrection.[29]

Through his vivid descriptions of death and dissolution, Donne brings his parishioners to the gates of death, but only in order to bring them home. He speaks to them, through even his most grotesque flights of discourse about disintegrating bodies, about the wages of sin, their lack of hope in themselves, and their need to depend solely on the love and power of God. In one aspect, the dissolution of the human body in the grave is the final working out of the consequences of sin, the final humiliation. Donne holds up pictures of that final humiliation before his congregation as salutary reminders of their true condition as sinners and of their inability to "hold themselves together" in body or soul without the continual grace of God. He reminds them to prepare now for their own approaching deaths. In its other aspect, however, Donne reminds them that this dissolution only brings them back to their true home: the earth from which they were made. Donne does in the passage what he does, and indeed directly states, in many others: the grave reaches back to creation and forward to resurrection. His emphasis on humiliation and disintegration simply returns his listeners to the *humus* from which God made them. He rhetorically returns them to the place where God will *literally* remake them at the resurrection of the dead so that God can remake them *spiritually* at the moment of the sermon through their remembrance, realization, and repentance.

Donne also represents the death of the righteous as the last of the ascetic practices through which the Christian prepares to meet God. In a late sermon, he tells his listeners,

He that begins with that mortification of denying himself his delights, (which is a dram of Death), shall be able to suffer the tribulations of this world, (which is a greater measure of death) and then Death itself, not only patiently but cheerfully; and to such a man, death is not a dissolution, but a redintegration; not a divorce of body and soul, but a sending of both divers ways, (the soul upward to Heaven, the body downward to the earth) to an indissoluble marriage to him, who, for the salvation of both, assumed both, our Lord and Savior, Jesus Christ.[30]

The disintegration of the human person is a necessary prelude to re-creation. God "forgets" the body in the grave, and allows Satan his dominion over it, only for a short time. In a Lenten sermon preached before the royal household in 1621, Donne says, "The punishment that God laid upon

Adam, '*In dolore & in sudore*, In sweat, and in sorrow shalt thou eat thy bread,' is but '*Donc reverteris*, till man return to dust': but when Man is returned to dust, God returns to the remembrance of that promise, 'Awake and sing ye that dwell in the dust.'"[31]

Donne goes on to say that although Satan has apparent dominion over the human body for a space, in fact the bodies of all of humankind have already been "sealed" to God's glory by his "pre-assuming" the human body of Christ to that glory.[32] God re-creates the redeemed, as he created the innocent body of Eden, after the pattern of Jesus, the eternal Word. The eschatological promise, which lay in Jesus' incarnation and will be fulfilled at the resurrection of the dead, allows Donne to reach back and reinterpret even the power of death. Donne tells his congregation,

> The Master of the house, Christ Jesus, is dead before; and now it is not so much a part of our punishment, for the first Adam, as an imitation of the second Adam, to die; death is not so much a part of our debt to Nature, or Sin, or Satan, as a part of our conformity to him who died for us . . . as the death of Christ Jesus is the Physick of mankind, so this natural death of the body is the application of that Physick to every particular man, who only by death can be made capable of that glory which his death hath purchased for us.[33]

Christ's resurrection changes "the whole frame and course of nature," Donne tells his congregation.[34] While Satan has apparent dominion over this world and over the bodies of humankind, the eschatological promise of Christ's resurrection reaches back even into the graves of the dead and transforms their *significance* and their trajectory. The grave actually "does not bury the dead man, but death himself."[35] For the elect, the grave forms the small and humble gate they pass through into Paradise.

While Donne reserves the actual transformation and re-creation of the dead for the general resurrection in his sermons, Donne often "reads back" this future eschatological transformation *into* the graves of the redeemed dead in the poetry written before his ordination. In his "Elegy on Mrs. Bulstrode," who died in 1609 at the age of twenty-five, Donne implies that her body (the "house") will not truly disintegrate, even though her soul (the "king") removes from it.

> As houses fall not, though the king remove,
> Bodies of saints rest for their souls above.
> Death gets 'twixt souls and bodies such a place
> As sin insinuates 'twixt just men and grace,

> Both work a separation, no divorce.
> Her soul is gone to usher up her corse,
> Which shall be almost another soul, for there
> Bodies are purer, than the best souls are here.[36]

Sin and death have such a temporary dominion over the subject of this poem that Donne changes the usual metaphor of divorce to a mere (temporary) separation. Her body, even in the grave, holds such a promise of heavenly purity that it merely "rests" instead of decaying. Fascinated as he is by the death and dissolution of the body, Donne never fixes his thoughts there. He looks at death as merely a stage in the process of transformation. He regards the graveyard as directly abutting the New Jerusalem, not lying within the territory of the "Prince of this World."[37] Paradoxically, the grave, which seems the very site of Satan's victory, does not truly lie in the kingdom of this world at all. In the poem "Obsequies upon the Lord Harrington," Donne writes,

> And churchyards are our cities, unto which
> The most repair, that are in goodness rich.
> There is the best concourse, and confluence,
> There are the holy suburbs, and from thence
> Begins God's city, New Jerusalem,
> Which doth extend her utmost gates to them.
> At that gate then triumphant soul, doest thou
> Begin thy triumph.[38]

The body of the dead Christian already is, potentially, what it will one day be in heaven.

The resurrection of the bodies of the redeemed depends on the sacrificial death of Christ and his resurrection. His is the prototype of the glorified body that all the saints will have on the last day. In "Resurrection Imperfect," Donne speaks of the resurrection of Jesus,

> Whose body having walked on earth, and now
> Hasting to heaven, would, that he might allow
> Himself unto all stations, and fill all,
> For those three days become a mineral;
> He was all gold when he lay down, but rose
> All tincture, and doth not alone dispose
> leaden and iron wills to good, but is
> Of power to make even sinful flesh like his.[39]

Here, Donne pictures Christ saving all by becoming a microcosm of all, both heaven and earth ("that he might allow himself unto all stations, and fill all"). In the poem's main conceit, the grave becomes an alchemical alembic, a vessel alchemists employed in their quest to turn base metals into gold. Christ, already perfect (gold) when he goes into the "alembic" of the grave, emerges as "tincture," the essence of gold that has in itself the power to transform base minerals into gold.[40] Christ's perfect body attains the power in the grave to transform the very bodies of humanity, not just their sinful wills, into a like perfection.

Donne employs the metaphor of the alchemical transformation of the body in several poems to represent the graves of the redeemed as liminal territory, sites of miraculous transformation. In *La Corona* ("Resurrection"), Donne says that even in death,

> If in thy little book my name thou enroll,
> Flesh in that long sleep is not putrefied,
> But made that there, of which, and for which 'twas;
> Nor can by other means be glorified.[41]

In this passage, Donne obliquely recalls the alchemical process through which base metal is reduced to ash (or more specifically here, the original dust of creation) before being transformed ("glorified") into another substance. In "Epitaph on Himself: To the Countess of Bedford," Donne rhetorically paints a picture of his own body in the tomb to remind the Countess to "mend herself" in contemplation of death. The poem works a brilliant reversal of the conventions of the tradition of *memento mori*. In this tradition, a representation of a moldering body (in a picture, a literary work, or even a tomb sculpture) reminds onlookers of their own mortality and urges repentance while there is still time. Donne points to his "dead" body and asks the Countess to consider that her current position, living, is inferior to what his will be in death.

> In my grave's inside seest what thou art now:
> Yet thou'art not yet so good, till death us lay
> To ripe and mellow here, we are stubborn clay.
> Parents make us earth, and souls dignify
> Us to be glass; here to grow gold we lie.
> Whilst in our souls sin bred and pampered is,
> Our souls become worm-eaten carcasses.[42]

In this startling poem, the actual dead body "grows gold," undergoing an alchemical transformation into perfection while awaiting the eschatological fulfillment of the resurrection. The "worm-eaten carcass" of the poem, the *memento mori,* is not a dead body, but the still living and sinful soul.[43]

In "Elegy on Mrs. Bulstrode," Donne writes that her soul has gone up to God, but

> Her body left with us, lest some had said,
> She could not die, except they saw her dead;
> For from less virtue, and less beauteousness,
> The gentiles frame them gods and goddesses.
> The ravenous earth that now woos her to be
> Earth too, will be a lemnia; and the tree
> That wraps that crystal in a wooden tomb,
> Shall be took up spruce, filled with diamond.[44]

"Lemnia" refers to *terra lemnia,* another alchemical term indicating a clay the alchemist used in the process of changing nonprecious substances into precious ones.[45] Donne pictures the ravening earth of the grave, which wants to dissolve the dead woman's body into elements, becoming instead the agent of a transformation of her pure body (a clear crystal) into a precious diamond, wrapped in spruce (an evergreen tree indicating everlasting life).

In "An Elegy on the Lady Markham," Donne represents the dead body of a saintly woman in imagery that parallels his presentation of the body of Jesus in "Resurrection Imperfect." Not only does her body undergo an alchemical transformation to perfection, but it has redemptive potency for others. These themes of perfection joined with salvific power are similar to those I have already examined in Donne's treatment of the living bodies of Jesus and those of redeemed women. Donne writes,

> In her this sea of death hath made no beach
> And leaves embroidered works upon the sand,
> So is her flesh refined by death's cold hand
> As men of China, after an age's stay,
> Do take upon porcelain, where they buried clay;
> So at this grave, her limbeck, which refines
> The diamonds, rubies, sapphires, pearls, and mines,
> Of which this flesh was, her soul shall inspire
> Flesh of such stuff, as God, when his last fire
> Annuls this world, to recompense it, shall,
> Make and name then, th'elixir of this all.[46]

As he does in "Resurrection Imperfect," Donne calls the grave a "limbeck," or alembic. He also refers in this poem to the belief that the Chinese made porcelain by merely burying clay vessels for a hundred years and awaiting their transformation.[47] Donne refers to Jesus' body in "Resurrection Imperfect" as the tincture that will make all bodies like his. Here he says that Lady Markham's body will become the elixir (another alchemical term) through which the material world will be refined at the last day when the world is destroyed and recreated in fire. Donne also uses this motif of the redemptive power of the dead body of a saintly woman extensively in *The Anniversaries*, to which I will turn in detail in the next chapter.

Donne represents the eschatological body not only in his poetry and sermons, but in one final and dramatic gesture: posing for a final portrait in his own shroud.[48] Donne offers the representation, in the form of a marble effigy that still stands in St. Paul's Cathedral, as a final and eloquent "sermon" on death and resurrection. According to his contemporary and earliest biographer, Izaac Walton, Donne himself decided the form the monument would take. He actually rose from his deathbed to pose for an artist. Stripped naked and holding his own funeral shroud about him, Donne modeled his expectation of his own resurrection.[49] Although later critics have tended to dismiss this tale as overly dramatic, Walton's account is not so unlikely. Donne loved drama and the grand gesture, and he probably did so to the last.

The effigy commissioned from the artist's sketch occupies an ambiguous and suggestive border region, representationally, historically, and theologically. The sculpture is a life-sized representation of Donne standing upright on his funeral urn, draped in his grave clothes. The upright position indicates Donne's wish to depict his body in the very instant of its rising from the grave at the last day.[50] The figure stands on the cusp of life and death, past and future, heaven and earth. Historically and artistically, Donne's effigy also seems to stand between styles and periods. During the early Middle Ages, a typical effigy showed "a recumbent person in a state of frozen alertness," or, if standing, the image stood for the person "in life," dressed to the hilt and with all their marks of office and honors about them.[51] A later medieval fashion in tomb sculpture was the *transi* tomb. This kind of tomb juxtaposed two sculptured or bas-relief figures: one a model of the deceased in life, usually with indication of all rank and honors, and the other a skeleton or moldering, naked corpse representing the state of the body of the deceased in the tomb. This called attention to the contrast between the states of life and death. These tombs were meant to function as *memento mori*, reminders to the individual who would lie there, or to onlookers, of the fate that awaited them in death. The use of *transi* tombs extended through the Renaissance until Donne's day, although the later version tended to be a bit less gruesome.[52] Kneeling or semirecumbent figures were also popular during Donne's time, but there seems to be little precedent for Donne's ambiguous standing figure gesturing toward the resurrection.[53]

Donne's effigy represents visually the point he makes in many sermons, including this one from 1621 on the destruction of death:

> As long as we put it off, and as loath as we are to look this enemy in the face, yet we must, though it be Death. . . . *Surge & descende in domum figuli*, says the Prophet Jeremy, that is, say the Expositors, the consideration of thy Mortality. It is *Surge, descende,* Arise and go down: a descent with an ascension: Our grave is upward, and our heart is upon Jacob's Ladder, in the way, and nearer to heaven. . . . We rise in the descent to death, and so we do in the descent to the contemplation of it.[54]

Donne offers the representation of his own body on the borderline between death and resurrection as an object of contemplation. Like his sermons, Donne's monument asserts the intimate interconnection between death and new life, pointing to the body's path of descent and ascent that makes up God's circle.

The Resurrection of the Body as a Representation of God's Love, Knowledge, Will, and Power

Donne's effigy represents his faith that he will continue to exist not primarily because of his own nature, but because of God's nature. The epitaph under the shrouded likeness on the monument in St. Paul's reads, "Having been invested with the Deanery of this Church, / November 27, 1621, / he was stripped of it by Death on the last day of March 1631: / and here, though set in dust, he beholdeth Him / whose name is the Rising [*Oriens*]."[55] Given both the style and content, it seems likely that Donne himself wrote the passage. It speaks volumes about his thoughts on his own identity and on the significance of the body. First, he notes on his monument not the date of his birth, but the date of his investiture as Dean of St. Paul's. Donne closely associated identity with vocation, as was common in his time. He was particularly sensitive to this issue, since his struggle to find a vocation, and with it a stable identity and place in the world, proved difficult and prolonged. He sometimes told friends that he dated his life from his ordination. Through the words "invested" and "stripped," he further associates his position and vocation with his body, since he often speaks of the embodiment of incarnation and the disembodiment of death in these terms, relating them to the Platonic image of the body as a garment. On one level Donne refers to his "disembodying": loss of position, vocation, life, bodily integrity, and identity all in one metaphor. He then makes a rather radical claim. Christians have tended to tie personal identity more closely to the soul, which after death and perhaps a necessary cleansing in purgatory is able to enjoy the *visio Dei* in heaven while the inert body awaits resurrection. Donne, to the contrary, refuses to link his continued identity with his soul in heaven, insisting instead that he is *here*, "*hic licet in occiduo cinere aspicit eum cujus nomen est Oriens.*" He has made his grave into a statement of a realized eschatology. Even in his grave, in his fragmented state, he asserts that he *beholds* the Risen One. He presents his hidden, fragmented body as a sign that both points to and participates in the hope represented by the visible effigy.

Donne believes that dead bodies may fall apart, but they never fall out of God's hands. God never truly turns away from the dead body; therefore, the dead never "fall away" into meaninglessness.[56] Donne lives and preaches in a world where *nothing* falls outside the ambit of God's love, knowledge, and power. God is Lord of all being and Lord of all signs. Even dead bodies have material existence, present significance, and future promise.

In spite of Satan's seeming power over human bodies, God's love and attention never stray far from the bodies he creates. Even though he allows them to suffer the sickness, pain, death, and dissolution that flow from sin, he never abandons them. Donne tells his congregation that just as the divine nature (or Godhead) did not "depart" from the body of Christ in the grave, "so neither doth the love and power of God depart from the body of a Christian, though resolved to dust in the grave, but, in his due time, shall recollect that dust, and recompact that body, and reunite that soul, in everlasting joy and glory."[57] The love that underlies this attention does not depend on the qualities or worthiness of the human person. God protected Christ's body from putrification not because he was sinless or because of the union of divine and human nature, but simply because of his own good pleasure.[58] The resurrection of all human bodies depends on that same will. During the first sermon he preached at St. Dunstan's after the congregation had been disbursed for weeks by a terrible outbreak of plague in the spring and summer of 1625, Donne assures his grieving listeners that "the soul of man is not safer wrapt up in the bosom of God, than the body of man is wrapt up in the Contract, and in the eternal Decree of the Resurrection."[59] God will resurrect "the creature, who, because he hath made him, he loves, for his own glory."[60]

The "potential" for a resurrected and glorified human body depends not only on God's love and will, but on his knowledge of the fragmented parts and his power to re-create the disintegrated body and reunite it with the soul. The idea that God knows (and cares) where every fragment of every dead body resides is a theme Donne loves to explore in his sermons. It also appears in his early work in "Obsequies upon the Lord Harrington." In that poem, Donne says that even if "man feed on man's flesh, and so / Part of his body to another owe, / Yet at the last two perfect bodies rise, / Because God knows where every atom lies."[61] He pursues the same themes and images in an Easter Day sermon preached at St. Paul's in 1626. Donne says that even though the flesh of dead men has been buried,

> and hath brought forth grass, and that grass fed beasts, and those beasts fed men, and those men fed other men, God that knows in which Box of his Cabinet all this seed Pearl lies, in what corner of the world every atom, every grain of every man's dust sleeps, shall recollect that dust, and then recompact that body, and then re-inanimate that man, and that is the accomplishment of all.[62]

From a human perspective, it may appear that human bodies are dispersed, lost and forgotten. From God's perspective, however, the whole earth simply makes up the strongbox where he keeps his precious jewels, including every fragment of every human body.[63] While human beings may forget the dead, God never does. His memory of them and his knowledge of the identity and location of every fragment holds their future. That memory and knowledge make God *present* to the human body, even in its most unrecognizable form, even as God is present to the soul in the *visio Dei*.[64] That presence is life even in death and contains the promise that Ezekiel's dry bones will sing and dance.

The resurrection of the human body also depends on God's power. Donne says in his 1626 Easter sermon, "For after such a scattering, no power, but of God only can recollect those grains of dust, and recompact them into a body, and re-animate them into a man."[65] Donne often associates such power with God's original act of creation. He says in the sermons that "recompacting" the body from disparate parts is surely less complicated than its original creation *ex nihilo*. He quotes Tertullian to this effect in an early sermon that deals with the ravages of death.

> Fall as low as thou canst, corrupt and putrefy as desperately as thou canst, *sis nihil*, think thy self nothing; *Ejus est nihilum ipsum cujus est totum*, even that nothing is as much in his power, as the world which he made of nothing; And, as he called thee when thou wast not, as if thou hadst been, so will he call thee again, when thou art ignorant of that being which thou hast in the grave, and give thee again thy form, and glorify it with a better being.[66]

This same thought appears in a 1613 letter to the Viscount of Rochester in which Donne says, "It is easier for God to recollect the Principles, and Elements of our bodies, howsoever they be scattered, than it was at first to create them of nothing."[67]

Conclusion

While some modern critics have tended to identify what one has called Donne's "needy fascination with the promise of bodily resurrection" with the psychoanalytic category of narcissism,[68] Donne's approach to death and resurrection indicate, instead, a profound acceptance of limitation, death, and powerlessness. In refusing to identify the human person with soul alone, and in further denying purity and even immortality to the soul,[69] Donne hews closely to a strictly biblical view of the human as *humus:* earthy, humble, limited, bounded, and contingent. In his eschatological representations of death and resurrection, Donne reads in the body the story of human limitation on the one hand and God's limitless power on the other: they are two sides of the same coin. Only God's love, will, knowledge, and power suffice to bring the disintegrated human person back together into a transformed and glorified integrity even as they were instrumental in human creation and redemption.

Notes

1. Several of these have explicitly eschatological themes and depend on imagery of the "recompacting" of the scattered body, and the body with the soul, on the last day. They include "The Relic," "The Funeral," and "A Valediction of My Name in the Window."

2. John Donne, *The Sermons of John Donne,* 10 vols., ed. Evelyn M. Simpson and George R. Potter (Berkeley and Los Angeles: University of California Press, 1953–62), 10:230.

3. Ibid., 236.

4. Ibid.

5. Frank J. Warnke, one of Donne's biographers, finds his "obsession with death and decay and the certainty thereof" unedifying, although he concedes that "that emphasis is to some extent balanced by the preacher's repeated and impassioned insistence on the doctrine of the resurrection of the body." *John Donne* (Boston: Twayne Publishers, 1987), 92. Another of Donne's eminent critics, Evelyn M. Simpson, calls his final sermon "a strange mingling of intense devotion to Christ with a gloomy morbidity of fancy which delights in picturing the physical corruption of the body, with the accompaniment of worms and dust." *A Study of the Prose Works of John Donne,* 2nd ed. (Oxford: Clarendon Press, 1948), 10. She further criticizes the effigy Donne chose for his tomb in St. Paul's, put off by the effigy's "horrible suggestion of mortality" (10). Noting regretfully that Donne had certain obvious psychological flaws, she identifies as the "chief of these . . . a morbid obsession with the idea of death. One is tempted to think that Donne had seen some horrible sight in childhood which left its mark on his highly sensitive nature" (65). John Carey, in *Life, Mind, and Art* (New York: Oxford University Press, 1981), eschews a psychological explanation for a rhetorical one, speculating that Donne "enjoyed giving his congregations the horrors. . . . Terror afforded him a histrionic tri-

umph" (134). Deborah A. Larson, in her review of twentieth-century Donne criticism, notes a more accepting attitude toward his "alleged melancholy, morbidity, and death-wish" in some more recent criticism. Still, she says that these traits "throughout this century turned some readers away from Donne. . . . The prevailing opinion has been that Donne's melancholy and morbidity are different from, more extreme than, these attitudes as they appear in other Jacobean writers." *John Donne and Twentieth Century Criticism* (London and Toronto: Associated University Presses, 1989), 154–56.

6. Caroline Walker Bynum has detailed the patristic and medieval arguments about bodily resurrection in "Material Continuing, Personal Survival and the Resurrection of the Body: A Scholastic Discussion in Its Medieval and Modern Contexts," in *Fragmentation and Redemption: Essays on Gender and the Human Body in Medieval Religion* (New York: Zone Books, 1992), and in *The Resurrection of the Body in Western Christianity: 200–1336* (New York: Columbia University Press, 1995).

7. According to Paul Binski in *Medieval Death: Ritual and Representation* (Ithaca, N.Y.: Cornell University Press, 1996), there was a long medieval devotional tradition that exploited the macabre as the "mirror image" to the redemptive body of Christ in the symbolism of transformation (126). Binski gives an illuminating analysis on the subject of anxiety and the macabre in medieval representations of death and the relevance of these representations to understanding medieval views of the body.

8. Donne, *Sermons*, 4:47.

9. Ibid., 8:97.

10. Ibid., 8:97.

11. Ibid., 4:45. Norman O. Brown has identified this kind of materiality as the distinctive characteristic of Christian eschatology. He says that the distinctive nature of Christian eschatology "lies precisely in its rejection of the Platonic hostility to the human body and to 'matter,' its refusal to identify the Platonic path of sublimation with ultimate salvation, and its affirmation that eternal life can only be life in a body." *Life against Death: The Psychoanalytical Meaning of History* (New York: Vintage Books, 1959), 309.

12. Donne, *Sermons*, 4:357.

13. Ibid., 4:358.

14. Ibid., 2:63; 7:103.

15. Ibid., 3:109. Walker Bynum argues in *Resurrection of the Body* that it is just this preoccupation with identity that fueled centuries of discussion on what happened to the fragments of the dead bodies of the saints.

16. Donne, *Sermons*, 5:250; 7:103.

17. Ibid., 4:61.

18. Ibid., 4:168.

19. See, for instance, the passage in which Donne likens the body in heaven to a well-loved child whom its indulgent parent-soul brings along with it to see the king. Ibid., 3:112.

20. Ibid., 3:118.

21. Ibid., 3:112.

22. Ibid., 3:121.

23. See, for instance, his statement in "Obsequies upon the Lord Harrington": "I do not wear / Those spirits, humours, blood I did last year." John Donne, *John Donne: The*

Complete English Poems, ed. A. J. Smith, (London: Penguin Books, 1971; repr., London: Penguin Classics, 1986), 157, lines 45–46.

24. Ibid., "This is my play's last scence," 311, lines 5–6.
25. Ibid., "At the round earth's imagined corners," lines 1–7.
26. Donne, *Sermons*, 10:239.
27. Ibid., 2:209.
28. Ibid., 6:212–13.
29. Ibid., 6:213.
30. Ibid., 8:168.
31. Ibid., 4:62.
32. Ibid. See also 10:52.
33. Ibid., 6:357.
34. Ibid., 9:203, quoting Severianus.
35. Ibid., 9:203. See also 4:62; 8:91.
36. Donne, *Poems*, 249, lines 37–44.
37. Donne wrote many sermons on the theme of the defeat of death. The same theme appears consistently in his early work. Two examples are the famous "Death be not proud" and "An Elegy on the Lady Markham," in which he says, "If carnal death (the younger brother) do / Usurp the body, or soul, which subject is / To th'elder death, by sin, is freed by this; / They perish both, when they attempt the just; / For graves our trophies are, and both deaths' dust" (ibid., 248, lines 30–34).
38. Ibid., 261, lines 171–78.
39. Ibid., 327, lines 8–15.
40. A. J. Smith discusses the poem's alchemical imagery in his notes. Ibid., 327–28.
41. Donne, *Poems*, 308, lines 8–11.
42. Ibid., 233, 10–16.
43. Perhaps the closest passage in the sermons to this kind of alchemical imagery is a delightfully metaphysical conceit from an early sermon Donne preached at the Temple Church in London. Donne says, "Though I perish, I do not perish; though I die, I do not die; but as that piece of money, which was but the money of a poor man, being given in subsidy, becomes a part of the Royal Exchequer: so this body, which is but the body of a sinful man, being given in subsidy, as a contribution to the Glory of my God, in the grave, becomes a part of God's Exchequer; and when he opens it, he shall issue out this money, that is, manifest it again cloth'd in his Glory: that body which in me was but a piece of copper money, he shall make a talent of gold" (*Sermons*, 5:230). Here God performs an alchemical transformation from copper to gold, but (as is typical of the sermons) Donne keeps the transformation firmly placed at the time of the resurrection of the dead ("when he opens it . . ."), not, as in the poems, before the resurrection.
44. Donne, *Poems*, 253, lines 53–60.
45. Ibid., A. J. Smith's commentary, 580.
46. Ibid., 248, lines 18–28.
47. Ibid., A. J. Smith's commentary, 574.
48. In addition to serving as the model for the effigy that Donne commissioned for St. Paul's, the portrait was used as the frontispiece to the publication of Donne's final sermon. For a discussion of this portrait and epigraph, see Catherine J. Creswell, "Reading

Subjectivity: The Body, the Text, the Author in John Donne" (Ph.D. diss., State University of New York at Buffalo, 1993), 109–14.

49. Izaak Walton, *The Lives of Dr. John Donne, Sir Henry Wotton, Mr. Richard Hooker, Mr. George Herbert and Dr. Robert Sanderson* (London: John Major, 1825), 72–73.

50. Donne's biographer, R. C. Bald, says of the effigy, "It seems to have been Donne's intention to represent the resurrection of the body; the shrouded figure is rising from the funeral urn, and what seems at first glance to be a crouching attitude suggests rather that he is still emerging, and has not yet drawn himself erect. That the resurrection was in Donne's mind is clear from Walton's statement that he faced east while the drawing was being made." *John Donne: A Life* (New York: Oxford University Press, 1970), 535–36.

51. Binski, *Medieval Death*, 93–94. As he notes, these effigies tended to deny or cancel out the state of the dead body in the tomb, and indeed the state of death itself (94). My account of the changing fashions in monuments is drawn from Binski and Erwin Panofsky, *Tomb Sculpture: Four Lectures on Its Changing Aspects from Ancient Egypt to Bernini* (New York: Harry N. Abrams, 1964).

52. Panofsky points out that such sculptures tended to leave out depictions of worms and vermin feeding on the body after about 1550 (*Tomb Sculpture*, 79).

53. Bald points out that Donne's monument attracted a good deal of attention among his contemporaries, and that engravings of it appeared in the second edition of Holland's *Ecclesia Sancti Pauli Illustrata* (1633) and in Dugdale's *History of St. Paul's Cathedral* (1658). He also states that people soon began copying it and that shrouded figures appeared on a number of tombs throughout England during the thirty years after Donne's death (*Donne: A Life*, 533). See also Katharine A. Esdaile, *English Church Monuments, 1510–1840* (London and Malvern Wells, Worcestershire: B. T. Batsford, 1946).

54. Donne, *Sermons*, 4:51.

55. Translation by Archdeacon Francis Wrangham from the Latin, quoted by Walton in *Lives*, 467. According to an account of Donne's life included by his son in his edition of some of the poems, Donne wrote the epitaph himself. John Donne, *Poems on Several Occasions, Written by the Reverend John Donne, D.D., Late Dean of St. Paul's, with Elegies on the Author's Death* (London: printed for J. Tonwon, 1719), 10. See also Bald, *Donne: A Life*, 535.

56. Julia Kristeva notes that modernity sees the corpse precisely as that which has fallen away. Such a way of seeing assumes the absence of God. She speaks of the dead body as the ultimate example of the abject, the "jettisoned object," the place where "meaning collapses." She says, "The corpse (or cadaver: cadere: to fall), that which has irremediably come a cropper, is cesspool, and death. . . . In the corpse, that thing that no longer matches and therefore no longer signifies anything, I behold the breaking down of a world that has erased its borders: fainting away. The corpse, seen without God and outside of science, is the utmost in abjection. It is death infecting life." *Powers of Horror: An Essay on Abjection*, trans. Leon S. Roudiez (New York: Columbia University Press, 1982), 2, 4–5. Her view of the horrible as the abject goes some way toward explaining why modern critics tend to see Donne's dead bodies through the lens of horror. Many of them assume the absence of God and thus read Donne's images of death through a psychoanalytic rather than theological point of view.

57. Donne, *Sermons*, 10:188. See also 3:106; 7:277.

58. Donne says that "we look no further for causes or reasons in the mysteries of religion, but to the will and pleasure of God. . . . Christ's body did not see corruption, therefore, because God had decreed that it should not" (ibid., 10:236).

59. Ibid., 6:363.

60. Ibid., 3:96.

61. Donne, *Poems*, 256, lines 53–56.

62. Donne, *Sermons*, 7:115.

63. In another similar passage, Donne says that "all the world is God's cabinet, and water, and earth, and fire and air, are the proper boxes, in which God lays up our bodies, for the Resurrection" (ibid., 4:359).

64. Ibid., 6:66.

65. Ibid., 7:114.

66. Ibid., 3:98.

67. Donne, *Letters*, 247.

68. Robert N. Watson, *The Rest Is Silence: Death as Annihilation in the English Renaissance* (Berkeley: University of California Press, 1994), 208. Another example of this sort of psychoanalytic reading is John Carey in *Life, Mind, and Art*, 220–30.

69. Donne seems to take the position that the soul is not immortal in nature any more than the body is, but that both are preserved in being by the will of God. See, for instance, *Sermons*, 8:144.

READING THE TRAJECTORY OF SALVATION IN THE BOOK OF THE BODY

I know that in the state of my body, which is more discernible than that of my soul, thou dost effigiate my soul to me.
DONNE, *Devotions*

In this final chapter, I will suggest a reading of the themes of creation, fall, redemption, and eschatological salvation as Donne represents them through the figure of the body in two of his major works: the early *Anniversaries* and the late *Devotions upon Emergent Occasions*. Such an analysis will serve as a fitting summary of my exploration of the body in Donne's thought. Although the first was written long before his ordination and the second at the height of his power and prestige as Dean of St. Paul's, these two works exemplify Donne's predilection for using the human body as the primary touchstone of his theological imagination. These two significant works represent explicitly what Donne was implicitly doing with the body throughout his career: lifting it from the realm of the created into the realm of sign and sacrament.

The Anniversaries

Donne's *Anniversaries* consists of two long poems, *An Anatomy of the World: The First Anniversary,* published in 1611, and *Of the Progress of the Soul: The Second Anniversary,* published in 1612, as well as a shorter poem called "A Funeral Elegy."[1] Donne wrote the poems to commemorate the death in December 1610 of Elizabeth Drury, the daughter of a wealthy and influential London landowner. In the poems, Donne represents the decay of the fallen world through her death and holds her up as an example, indeed an elixir, of virtue through which the world might be re-created. The poems give a significance to the body and soul of a dead fourteen-year-old girl that some of Donne's contemporaries considered ridiculous or scandalous. Ben Jonson, for one, said that "Donne's Anniversary was profane and full of blasphemies; . . . he told Mr. Donne, if it had been written of the Virgin Mary it had been something."[2] Donne significantly answered Jonson by saying "that he described the Idea of a Woman, and not as she was." Many of Donne's readers, then and since, may have misread the poems, interpreting the importance he attached to the slight figure of Elizabeth too literally.

Donne deploys the familiar conceit of the human person as a microcosm of the universe as the master trope of *The Anniversaries*. The figure of Elizabeth Drury is complex, but Donne roots all of the facets of that representation in the motif of microcosm and macrocosm and thus in his doctrine of creation. On one level, her soul and body simply parallel the larger soul and body of the cosmos. By describing the departure of her soul from her body, Donne refers to the departure of spirit (virtue and union) from the larger world. On another level, Donne claims that she *is* the world-soul: the epitome of virtue and beauty that enlivens an otherwise dead world. She is (in Aristotelian terms) "the form, that made [the world] live."[3] She is the "rich soul" whose departure from the earth made it quake, like a body with ague.[4] In "A Funeral Elegy," Donne also uses the image of the body to represent the social world, with

> Princes for arms, and counsellors for brains,
> Lawyers for tongues, divines for hearts, and more,
> The rich for stomachs, and for backs, the poor;
> The officers for hands, merchants for feet
> By which remote and distant countries meet.
> But those fine spirits which do tune and set
> This organ, are those pieces which beget
> Wonder and love; and these were she; and she
> Being spent, the world must needs decrepit be.[5]

With Elizabeth's death, the soul or vital spirits have left the social and cosmic worlds. Donne depicts the abandoned "body" of the world as sick, dying, or already dead. In *The First Anniversary,* Donne "anatomizes" the decaying world, using Drury's death as an occasion to criticize at length the sorry state of the fallen cosmos and the society that reflects that fall. In *The Second Anniversary,* he continues this anatomy of the carcass of the "body" and follows the progress of Elizabeth's soul to heaven. In this, as in many of his other works, Donne sees the relationship of microcosm to macrocosm as more than metaphorical. The correspondences are both realities and signs, rooted in God's original and ongoing act of creation.

The perfection of creation, and of the created body, appears in the poems only in glimpses of a paradisal state in which "every soul / Did a fair kingdom, and large realm control [the unfallen body].[6] The only body in the world of *The Anniversaries* that recalls the unfallen world is Elizabeth Drury's remembered body. Donne represents it as beautiful, young, and virginal. Untouched by the fall and the decay that haunt the rest of the world, her body reflects the perfection and beauty of her soul. As an unmarred example of some of God's original creative principles, it reflects proportion, harmony, and color.[7] Symmetrical and harmonious, it contained a perfect balance of all the elements.[8] In her the colors that are "beauties ingredients" grew naturally, "as in an unvexed paradise."[9] She embodies the unity of Eden: the union of person with God and of material with spiritual natures. When the original union with God, which she represents, dies, so does all that is best in the world. Lacking its vital spirit, the world loses its beauty, its health, and finally its very life. All the correspondences between heaven, earth, soul, and body are broken.

Donne speaks of the fallen "body" of the world that remains through images of deformity, barrenness, disease, and death. With the soul sundered from the "body" of the world, "the world's beauty is decayed, or gone,"[10] and its proportion is disfigured.[11] The earth has become an ugly monster, its face marred by warts and pockmarks.[12] The body of this earth is also barren: springtimes that "were common cradles" become tombs and fiery meteors rather than life-giving rainfall from the sky.[13] Donne also portrays the fallen world as diseased. Its sickness "doth not lie / In any humour, or one certain part; / But as thou sawest it rotten at the heart, / Thou seest a hectic fever hath got hold / Of the whole substance."[14]

Among all the images of the fallen body in *The Anniversaries*, the dead body dominates. With Elizabeth as the world-soul gone to heaven, the body of the world is simply a carcass. Donne bases the whole of *The First Anniversary* on the trope of the dissection of a dead body: the decaying body of the world. The fact that the world in *The Second Anniversary* has apparently survived Elizabeth's death is, Donne tells the reader, deceptive. He explains the continuing motions of the world through the following horrifying image.

> . . . as sometimes in a beheaded man,
> Though at those two red seas, which freely ran,
> One from the trunk, another from the head,
> His soul be sailed, to her eternal bed,
> His eyes will twinkle, and his tongue will roll,

> As though he beckoned, and called back his soul,
> He grasps his hands, and he pulls up his feet,
> And seems to reach, and to step forth to meet
> His soul. . . .[15]

Divorced from the soul, the body is out of control. Its motions are meaningless, although onlookers may seek to ascribe meaning to them. It stands in opposition to the paradisal body Donne describes in *The First Anniversary*, a "fair kingdom" ordered and controlled by the virtuous soul.[16] Once the soul departs, in the person of Elizabeth, the world's body is in the process of decay, even though it seems to live. Eventually its decay becomes apparent, until the dead carcass "is crumbled out again to his atomies" and loses all coherence and meaning.[17] It is at this juncture that Donne's famous lines, "And new philosophy calls all in doubt. . . . 'Tis all in pieces, all coherence gone," appear.[18] Scholars often read these lines as a crisis of faith that the new sciences, particularly the new astronomy, have thrust on Donne and his contemporaries. While this may be a plausible reading, looking at the passage in context reveals that Donne uses the images in the service of his larger point in these poems. The loss of coherence he speaks of generally is the decay of the world/body because of the departure of virtue and purity in the person of Elizabeth, the "world-soul." The decay of planetary orbits was only an image for the decay that concerned Donne and his contemporaries more: the decline of the world from a golden age of beauty, unity, and virtue. For Donne the parallel losses of original coherence between body and soul and between human person and God lie at the root of the disintegration of all worlds: bodily, social, epistemological, and cosmological.[19]

Faced with the dead body of the world, Donne positions himself as its anatomist. Traditionally, the early modern anatomist was an almost priestly figure: one who sought knowledge of the mysteries of the human body, drew attention to the hand of God as creator of those mysteries, and tried to use the knowledge gained from the anatomy to cure the sick. Thus, "anatomizing" could be a redemptive activity, bringing knowledge and cure out of death. In this case, however, Donne says that it is too late to succor this sick world,

> . . . yea dead, yea putrefied, since she
> Thy'intrinsic balm, and thy preservative,
> Can never be renewed, thou never live,
> I (since no man can make thee live) will try,
> What we may gain by thy anatomy.[20]

Donne hopes, however, to gain knowledge of what killed the old, fallen world. In his evocation of Elizabeth's redeemed body and soul, he seeks a pattern for the re-creation of a new and redeemed world.[21]

If the disease of the old world was sin that broke humanity's union with God, Elizabeth (soul and body) serves as an example of a reunited life. Donne urges the reader to make new bodies for the new world in the Aristotelian manner, by giving form through their own practice to the "matter" of his poem (Elizabeth's virtue).[22] She is another of Donne's redeemed women. Donne often holds up virtuous women as objects of contemplation. The bodies of these virtuous women reflect the beauty and purity of their souls. They can inspire, and sometimes enable, the salvation of others. In Elizabeth's case, Donne says that her

> ... clear body was so pure, and thin,
> Because it need disguise no thought within.
> 'Twas but a through-light scarf, her mind to enrol,
> Or exhalation breathed out from her soul.
> One, whom all men who durst no more, admired,
> And whom, whoe'er had worth enough, desired.[23]

Because of her virtue, her body was not a prison, but a temple. Donne likens her soul to gold, the perfect metal of the alchemists, and her body to electrum, an alloy of gold and silver that was scarcely less pure or precious than gold.[24] Not tainted by sin, "a soul might well be pleased to pass / An age in her [body]."[25] Elizabeth's harmony of soul and body in life signifies the harmony of union with God.

Donne represents Elizabeth as a book in which onlookers can read of the possibilities of harmony with God and the resultant harmony between the human body and soul. When she was alive, her virtue made her "our best, and worthiest book."[26] Even in life, her soul and body were like "two souls / Or like to full, on both sides written rolls, / Where eyes might read upon the outward skin, / As strong records for God, as minds within."[27] In this passage, Donne reinforces the idea of the body as scripture through the similarity of the animal skins or parchment on which scrolls were written and the "outward skin" or body of Elizabeth.[28] Donne uses the same image of the virtuous woman as a book two years later in his verse letter to the Countess of Salisbury, which I discussed in chapter 3. Both Elizabeth and the Countess provide new scriptures to replace the defaced or decaying book of nature.

Does the death of her body close or destroy the book? Donne traces the progress of Elizabeth's soul to heaven, while her body lies in sundered pieces, like a clock "not to be lost, but by the maker's hand / Repolished."[29] She was so close to perfection when she died that her "book" has been reissued "in a far fairer print," but still basically "reads the same."[30] She continues to serve as a book in which those still on earth can read God's will for human life. Now dead, Elizabeth represents eschatalogical union with God and reaches back to draw those still in the world forward to heaven through her example.

While she awaits the eschatological resurrection of the dead at the last day, Donne provides her with his own sort of resurrection. He offers up his poems, his evocations of her soul and body in memory, as a re-created and substitute body that a part of her soul (her fame or memory) can inhabit. Playing on the imagery of paper as skin, he asks,

> Can these memorials, rags of paper, give
> Life to that name, by which name they must live?
> Sickly, alas, short-lived, aborted be
> Those carcass verses, whose soul is not she.
> And can she, who no longer would be she,
> Being such a tabernacle, stoop to be
> In paper wrapped . . . ?[31]

He admits his poems are a defective sort of body. He asks whether she, having left such a rich and beautiful body behind in death, would humble herself to take another body in his poems. Realizing that verse has a "middle nature" in between the heaven to which her soul has gone and the grave where her body lies, he presents his poems as a body in which she can again become incarnate and redemptive.[32] It is instructive to recall that one poem in his *Divine Poems*, written at about the same time as the *Anniversaries*, refers to the Virgin Mary's womb as "a place / Of middle kind" through which Christ became incarnate.[33] Donne presents both his poems and the Virgin's womb as places in between earth and heaven in which the holy can find a body.

In these poems, Elizabeth Drury represents not only a microcosm of the world. She becomes, through the alchemy of Donne's poetry, a sign and sacrament of grace. In *The First Anniversary*, she is the "best and worthiest book," the book of Scripture that repairs the defects of the "book of creature," the fallen world in which signs of God grow faint. As the "best book," she reveals God's redemption and points the way to that redemption for others. At the end of *The Second Anniversary*, Donne says of Elizabeth, "Thou art the proclamation; and I am / The trumpet, at whose voice the people came.[34] Donne entered Holy Orders three years after this was published, and in his sermons he often refers to the preacher as the trumpet or tuba who called the people to hear the voice of God manifest in Scripture and preaching. For Donne, Elizabeth becomes a word from God that he incarnates in the "poor rags" of his verse while she awaits God's own resurrection.

Devotions upon Emergent Occasions

Much later in his career, in the winter of 1623, Donne was Dean of St. Paul's Cathedral in London and found himself suddenly in the grip of a serious illness. Dizziness, fever, and other disturbing symptoms rapidly confined him to bed, cutting him off from the activities that were the main focus of his life: the days of biblical study and interpretation and other theological reading that culminated in the sermons for which he had become increasingly renowned.[35] Deprived of his library, Donne turned to a different book as the focus for his usual activity of reading and interpretation: his own body. By looking to his body and its unfolding symptoms as the text God had "set" for him, Donne proceeded to read it for his own salvation and for the edification of a new congregation, his prospective readers. The result of this reading was *Devotions upon Emergent Occasions,* which Donne conceived during his illness, wrote during his convalescence, and published within two months of the onset of the disease.

The *Devotions* begins dramatically, *in media res,* with Donne's sudden realization that he is sick. "Variable, and therefore miserable condition of Man," he says, "this minute I was well, and am ill, this minute."[36] He proceeds from this point to describe in great detail the progress of his illness, its treatment, and his meditations on its meaning in a series of twenty-three devotions, each divided into three parts: a meditation, an expostulation, and a prayer. Many books in the history of Christian devotion up to that point had dealt with comfort in illness and preparation for death in general terms, always paying careful attention to the state of the suffering soul. Few, if any, shared Donne's interest in the body and its unfolding symptoms.[37]

The weight of attention Donne gives to bodies, his own in particular, and the way in which the body functions in the *Devotions* are distinctive in the context of the theological and devotional literature of the time.[38] By elevating his own body to the status of a "text" through which God speaks, Donne diverges from the emerging trend in Protestant thought that identified revelation solely with Holy Writ.[39] By elevating the body to the status of sacrament, he transgresses the Protestant tendency to turn away from the material as the locus of God's presence and grace. My reading of the *Devotions* explores three interrelated sets of images—bodies, books, and sacraments—and their place in the narrative of salvation history of creation, fall, redemption, and eschatalogical fulfillment that Donne adumbrates here in the narrative of his illness.

Although images of books fill the *Devotions,* Donne lays out the most comprehensive list of the "books" with which he is concerned in the ninth meditation and expostulation.[40] As is the pattern in this work, the ninth meditation opens with Donne's own bodily situation. Here his physicians have gathered in consultation. Donne has "anatomized" (or opened) his body to them, and they proceed to "read" it like a book.[41] When they are finished reading and are ready to prescribe, they write their orders down "so there is nothing covertly, disguisedly, unavowedly done."[42] In the expostulation that follows, he imports the images of anatomizing, reading, and writing to describe the interrelationship between God and the soul. He "anatomizes" his soul to God by confession. The Trinity, like his several physicians, holds consultation over the miserable state of that soul. The persons of the Trinity, again like his physicians, "prescribe" for him in writing, which he must then read for his salvation. He tells God that he has hope that "if you refer me to that which is written, you intend my recovery: for all the way, O my God, (ever constant to thine own ways) thou hast proceeded openly, intelligibly, manifestly, by the book."[43] Donne then lists all the "books" through which God manifests himself, all of which he intends as "physick": the book of life (or election), the book of nature, the book of Scripture, the book of laws, the book of indiviual conscience, the books of personal and particular sins, and the book of the seven seals (judgment). This complex of images centers on the master trope of reading as a salvific act: the physicians try to read the body in order to heal it, God reads the soul and heals it, and Donne reads the will of God through his manifest books as mercy and appropriates it to his own healing of body and soul. The books represent the prodigality of God's desire to be known and of humanity's opportunity to know him and to know themselves in relation to him.

I would like to focus on three ways Donne reads his body in the *Devotions:* (1) as a book of nature, (2) as a book of Scripture, and (3) as the book of the Lamb. First, Donne reads his body as a material object and abridgment of the book of nature. Donne sees his body as a microcosm of the universe that God created. That "world" has fallen and is suffering the consequences of the fall in his illness. Second, he reads his body as a book of Scripture, a collection of signs God writes with specific and salvific intent. In his physical condition and symptoms, Donne discerns the "letters" through which God inscribes his presence and his will on the body's fragile page.[44] Third, he rereads his body as the book of the Lamb: the liminal point at which his suffering body meets the body of Christ as sacrifice. In this rereading, the body becomes not only a sign, but a sacrament that conveys the presence of the eschatological promise of salvation.

These three books sketch the trajectory that I have examined through all of Donne's religious writing: the line that moves from creation and fall, through revelation, to eschatological salvation. In the first expostulation of the *Devotions,* just after he has lamented the miserable condition of humankind generally and his own in particular, he finds hope in his ability to address God out of the depths. He says,

> If I were but mere dust and ashes, I might speak unto the Lord, for the Lord's hand made me of this dust, and the Lord's hand shall recollect these ashes; the Lord's hand was the wheel, upon which this vessel of clay was framed, and the Lord's hand is the urn, in which these ashes shall be preserved. I am the dust and the ashes of the temple of the Holy Ghost; and what marble is so precious?[45]

He transforms the Jobean dust and ashes of his illness into the dust of creation and the ashes of his hopeful resurrection. He trusts that even in its present decaying state, his body is still God's temple. Looking backward to his creation and forward to his resurrection, he trusts God's hand to hold his body through his present crisis. The body is the living vessel of God's signifying work: in it the past, present, and future of salvation history meet. The body lies at the nexus of the web of speech-acts through which God works and reveals himself. As I will discuss in greater detail below, God figures the body in creation, reconfigures it through revelation, and transfigures it through the body of Christ.

The Body as a Book of Nature

Donne grounds his reading of the body as a book of nature in his belief that God figures the body and the world both as creation and representation. God first figured matter in his creation; he gave it form from nothingness. As the culmination of that creation, he formed the human person out of the earth as a sculptor gives shape to a figure from clay or marble. God also figures forth his existence and attributes (his existence, his goodness, his power, and his glory) in the more poetic sense of representing them through the signs of world and body. Donne espouses the traditional Christian notions that God creates human being in his image and that this image resides in the human spirit or intellect. He also sometimes espouses the less traditional idea that the body in a sense became an image of God since Christ assumed it and redeemed it. He further expresses in the *Devotions* the more unusual idea that the world itself is in God's image. He refers to the book of nature "where though subobscurely, and in shadows, thou has expressed thine own Image."[46]

The link Donne exploits in the *Devotions* to explore God's figuration in world and body is the image of the human being as a microcosm of the world. As has become evident in previous chapters, the image fascinated Donne throughout his career. He states the traditional idea succinctly in one of his sermons: "Man is not only a contributary creature, but a total creature. . . . He is not a piece of the world, but the world itself; and next to the glory of God, the reason why there is a world."[47] When Donne suddenly fell ill, he was predisposed to reading his body as a microcosm; reading it for signs of creation, sin, and redemption; and linking his illness to the decay and mutability of the fallen world.

On the first page of the *Devotions,* he considers the symptoms he is suffering: the shaking, the fever, the blood in his urine. In an ironic turn on the Renaissance picture of man as the epitome and glory of the world, he asks, "Is this the honor which man hath by being a little world, that he hath these earthquakes in himself, sudden shakings; these lighting, sudden flashes . . . these rivers of blood, sudden red waters?"[48] In the first meditation, of which this is a part, Donne ties his sudden fall into dizziness and fever with humanity's fall into sin and with the general decay of the world, a popular motif in his day. Donne intertwines all these metaphorically, but the images grow out of what were, for him, actual metaphysical connections. Original sin lies behind the decay of nature and of the human body, which otherwise would have been free from illness and death. Donne interprets his symptoms as reflections of this general decay and as indications of his own sinful life.

He returns again and again in the course of the *Devotions* to images that link the human person, especially the human body, with nature. What he reads most clearly in the body and in nature is their radical dependence on their Creator. Since they were created out of nothing, when separated from God they tend to fall into disorder and, eventually, annihilation. Donne bases one meditation on the traditional cosmological picture of earth as the center of a universe of concentric spheres. He says, "This is Nature's nest of boxes; the heavens contain the earth, the earth, cities, cities, men. And all these are concentric; the common center to them all, is decay, ruine."[49] This image relies on the traditional cosmological model in which the center of the cosmos is the most "dense" and corrupt, while the outer spheres are more ethereal and closer to God. Donne takes the tradition model one step further, replacing the ruinous center of earth with fallen man himself. In another meditation, Donne likens the body to a "ruinous farm," the house falling down, the ground spread over with weeds as the body is with diseases.[50] In another, after waxing eloquent on the traditional Renaissance theme of the greatness and glory of man the microcosm, Donne says,

> Call back therefore thy meditations again, and bring it down; what's become of man's great extent and proportion, when himself shrinks himself, and consumes himself to a handful of dust; what's become of his soaring thoughts, his compassing thoughts, when himself brings himself to the ignorance, to the thoughtlessness of the grave?[51]

In addition to using the traditional picture of man as a microcosm and the old cosmology on which that picture is based, Donne plays with the new cosmology emerging from the work of Kepler and Tycho Brahe as another set of metaphors through which to "read" humanity's dependence on God. In a nod to the old cosmology, Donne pictures the human person as the "middle term" of the great chain of being, standing upright, "naturally disposed toward contemplation of heaven." The human person also is tied to the earth, both as origin and as intermediate end (the grave).[52] In the same meditation, Donne incorporates the uncertainties that the new sciences have cast upon this ontological picture, noting that, in his illness, "God suspends me between heaven and earth, as a meteor; and I am not in heaven, because an earthly body clogs me, and am not in the earth, because a heavenly soul sustaines me."[53] He also uses the new cosmological argument that the earth goes around the sun as a link with his own bodily condition. Beset by dizziness when he tries to get out of bed, he says, "I am up, and I seem to stand, and I go round; and I am a new argument for the new philosophy, that the earth moves round. . . . I am carried in a giddy, and circular motion, as I stand." Donne concludes from his reading of the body as rotating earth that "man hath no center, but misery; there and only there he is fixed, and sure to find himself. . . . Everything serves to exemplify, to illustrate man's misery; but I need go no farther than myself."[54] In his reading of the body as the earth of the new cosmology, Donne emphasizes the uncertainty of his physical and spiritual state and links it to the condition of a lost humanity that is not "fixed" in God.

The Body as a Book of Scripture

Since both nature and the human body have been disfigured in the fall, reading them as figures of God's intent proves inadequate to Donne's situation. He can read in them his dependence on God and his own mortality, but he needs a clearer book in which to discern God's working and his redemption of soul and body. Donne turns to his own fallen body as a personalized book of "Scripture" evincing specific signs from God about his own spiritual state and God's presence in his illness. The marks of the fall manifest by his illness, and the death and damnation they portend, take on a new figuration as redemptive signs of God's will, presence, and grace.

Donne's elevation of his body to the status of Scripture, while radical, rests on several orthodox beliefs. First, Donne believes that God works and speaks through outer and physical means, most specifically in Scripture, sacraments, and sermons. Donne is always suspicious of claims of mystic enlightenment or direct spiritual knowledge divorced from external modes of God's representation of himself. Second, Donne believes that God communicates with human beings "openly, intelligibly, manifestly" through signs.[55] Donne's God is a "metaphorical" God, a poet, who loves the poetic means of representation and communication. God wants people to know him and his will, and he uses material things to refer to and embody spiritual reality. Third, Donne believes that God operates providentially and directly in the lives of the elect. Among other things, God visits diseases of the body on his saints as punishment and as correction. Donne specifically understands his malady as a correction from God's own hand.[56] In the immediate circumstances of his illness, these beliefs meet his lifelong fascination with the human body, as well as his immediate need to know his own spiritual state and God's will for him.

Donne gives a pointed reason for turning to his body for information in the first expostulation of the *Devotions*. Connecting his ill health with the sinful state of his soul, he laments that his body is more sensitive to the symptoms of physical infirmity than his soul to the symptoms of its sinful condition.[57] The *Devotions* are full of metaphors that link sin and sickness. These images rest on the belief, which Donne held in common with many Christians of his time, that there is an actual connection between the two. Ill health could be a judgment of God for sin or a trial intended for spiritual purification. For the Donne of the *Devotions*, the relationship between soul and body is not mere allegory or even analogy. Soul and body are interconnected. Spiritual "illness" can manifest in the body, and spiritual attitude (of hope or fear) can affect healing.

Where most devotional works of Donne's day leap quickly from the simple condition of illness to an examination of the soul, leaving the body behind, Donne does not move so expeditiously. His illness has presented him with an urgent need to examine his soul in preparation for death, but he finds that he cannot "read" its state. It gives no sign to him of his true condition. He needs a more accessible book, and he finds it in his body. He believes that God is at work in his illness, not only as judge and teacher but as creator/poet. He expresses late in the *Devotions* a belief that undergirds this radical view of his own body: "I know that in the state of my body, which is more discernible than that of my soul, thou dost effigiate my soul to me."[58] This belief reveals the inner logic of the *Devotions*. God, through his illness and its specific signs and symptoms, represents his soul to him in a visible form. God as creator, poet, and artist conveys spiritual realities through physical means.

This connection appears most directly in the nineteenth meditation and expostulation, entitled "At last, the Physicians, after a long and stormy voyage, see land; They have so good signs of the concoction of the disease, as that they may safely proceed to purge."[59] Donne employs an extended and elaborate figure in which his physicians are explorers, navigating the stormy and uncertain seas of his illness. They sight "land" in the "concoctions" given off by Donne's body, which signal that the disease had reached its crisis and they can now take action to treat him. Although Donne is somewhat vague as to the nature of these concoctions, it seems likely from the context that they were clouds appearing in his urine, which the medical men of his time believed were "solid" matter, bad humors that the body discharged at the high point of a disease.⁶⁰ This sight of land gives him and his physicians hope that he may be saved.

Donne then follows his typical pattern of moving from a meditation that deals with his body and its situation to the "spiritual" truth he wishes to explore. Here he moves abruptly from his bodily secretions to a rhapsody on the way God writes in Scripture. The connection between the two is not immediately apparent. He begins,

> My God, my God, Thou art a direct God, may I not say, a literal God, A God that wouldest be understood literally, and according to the plain sense of all that thou sayest.... But thou art also ... a figurative, a metaphorical God too: A God in whose words there is such a height of figures ... remote and precious metaphors ... curtains of allegories, such third heavens of hyperboles.... Neither are thou thus a figurative, a metaphorical God, in thy word only, but in thy works too. The style of thy works, the phrase of thine actions, is metaphorical. The institution of thy whole worship in the old Law, was a continual allegory; types and figures overspread all.⁶¹

He goes on to say that God's way of writing in Scripture inspired early commentators as well as those who wrote prayers and liturgies for the Church to "make their accesses to thee in such a kind of language, as thou wast pleased to speak to them."⁶² He proceeds in the same manner to speak of his own illness.

He then extends the metaphor. The waters become all the "afflictions and calamities" of human life, while the "land" becomes the outward means available through the Church that give hope of salvation: baptism, Scripture, and preaching.⁶³ For Donne, these outward means are signs of future mercy, but assurance of future mercy "is present mercy."⁶⁴ Thus, the signs become seals, a word associated with the sacraments. For Donne, the physical signs that indicate hope for a cure become signs of God's future mercy as well as seals (sacraments) of God's promises and thus of his presence. Donne asks,

> What is my seal? It is but a cloud; that which my physicians call a cloud, is that, which gives them their Indication. But a Cloud? Thy great Seal to all the world, the rainbow, that secured the world for ever, from drowning, was but a reflection upon a cloud. A cloud it self was a pillar which guided the church.... None of thy indications are frivolous; thou makest thy signs, seals; and thy Seals, effects; and thy effects, consolation, and restitution.⁶⁵

A close reading makes clear the reason for the previous discussion of Scripture, which on first sight appears to be a non sequitur. For Donne, the language of Scripture epitomizes the way God works in the world and reveals himself to his saints. God, Lord of both the material and spiritual realms, creates and signifies. His words and works not only signify spiritual reality, but sacramentally connect the believer to salvific reality through his promises. Although Scripture is the epitome of God's word, it by no means encompasses God's speech. Donne is confident that the same God who wrote Scripture extends his creative and metaphorizing ways to the lives and even the bodies of his saints. Thus, Donne tells God that he can read the "declaration of thy self in this my sickness" and the "seal of bodily restitution" as God's work and as "a manifestation of heaven to me here upon earth."[66]

Although the nineteenth meditation, expostulation, and prayer contain the clearest indication of the relationship Donne sees between Scripture, sacraments, and the body, he looks throughout the *Devotions* to his body as a collections of signs, written by the "metaphorical" God. He reads the signs of his bodily conditions as he does the signs of Scripture: on a literal and historical level as events under the control of God's providence and on a spiritual level as metaphors, types, and prophecies of God's mercy and salvation.[67]

The Body as the Book of the Lamb

Reading his body as a book of Scripture allows Donne to discern in the signs of his illness evidence of God's working and salvific intent, but these signs only promise the redemption of his body and soul. Although he has cause for hope, he cannot read his own personal salvation in the books of nature and Scripture, even as abridged in his body. His final redemption lies hidden in the books of election and judgment. The first book through which God speaks is the book of life, God's decree of election, "never shut to thee but never thoroughly open to us." The last book is the book of the seven seals, "which only the Lamb which was slain was found worthy to open."[68] Donne expresses his faith that God has written his name in the book of election and, in Christ's own blood, in the book of the Lamb. However, those books are closed to Donne in his present crisis. Further, the deluge of his sins has swamped the ordinary means that should have helped him toward salvation: his natural faculties, the Church, the Word, and the sacraments.[69] They have all proved inadequate to overcome his propensity to sin.

The fulfillment of God's promise of Donne's redemption requires further reading: a reading of redemption and eschatalogical salvation in the book of the Lamb. This reading involves one final figuration of Donne's body, or rather a *transfiguration*. The word *transfiguration* can mean to alter the figure or appearance (most specifically applied to Christ's change of visage on the mountain in the gospel account), to elevate or glorify, or (in a now obsolete sense) to transfer by a figure. All these senses have resonance with the final figuration of Donne's body in the *Devotions*.

In one sense of figuration harking back to his creation of the human person, God transforms Donne's body and soul through physical suffering. God's inscriptions on his body are not merely signs. They are efficacious. In the sixth prayer of the *Devotions,* Donne asks God that "when thou shalt have inflamed and thawed my former coldnesses, and indevotions, with these heats, and quenched my former heats, with these sweats, and inundations, and rectified my former presumptions, and negligences with these fears, be pleased . . . as one made so by thee, to think me fit for thee."[70]

Donne believes that God is purging him of his sinful tendencies through the corrections of his illness. Donne sees these corrections as both signs and sacraments. He calls them "cordials" that purge him of sin, just as the "cordial water" of baptism purged him from original sin and the "cordial blood" of the Eucharist purges him of habitual sin.[71] He also calls the pains of his body his manna in the wilderness and further associates them with the bread of the Eucharist through a complex play on the words *elements, substance,* and *accidents.*[72] He speaks of the corrections of his illness as "the elements of our regeneration, by which our souls are made thine."[73] At the end of the *Devotions,* Donne says that God's correction, the illness, has brought him to a participation in and "entire possession" of God.[74] How has this "entire possession" come about? How are the promises of God which Donne reads in his body fulfilled?

They are fulfilled by a sacramental chain of signifiers in which Donne "trans-figures" his represented body as the body of Christ, echoing poetically what he trusts is God's actual transfiguration of his body through the blood of Christ. In Donne's sacramental theology, God "makes little things to signify great" and conveys the "infinite merits" of Christ through the elements of those sacraments.[75] Donne believes that signs are the beginning of a chain of signification that lead to the reality of the things they signify. Describing the sacraments in the *Devotions,* Donne asks God

> that I may associate the Word, with thy Sacrament, thy Seal with the Patent; and in the Sacrament associate the sign with the thing signified, the Bread with the Body of thy Son, so as I may be sure to have received both, and to be made thereby . . . the Ark, and the Monument and the Tomb of thy most Blessed Son, that he, and all the merits of his death, may, by that receiving, be buried in me, to my quickening in this world, and my immortal establishing in the next.[76]

Donne reads his body as a sign of the body of Christ, which in turn conveys to him that which it signifies: the healing salvation of Christ's redemption for his body and soul. Donne associates his own body with the body of

Christ through both the experience and the metaphors of suffering. Throughout the *Devotions*, Donne links his travails to those of Christ's passion, sometimes explicitly and sometimes through a simple juxtaposition of images. In the second prayer, Donne asks God to appear to him in his illness. Evoking the imagery of God appearing to Moses, Donne asks God to make himself a light in a bush "in the midst of these brambles and thorns of a sharp illness." He asks God to do this for the sake of Jesus, "who was not the less, the King of Heaven, for thy suffering him to be crowned with thorns, in this world."[77] Through the simple juxtaposition of the two images of thorns, Donne associates his suffering with the suffering of Jesus and implicitly asks God to do the same. Donne makes this connection more explicitly in the third expostulation, contemplating the fact that God has chosen to cast him into his bed, flat on his back with fever. He says that God has cast him down

> that I might not be cast away; thou couldst take me by the head, as thou didst Abacuc, and carry me so; by a chariot, as thou didst Elijah, and carry me so; but thou carriest me thine own private way, the way by which thou carryedst thy Son, who first lay upon the earth, and prayed, and then had his exaltation, as himself calls his crucifying, and first descended into hell and then had his Ascension.[78]

Here Donne associates his bodily position and sufferings explicitly with those of Christ. He later associates his sadness and fear of death with those of Jesus in the garden of Gethsemane, and he sees the solution to both in submission to the will of God.[79] He also links his body in its sickbed with the sacrifice of Christ on the cross through figuring his sickbed as an altar and his body as the communion sacrifice.[80] In "trans-figuring" his body as the body of Christ, Donne attempts to find meaning and comfort in his suffering, as well as hope for deliverance from it.

Even more significantly, Donne holds up before God the image of his own body as Christ's body to suggest to God a possible transformative rereading of Donne's situation. He realizes that the recovery of his body and soul depends, finally, not on his reading, but on God's. Only God makes signs efficacious. Without his action, they are empty. In the second prayer of the *Devotions*, Donne declares,

> There is no soundness in my flesh, because of thine anger. Interpret thine own work, and call this sickness, correction, and not anger, and there is soundness in my flesh. There is no rest in my bones, because of my sin; transfer my sins, with which thou art so displeased upon him, with whom thou art so well pleased, Christ Jesus, and there will be rest in my bones.[81]

Immediately after this comes the passage, already discussed, in which Donne associates his body with that of Christ through the image of thorns. Donne subtly suggests to God that he see Donne as Christ (and Christ as Donne). While holding up a picture before God associating his suffering with that of Christ, Donne suggests to God that he "interpret" his workings in Donne's body as correction and that he "transfer" Donne's sins to Christ. Donne believes that he will then be healed both in body and soul. God's reading will accomplish what it signifies.

Donne holds his body up to God to be "trans-figured" as Christ in many passages, but the most significant are two that represent Donne's body as the eucharistic sacrifice. In the third prayer, Donne asks God,

> As thou hast made this bed, thine Altar, make me thy Sacrifice; and as thou makest thy Son Christ Jesus the Priest, so make me his Deacon, to minister to him in a cheerful surrender of my body and soul to thy pleasure, by his hands ... as I feel thy hands upon all my body ... and see all my corrections, and all my refreshings to flow ... from thy hand.[82]

Donne returns to this theme in the thirteenth expostulation. In this section of the *Devotions,* Donne finds his body covered in "spots" through which his sickness has declared its malignancy. He again evokes the image of his bed as God's altar and his body as the sacrifice. He associates the spots on his skin, through which the disease "declares itself," with human sins that Christ (the "spotted sacrifice" of Hebrews 9:14) took on himself.[83] Just as his sickness has declared itself in blotches on his skin, his illness (read as a correction from God) has led him to see and confess the spots on his soul. That confession has allowed God (and Donne) to reread the blots:

> Even my spots belong to thy Son's body, and are part of that, which he came down to this earth, to fetch, and challenge, and assume to himself. When I open my spots [confession], I do but present him with that which is His. . . . When therefore thou seest them upon me, as His, and seest them by this way of Confession, they shall not appear to me, as the pinches of death, to decline my fear to Hell . . . but these spots upon my breast, and upon my soul, shall appear to me as the constellations of the firmament, to direct my contemplation to that place, where thy Son is, thy right hand.[84]

This transfiguration of Donne's body as the body of Christ allows a double rereading. God sees in Donne the sacrifice of his Son. Donne claims that sacrifice through the chain of signification, starting in his own body, that connects the sign with the thing signified: Christ himself. In the prayer that ends his meditation, Donne says that his spots "are but the letters, in which thou hast written thine own Name, and conveyed thy self to me" and that the heats (fevers) God has brought on his body "are but thy chafing of the wax, that thou mightest seal me to thee."[85] In this passage, as in many others, Donne combines the language of signs and seals, Scripture and sacraments, to describe God's working in his body.

When this mutual rereading accomplishes its work, Donne is healed in body and soul. He sees it as a resurrection, saying that Gods calls "Lazarus out of his tomb, me out of my bed."[86] He asks,

> My God, my God, how large a glass of the next world is this? . . . We shall have a resurrection in heaven; the knowledge of that thou castest by another glass on us here; we feel that we have a resurrection from sin; and that by another glass too; we see we have a resurrection of the body, from the miseries and calamities of this life. This resurrection of my body, shows me that resurrection of my soul.[87]

He can look at the reflection of his promised resurrection in glory in the eschatalogical future through the image of his current restoration in body and soul. He realizes, however, that it is only a future possibility. He still lives subject to sin, in danger of a "relapse" of body and soul, and ends the *Devotions* with a prayer that God not forsake him.

Conclusion

In this examination of the *Anniversaries* and the *Devotions*, I have drawn together the strands of Donne's reading of the narrative of creation, fall, redemption, and eschatological fulfillment in the book of the body. In these works, and throughout his career, he turns to that which is closest to him—his own body and the bodies of his fellows—as books upon which God writes the large story of salvation history and the smaller chapters of his actions in individual lives. In a "macrocosm" of increasing political, intellectual, and religious uncertainty, Donne looks to the more easily accessible microcosm of the human person as a text in which to read God's will and work. Those who can interpret the signs of the body's narrative also can experience them in their own flesh as salvific.

Notes

1. *An Anatomy of the World: The First Anniversary, Of the Progress of the Soul: The Second Anniversary,* and "A Funeral Elegy," in *John Donne: The Complete English Poems,* ed. A. J. Smith (London: Penguin Books, 1971; repr., London: Penguin Classics, 1986). All quotations are from this edition and are referred to below as *First Anniversary,*

Second Anniversary, and "A Funeral Elegy." Critical editions of all three poems are available in *The Variorum Edition of the Poetry of John Donne, vol. 6, The Anniversaries and the Epicedes and Obsequies*, ed. Gary Stringer (Bloomington: Indiana University Press, 1995). To indicate the substantial nature of these works, *The First Anniversary* is 474 lines, *The Second Anniversary* runs to 528 lines, and "A Funeral Elegy" is 106. Most of Donne's poems are much shorter, with only the unfinished *Metempsychosis* (520 lines) and *Lamentations of Jeremy* (390 lines) being comparable.

2. Quoted by A. J. Smith in his notes to the poem, in Donne, *Poems*, 594.

3. Donne, *Second Anniversary*, 289, line 72. See also *The First Anniversary*, in which Donne says, "Her name defined thee, gave thee form, and frame," 271, line 37.

4. Donne, *First Anniversary*, 270–71, lines 1–22.

5. John Donne, "A Funeral Elegy," 283–84, lines 22–30.

6. Donne, *First Anniversary*, 273, lines 123–24.

7. Ibid., 278, lines 306–20.

8. Ibid., 279, 320–24.

9. Ibid., 280, lines 361–64.

10. Donne, *First Anniversary*, 277, line 249.

11. Ibid., 278, line 302.

12. Ibid., 279, line 326.

13. Ibid., 280, lines 380–89.

14. Ibid., 277, lines 240–48.

15. Donne, *Second Anniversary*, 287–88, lines 9–16.

16. Donne, *First Anniversary* 273–74, lines 123–27.

17. Ibid., 276, lines 210–19.

18. Ibid., 205–18.

19. See especially ibid., 275–76, lines 183–219, for a succinct expression of the consequences of the fall of humankind for all these disparate realms.

20. Ibid., 272, lines 55–60.

21. Ibid., lines 67–77.

22. Ibid., lines 86–88.

23. Donne, "A Funeral Elegy," 284, lines 59–64.

24. Donne, *Second Anniversary*, 293, lines 241–42.

25. Ibid., lines 221–23.

26. Ibid., 296, 319–20.

27. Ibid., 300, lines 503–6.

28. The scroll written on two sides may also be a reference to Ezek 2:8–10 and Rev 5:1, where the book of the seven seals that holds the future of humanity is referred to as "a scroll written within and without" or "with writing on both sides." If Donne had this in mind, the image is an extravagant one, equating Elizabeth with the eschatalogical drama of the end times and the election of the saints.

29. Donne, "A Funeral Elegy," 284, lines 39–40.

30. Ibid., 295, lines 310–14.

31. Ibid., 283, lines 11–17.

32. Donne, *First Anniversary*, 283, lines 471–74.

33. Donne, "A Litany," *Poems*, 322, lines 154–57.

34. Donne, *Second Anniversary,* 301, lines 527–28.

35. Izaak Walton, Donne's friend and first biographer, says in his notes to Donne's *LXXX Sermons* (London, 1640) that "the later part of his life was a continued study, Saturdays only excepted" (page not numbered). Donne's own letters, as well as his comments in the sermons, confirm the fact that his life at this point was spent almost exclusively in study and sermon preparation, and that his sense of identity and vocation were centered there.

36. John Donne, *Devotions upon Emergent Occasions,* ed. Anthony Raspa (New York: Oxford University Press, 1987), 7.

37. Although many of Donne's commentators have attempted to relate the *Devotions* to various Catholic or Protestant meditative traditions, others have noted that it is an unusual contribution to the genre, actually having little to do with traditional devotional conventions. P. M. Oliver even argues that the *Devotions* aren't really devotions, since Donne's obsessive self-reference would "minimize their devotional value to others." *Donne's Religious Writing: A Discourse of Feigned Devotion* (London and New York: Longman, 1997), 228. Anthony Raspa, in the introduction to his edition of the work, says, "There is no other work even remotely like *Devotions* in [the Anglican devotional] tradition" (Donne, *Devotions,* xxxix). In fact, Donne's contribution to the devotional genre is just as revolutionary as was his contribution to love poetry in the 1590s (although his poetry was much imitated and his devotional work was not).

38. Somewhat surprisingly, since the *Devotions* deal most immediately with an illness, commentators on the work often overlook or give short shrift to Donne's central focus on his own body and the implications of that focus. The most active line of criticism has attempted to assign the *Devotions* a place in either Catholic or Protestant meditative traditions. Three exceptions to the general tendency to ignore the body in the *Devotions* are Elaine Scarry's essay "Donne: 'But yet the body is his booke'"; Jonathan Sawday's consideration of the *Devotions* in his *The Body Emblazoned: Dissection and the Human Body in the Renaissance Culture* (London and New York: Routledge, 1995); and Catherine Creswell's "Reading Subjectivity: The Body, the Text, the Author in John Donne" (Ph.D. diss., State University of New York at Buffalo, 1993), 62–107. Scarry briefly examines the body in the *Devotions* in relationship to Donne's (and God's) "volitional materialism" (71–75). Sawday considers the *Devotions,* passim, in relationship to his theories about the significance of the imagery of bodily anatomy. Neither of these works offers a full account of the historical context and theological implications of Donne's use of the body in the work. Creswell's dissertation contains a substantive analysis of Donne's representations of the body in the *Devotions.* While I agree with her emphasis on "conversionary reading" of the bodily text (92–93), I question the interpretive value of reading Donne's "text" through the postmodern lenses of violence, alterity, and undecidability.

39. For an analysis of this trend and its implications for spirituality, see David S. Pacini, "Excursus: Reading Holy Writ: The Locus of Modern Spirituality," in *Christian Spirituality: Post-Reformation and Modern,* ed. Louis Dupre and Don E. Saliers, vol. 18 of *World Spirituality: An Encyclopedic History of the Religious Quest* (New York: Crossroad, 1991).

40. Anthony Raspa, in his introduction to the critical edition of the *Devotions,* identifies three books as important to Donne's theology: the book of election, the book of

nature, and the book of Scripture (xx, xxvii – xxx). Several commentators have pointed to biblical exegesis as the crucial model for understanding Donne's procedure in the *Devotions,* including Raspa, xxxix, and Janel Mueller, "The Exegesis of Experience," *Journal of English and German Philology* 67 (1968): 1–19.

41. Donne, *Devotions,* 45–46.
42. Ibid., 47.
43. Ibid., 49.
44. Ibid., 70.
45. Ibid., 8.
46. Ibid., 49.
47. John Donne, *The Sermons of John Donne,* 10 vols., ed. Evelyn M. Simpson and George R. Potter (Berkeley and Los Angeles: University of California Press, 1953–62), 7:297.
48. Ibid., 7–8.
49. Ibid., 51.
50. Ibid., 116–17.
51. Ibid., 20.
52. Ibid., 14.
53. Ibid., 17.
54. Ibid, 111.
55. Ibid., 49.
56. Ibid., 13.
57. Ibid., 8–9.
58. Ibid., 119.
59. Ibid., 97.
60. In his commentary on the *Devotions,* Raspa identifies "concoctions" in the physiology of the time as secretions or digestions (sweat, tears, urine, spittle, and other excretions) through which bad humors left the body (177).
61. Ibid., 99–100.
62. Ibid., 100.
63. Ibid., 101.
64. Ibid., 102.
65. Ibid., 102–3.
66. Ibid., 103–4.
67. While commentators on the *Devotions* have rightly noted biblical exegesis as the model for the structure of the work, they have overestimated the extent to which this aligns Donne with "Protestant" sensibilities. The structure of the *Devotions* does relate directly to Donne's methods of (and opinions about) biblical exegesis as reflected in his *Sermons,* but the "text" he is explicating is not Scripture and his method of exegesis is not the accepted Protestant reading for literal and typological meaning. The text Donne reads in the *Devotions* is the "emergent occasions" of his own illness: most often his own body and its symptoms. His exegetical method, in the *Devotions* as in his sermons, is often a form of the medieval fourfold interpretation. In doing exegesis, Donne states specifically that one should always start with the literal interpretation (the standard Protestant position). However, unlike most other Protestants who collapsed the other three senses into a

typological reading that was tied to the literal, Donne not only uses the language of typology, but proceeds unabashedly into readings that are allegorical (spiritual), tropological (having to do with ethical and moral lessons, recommending action to the faithful), and anagogical (having to do with heaven and the last things). Donne's three levels in the *Devotions* proceed exactly as does this sort of exegesis. He divides each devotion into three parts: (1) the meditation, in which he deals primarily with his body and the historical and material reality of his situation (or sometimes the state of humanity as a whole in the body, the "body" of society, or the "body" of state); (2) the expostulation or "debatement with God," in which he takes the body images he established in the first division as ways to talk about the soul (and/or spiritual realities); and (3) the prayer, in which he moves beyond the level of allegory to join body and soul in a lesson or reflection that embodies their unity. Thus, he begins with the "literal" (usually his own body or the human body generally), moves to the "allegorical" (usually the condition of the soul), and ties them together in a reading that unites body and soul in a discussion about ethical and moral demands posed to him by his previous reading or in reflections on the unity of the body and soul at the resurrection of the dead in the last days.

68. Donne, *Devotions*, 49.
69. Ibid., 109.
70. Ibid., 34.
71. Ibid., 61.
72. Ibid., 39–40.
73. Ibid., 40.
74. Ibid., 126.
75. Ibid., 114.
76. Ibid., 39.
77. Ibid., 14.
78. Ibid., 17.
79. Ibid., 34, 61.
80. Ibid., 18, 68–69.
81. Ibid., 14.
82. Ibid., 18.
83. Ibid., 68.
84. Ibid., 69–70.
85. Ibid., 70.
86. Ibid., 110.
87. Ibid., 112.

APPENDIX A
Literature Review: The Body in the Context of Donne Scholarship

The sheer mass of the critical literature on John Donne must give pause to anyone interested in contributing to the study of his work. The portion of Sir Geoffrey Keynes's Donne bibliography that lists biographical and critical works from 1594 to 1971 runs to ninety crowded pages, which Keynes says are by no means exhaustive but "surely already as long as anyone can wish."[1] John Roberts's two-volume annotated bibliography of modern Donne criticism from 1912 through 1978 is over seven hundred pages long and runs to some twenty-three hundred entries.[2] Although scholarly zeal has flagged somewhat since the heyday of New Criticism, studies of Donne's work continue to appear regularly. Two questions stand at the threshold of any work on Donne's religious thought. First, why another study of Donne? Second, why a *theological* study of Donne, since the weight of the critical literature suggests that he is of interest almost exclusively to those in English studies, not to historians of religion? In answer to the first question, there is an increasing awareness in the field of Donne studies that in spite of the sheer numbers of critical books and articles, there has been an imbalance in the focus of scholarly attention. First, the bulk of critical attention has been focused on Donne's poetry, not on his prose (and actually on less than half the poetic canon).[3] One recent critic has pointed out that this imbalance is even more acute in regard to Donne's prose, that "despite the lip-service paid to the importance of the sermons, Donne criticism is still focused on a mere fraction of a fraction of his total output."[4] Even among critical works that do deal with Donne's religious prose, the emphasis has until recently been weighted toward analyses of style and rhetoric, not theological content.[5] Most studies that do try to deal with theological content have been written by literary, not religious, scholars.[6]

Although there has been an increasing interest in Donne's religious thought and sensibilities, there is a definite sense among Donne scholars that, as one writer put it, "the essential nature of his religiosity remains at issue."[7] Another says that "Donne's religious life—and the imaginative works that his religion inspired—are among the most troublesome paradoxes and problems to emerge from the English Renaissance."[8] There is also a recognition, one with which I concur, of a certain innate undecidability about Donne's work. In 1925, Robert Sencourt aptly said that "no knowledge of Donne could even present one with anything but tantalizing complexity."[9] In 1995 Jeanne Shami echoed, "It cannot be said too often that Donne's views on any subject are complex and elusive."[10] Deborah Larson points out that "the problem with determining Donne's thoughts, attitudes, and beliefs is similar to the problem in other areas of Donne scholarship: it is difficult to decide how committed Donne was to the ideas that appear in his works, how often he believed in a theological or philosophical idea, and how often he merely played with that idea."[11] Donne seems, more than most poets and thinkers, to remain elusive.

The disciplines of church history and historical theology in the twentieth century have largely ignored Donne. Many surveys of Christian history fail to mention him at all. Even histories of Anglicanism and the English Reformation give him short shrift.[12] Those who do discuss him usually note that he was an eloquent preacher, with little discussion of what he preached. This lack of attention deviates markedly from that accorded to Donne and his work in the seventeenth century. In Donne's own time, and for many years after his death, he was esteemed both as a great preacher and as a "learned divine." His son published editions of 154 of the sermons in 1640, 1649, and 1660.[13] From contemporary accounts, it is clear that Donne's preaching, both in performance and content, struck a chord in the religious sensibilities of the seventeenth century. It is just as clear that those sensibilities changed. The next reprint of Donne's sermons was in 1839. After that, there was not another until the current scholarly edition of Simpson and Potter, published from 1954 to 1962. Opinions about Donne after the seventeenth century, when expressed at all, tended to be similar to T. S. Eliot's evaluation that "for the theologian, even the high-sounding Bramhall and the depressive Thorndike are more important names than Donne's. His sermons will disappear as suddenly as they have appeared."[14] With a few exceptions, notably Coleridge,[15] theologians and church historians have not taken Donne seriously as a religious thinker. Most concluded that Donne was not an original theologian and did not influence the history of theology. Their unstated premise equates theology with systematic theology, and given that premise, they are basically correct. Donne tends to think poetically, not systematically. To the extent that he speaks from any systematic theology at all, he is quite orthodox and derivative. A religious historiography preoccupied for many years with seminal thinkers and systematic theology would naturally bypass Donne.

Only two published, book-length studies have attempted to present a systematic view of Donne's theology as a whole, or to present Donne's theology as systematic.[16] The first is Itrat Husain's *The Dogmatic and Mystical Theology of John Donne*.[17] In this curious work, Husain manages to lay out a systematic theology for Donne while getting at very little of the flavor of Donne's religious sensibility, since Donne is actually neither systematic, nor "dogmatic," nor "mystical." The most recent attempt at a comprehensive interpretation of Donne's theology is Jeffrey Johnson's *The Theology of John Donne*. Johnson correctly notes that "with surprisingly few exceptions, John Donne has not been treated seriously as a religious thinker." He recognizes that Donne does not have a systematic theology but does "present a clear theological vision (Donne's own eclectic *via media* as it were)."[18] Johnson's interpretation of Donne's theology through the categories of Trinity, Church, repentance, and grace is a valuable and long overdue contribution to understanding Donne as a theologian. My interpretation of the nature of Donne's religious imagination and the distinctive nature of his theology differs from Johnson's, however. Neither Husain nor Johnson considers the human body as a significant part of Donne's religious thought.

Apart from the two questions of why another study of Donne and why a *theological* study, another question arises. Why study the body and its religious significance in Donne's work? As with most questions in the study of Donne, literary scholars have speculated on the significance of the body in Donne's work while religious scholars have given it scant attention.[19] Even those studies that have attempted to grapple with the religious significance of his views on the body have so far failed to give a full and integrated account of it. By this I mean specifically that no scholar has proposed a reading of Donne's use of the body that (1) takes into account all of the fragments of his discourse, (2) relates it to its larger context in his religious sensibilities, and (3) places his account of the body within a history of religious anthropology.

Studies from literary and cultural scholars that deal with Donne's representations of the human body fall into two basic categories. One is the plethora of short articles on individual works that deal with Donne's representations of the body as a secondary point. Many of these articles deal with Donne's embrace or rejection of Neoplatonism in individual poems, especially in "The Ecstasy" and "Air and Angels." One excellent recent example of this extensive literature on individual poems is Frances Malpezzi's "As I Ride: The Beast and His Burden in Donne's 'Goodfriday,'"[20] which puts forward a perceptive reading of Donne's views of the body. The second category of work is the more substantive studies that deal directly with the body in

Donne's thought. Mary Paton Ramsey's *Les Doctrines Medievales Chez Donne*, Coffin's *New Philosophy*, Sherwood's *Fulfilling the Circle*, Carey's *Life, Mind, and Art,* and Kathryn Kremen's *Imagination of the Resurrection*[21] contain relevant chapters or sections on Donne's view of the body. Catherine Creswell's dissertation, "Reading Subjectivity: The Body, the Text, the Author in John Donne," analyzes some of Donne's representations of the body from a postmodern, literary-critical stance. David Hirsh's essay "Donne's Atomies and Anatomies: Deconstructed Bodies and the Resurrection of Atomic Theory" and Elaine Scarry's essay "Donne: 'But yet the body is his book,' " make important points about Donne's representations of the body.[22] Rosalie Osmond's essay "Body and Soul Dialogues in the Seventeenth Century" and her related book *Mutual Accusation: Seventeenth-Century Body and Soul Dialogues*,[23] while not focused on Donne exclusively, contain considerable material on Donne's views of the body, as does Jonathan Sawday's *The Body Emblazoned.* Of the works I have mentioned, Ramsey's and Osmond's readings overemphasize Donne's Platonism, largely ignoring his many statements that undermine any Platonic interpretation and the whole tenor of his reaction to the breakup of the medieval synthesis. Sherwood's interpretation is comprehensive, balanced, and acute. In my view, he also tends to overemphasize the medieval and conventional side of Donne's thought while passing over ways in which Donne's views of the body were distinctive. Sherwood reads Donne's body almost totally through his references to the medieval world of correspondences, while glossing over the more fragmented and disturbing references to the body, especially Donne's fascination with the macabre and with death, as well as the influence of Protestant theology on Donne's representations of the body. Cresswell's dissertation on the body in Donne goes perhaps too far in the other direction. It is a postmodern reading of several of Donne's works with an emphasis on the production of the self through the reading of the body as text. She looks in particular at Donne's representation's of the body in some of his portraits, in the *Devotions,* and in certain of the poems. While I think her focus on Donne's "body as text" is a valuable and interesting one, her literary study does not attempt to place either "body" or "text" within the larger context of the history of Christian thought. Carey's chapter "Bodies" in *Life, Mind, and Art* points out Donne's fascination with material and organic life but does not discuss how that fascination fits into the context of Donne's religious thought and the broader history of theology. Coffin's and Kremen's books, Scarry and Hirsch's essays, and Jonathan Sawday's references to Donne within his larger work on the culture of dissection in the Renaissance are astute readings of Donne's images of and attitudes toward the body, but none of them purports to be a comprehensive review of the subject and none of them is fully situated in the history of Christian thought.

Notes

1. Sir Geoffrey Keynes, *A Bibliography of Dr. John Donne, Dean of Saint Paul's*, 4th ed. (Oxford: Clarendon Press, 1973), 280.

2. John R. Roberts, *John Donne: An Annotated Bibliography of Modern Criticism, 1912–1967* (Columbia: University of Missouri Press, 1973); and *John Donne: An Annotated Bibliography of Modern Criticism, 1968–1978* (Columbia: University of Missouri Press, 1982).

3. Roberts, *Bibliography, 1968–1978*, 82.

4. Jeanne Shami, "Donne's Sermons and the Absolutist Politics of Quotation," in *John Donne's Religious Imagination: Essays in Honor of John T. Shawcross*, ed. Raymond-Jean Frontain and Frances Malpezzi (Conway, Ariz.: University of Central Arizona Press, 1995), 382.

5. Examples of this sort of study include Evelyn Simpson, "The Literary Value of Donne's Sermons," in *John Donne: A Collection of Critical Essays*, ed. Helen Gardner (Englewood Cliffs, N.J.: Prentice-Hall, 1962); William R. Mueller, *John Donne: Preacher* (Princeton: Princeton University Press, 1962); and John Chamberlin; *Increase and Multiply: Arts-of-Discourse Procedure in the Preaching of John Donne* (Chapel Hill: University of North Carolina Press, 1976).

6. Major books or articles by scholars in English and cultural studies who deal with Donne as a religious thinker include Mary Paton Ramsey, *Les Doctrines Medievales Chez Donne, Le Poete Metaphysicien de l'Angleterre (1573–1631)* (London: Oxford University Press, 1917); Louis I. Bredvold, "The Religious Thought of Donne in Relation to Medieval and Later Traditions," in *Studies in Shakespeare, Milton and Donne* (New York and London: Macmillan, 1925); Evelyn M. Simpson, *A Study of the Prose Works of John Donne*, 2nd ed. (Oxford: Clarendon Press, 1948); Herschel Baker, *The Wars of Truth: Studies in the Decay of Christian Humanism in the Earlier Seventeenth Century* (Cambridge: Harvard University Press, 1952); Evelyn M. Simpson and George R. Potter in their extensive introductions to each of the volumes in their edition of Donne's sermons; D. W. Harding, "The *Devotions* Now," in *John Donne: Essays in Celebration*, ed. A. J. Smith (London: Methuen, 1972); Richard E. Hughes, *The Progress of the Soul: The Interior Career of John Donne* (New York: William Morrow, 1968); William H. Halewood, *The Poetry of Grace: Reformation Themes and Structures in English Seventeenth-Century Poetry* (New Haven and London: Yale University Press, 1970); Gale H. Carrithers, *Donne at Sermons: A Christian Existential World* (Albany: State University of New York Press, 1972); Barbara K. Lewalski, *Donne's Anniversaries and the Poetry of Praise: The Creation of a Symbolic Mode* (Princeton: Princeton University Press, 1973); John Carey, *John Donne: Life, Mind, and Art*; and Terry G. Sherwood, *Fulfilling the Circle: A Study of John Donne's Thought*. Two of the best of the more recent books that deal with Donne's religious thought, imagery, and imagination are Raymond-Jean Frontain and Frances Malpezzi, eds., *John Donne's Religious Imagination: Essays in Honor of John T. Shawcross* (Conway, Ariz.: University of Central Arizona Press, 1995); and James Baumlin, *John Donne and the Rhetorics of Renaissance Discourse* (Columbia, Mass., and London: University of Missouri Press, 1991).

7. Francis Malpezzi, "Donne's Transcendent Imagination: The Divine Poems as Hierophantic Experience," in *Donne's Religious Imagination*, 141.

8. Raymond-Jean Frontain in the introduction to *Donne's Religious Imagination*, ix.

9. Robert Sencourt, *Outflying Philosophy: A Literary Study of the Religious Elements in the Poems and Letters of John Donne and in the Works of Sir Thomas Browne and of Henry Vaughan the Silurist* (London: Simpkin, Marshal, Hamilton, Kent, 1925), 27.

10. Shami, "Donne's Sermons," 383.

11. Deborah Aldrich Larson, *John Donne and Twentieth Century Criticism* (London and Toronto: Associated University Presses, 1989), 136.

12. For instance, he receives scant mention in A. G. Dickens, *The English Reformation* (New York: Schocken Books, 1964); Owen Chadwick, *The Reformation*, vol. 3 of *The Penguin History of the English Church*, ed. Owen Chadwick (London: Penguin Books, 1964; repr., 1984); Horton Davies, *Worship and Theology in England from Andrewes to Baxter and Fox, 1603–1690* (Princeton: Princeton University Press, 1975); or Stephen Neill, *Anglicanism*, 4th ed. (New York: Oxford University Press, 1977).

13. Keynes, *Bibliography*, 31.

14. T. S. Eliot, "Donne in Our Time," in *A Garland for John Donne: 1631–1931*, ed. Theodore Spencer (Cambridge, Mass.: Cambridge University Press, 1931), 19. In Eliot's opinion, Donne's mind "was legal and controversial rather than philosophical and theological" (8).

15. Samual Taylor Coleridge reflected at considerable length on Donne's sermons. See Roberta E. Brinkley, *Coleridge on the Seventeenth Century* (Durham, N.C.: Duke University Press, 1955).

16. Two notable studies have attempted a systematic presentation of Donne's thought as a whole: Carey's *Donne: Life, Mind, and Art* and Sherwood's *Fulfilling the Circle*. Neither focuses on Donne's theology.

17. (London: SPCK and New York: Macmillan for the Church Historical Society, 1938; repr., Westport, Conn.: Greenwood Press, 1970).

18. Jeffrey Johnson, *The Theology of John Donne* (Cambridge, UK: D. S. Brewer, 1999), ix, x.

19. Husain gives no attention to the body in his systematic theology. Johnson's only consideration of the body comes in his discussion of the human faculties, especially sight.

20. In *Religion and Literature* 24 (1992): 23–31.

21. Kathryn R. Kremen, *The Imagination of the Resurrection: The Poetic Continuity of a Religious Motif in Donne, Blake, and Yeats* (Lewisburg, Pa.: Bucknell University Press, 1972).

22. David Hirsch, "Donne's Atomies and Anatomies: Deconstructed Bodies and the Resurrection of Atomic Theory," *Studies in English Literature: 1500–1900* 31 (1991): 69–94; and Elaine Scarry, "Donne: 'But yet the body is his booke,' " in *Literature and the Body: Essays on Populations and Persons*, ed. Elaine Scarry (Baltimore and London: Johns Hopkins University Press, 1988).

23. Rosalie Osmond, "Body and Soul Dialogues in the Seventeenth Century," *English Literary Renaissance* 4 (1974): 364–403, and *Mutual Accusation: Seventeenth-Century Body and Soul Dialogues in Their Literary and Theological Context* (Toronto: University of Toronto Press, 1990).

APPENDIX B
Donne's Representations of the Body in Their Historical Context

The body Donne spoke of, and spoke through, in his work was a creature both of a particular moment in history and of a unique religious imagination. It was an artifact of a rich history of Christian anthropology and of the perturbations of the dawning of a new age. Donne differed from the Christian past and from his contemporaries not so much in his theological anthropology as in the weight he gave the body and the way he deployed it in his writing. Donne's statements about the composition of the human person, the relationship of body and soul, and the relation of both to God harmonize with the orthodox views of the early Fathers and medieval theologians on most essential points. His particular mix of Aristotelianism and Platonism, Catholicism and Protestantism, medieval and Renaissance, scholasticism and poetry, alchemy and anatomy, piety and wit was, while unique to him, a reflection of the rich opportunities and conflicts of his age. It is not primarily what Donne said about the body that was unusual, but what he *did* with it theologically.

In order to understand the interplay between tradition and imagination in Donne's work, it is helpful to look at that work in its relationship to the history of philosophical and theological thinking about the human body. To provide such a context, I will pursue some themes and particular authors within that history that are of particular relevance for an understanding of Donne's representations of the body.[1]

Donne lived in a time and place where thinking about the body was multifaceted and fluid. There have been a multiplicity of "bodies" throughout the history of Western thought, although certain models dominate at various times and among various branches of the Christian world. These models of the human body multiplied even further, and met and mingled, within the kaleidoscopic world of postmedieval Europe in which Donne lived and wrote. The late sixteenth and early seventeenth centuries were times of extraordinary richness and flux in intellectual life. They supported many differing models of the universe, nature, and the human person. In regard to ideas about the human body, it was a time between orthodoxies. The old orthodoxy of traditional Christian anthropology that understood the body as God's good creation and as part of a web of correspondences that tied that creation together was yielding to the new orthodoxy of Cartesian and scientific mechanism that relegated the body to a separate realm of the material, devoid of meaning. Somewhere in between these two orthodoxies, humanism, Neoplatonism, the reforming movements, revivals of occult thought systems, and the growth of the "new" sciences all gave rise to new "bodies" or ways of thinking about the body that coexisted and interacted for a time with traditional Christian models. Donne absorbed all these influences, employing their ideas and images in his own construal of the human body.

Donne's age inherited a generally consistent theological anthropology from the patristic and medieval theologians, who in turn had developed their thinking about the human person from an amalgam of biblical sources and Hellenistic philosophy. Donne's basic views of the human person were consistent, in most ways, with the Christian orthodoxy of his age. In summary form, the components of this anthropology are (1) the belief that God created the human body out of the dust of the earth; (2) the view that the human being is a composite of body and soul; (3) the general agreement that the body did not cause humanity's fall but has suffered from it through subjection to sin and death; and (4) the hope that God will raise and glorify the human body in the resurrection of the dead. Most Christians in Donne's time, regardless of their doctrinal persuasion, also thought (1) that the human body was a microcosm of the whole universe and (2) that the soul and body reflected the hierarchy of that universe in which spirit is superior to matter.

Donne also shared the ambivalences and contradictions that haunted the orthodox picture of the human body. Donne could use the rhetoric of bodily denigration with the best (or worst) of them. He spoke sometimes of the body as the prison of the soul, railed against the susceptibility of the body to temptation, and sorrowed over its mutability. In the *Devotions,* he says that his body "clogs" him, and he refers to it as a narrow room and a "leprous house" that subjects him to the invasion of "malign and pestilent vapors."[2] He often spoke of the soul and body as marriage partners, with the body in the subordinate (wifely) position. When he addressed one of his favorite subjects, the dissolution and putrifaction of the body in death, Donne could send shivers up the spines of his congregations and can still manage to offend modern commentators who see his fascination with the decaying corpse as merely macabre.

On the other hand, Donne celebrated the body as did perhaps no other religious figure of his period. He believed that Christ redeemed the body when he took human nature upon himself. In a view uncommon for his time, Donne held that the image of God resided in the body as well as in the soul after Christ became human and redeemed humankind. He also thought that only through the bodily senses (and thus through the outward means of reading and hearing the Word, as well as through the sacraments) did the human person have access to knowledge leading to God and to God's grace. Finally, Donne placed great emphasis on the doctrine of the resurrection of the body and preached some of his most eloquent sermons on that topic.

Unlike many of his contemporaries, Donne never disregarded the body. The human body preoccupied Donne and was a ubiquitous presence in his work. He turned to it as a source of experience, a locus of meaning, a means of expression, and a key to understanding the human condition in relationship to God. Discernment of the way Donne deploys the body in his work is essential to an understanding of his theology and his religious aesthetic. Although Donne's doctrine of the body was orthodox, the pervasive presence of the body in his work, early and late, and the crucial role it assumes in his theology and in his religious imagination were novel.

I would like to take a brief look at those portions of the history of the human body most relevant to Donne's representations of it. I begin with the material that formed the foundation of all thought about the human person in Christian history and the source that was most significant for Donne himself: holy Scripture. I will then move through patristic and medieval influences and, finally, into a look at the many new ideas that clamored for attention in the intellectual milieu of late medieval and early modern Europe.

Biblical Material

Donne loved the Bible and immersed himself in its language and themes throughout his life. Naturally, much of his thinking and speaking about the body relates directly to this decisive source. As a preacher and theologian, he tended to connect the body to traditional Christian categories that have their origins in Scripture: creation, incarnation, healing, purification, death, resurrection. Even in his earliest work, he dealt repeatedly in these biblical categories and metaphors. While the significance Donne accorded to the human body, his obvious love for it, and the contradictions and dissonances in his representations of it probably have many sources (including his own life experience), they have roots in biblical materials.

Hebrew Scriptures tended to represent the human person as a psychosomatic unity. Any concept of a soul as an entity separable from the human body was a late and problematic development in Jewish culture. Jesus himself, in his teachings and miracles, seemed focused on the human person as a unity. His concern with present human life and problems, his celebration of marriage, his parables, and his healings seemed to draw no distinction between body and spirit. As Christianity grew as a religion separate from Judaism, its development of the doctrines of incarnation and resurrection of the body, as well as its sacraments, seems based on the intimate interconnection between body and soul, spiritual and material.

Even in Hebrew Scriptures, however, there was some room for the idea of body and soul as distinct entities. Genesis described God making man from clay, then breathing into him the breath of life. Exegetes later used this story to distinguish between body (clay) and soul (the breath of God). Since Genesis contains two separate creation stories, some commentators (notably Origen) claimed two creations for humanity, the first spiritual and the second physical. Further, although the dominant orthodox Judaism did not see a distinction of body and soul in the human person, Christianity in its beginning was surrounded by sects of ascetic and ecstatic Jews, such as the Essenes, who seemed to imply through their practices a distinction between body and spirit.

Next, Paul's theology, enormously influential in the formation of Christian thought, contained the seeds of a distinction between soul and body. One such seed was Paul's distinction between spirit and flesh. This dualism reflected, at least in part, Paul's appropriation of Hellenistic categories for his pastoral work. While Paul did not equate body (*soma*) with what he condemned as *sarx* ("flesh," or the human being as separate from God), he did associate his own body with sin and depicted it as warring with spirit. Christians have tended to conflate Paul's *soma* and *sarx*, reinforcing an adversarial picture of the relationship between soul and body.[3] Another aspect of Paul's thinking that supports the division of the person into body and soul was his distinction between law and gospel. He abrogated many of the customs of the Jewish law, such as circumcision and the dietary laws. This implies a separation between soul and body, since Paul claimed that what affects the body does not necessarily affect the spirit (something that an orthodox Jew never would have admitted). Precisely because they drew no essential distinction between body and soul, or between the material and the spiritual, purity and pollution of the body were of great significance to the Jewish people. Finally, Paul's picture of Christ as both divine and human, the God-man, also implied a radical distinction between body and soul that later haunted Christology and Christian anthropology.

The delay of the *parousia*, the second coming of Christ, was another factor favoring the adoption of the distinction between the human soul and body. Early Christians were concerned with purification of the body, first as a preparation for, and later as an anticipated participation in, a deferred kingdom. As Peter Brown argues in *The Body and Society*, early Christians saw virgin bodies in particular as eschatological signs of a kingdom that was absent but coming. In the longer term, when the reign of Christ failed to materialize and the majority of Christians had to adjust to continuing to live in the social world of marriage and property, the separation of soul from body served the practical function of enabling the body to go on living in the world while the spirit turned toward heaven.

Donne's representations of the body owed much to these biblical sources and the elaboration of their themes by later theologians. His propensity to read the body through the trajectory of creation, fall, redemption, and resurrection on one level simply reflected the grand narrative of the Scriptures themselves. His use of bodily metaphors for spiritual realities, as well as his tendency to read spiritual significance into bodily conditions and signs, came, at least in part, from his immersion in biblical language. Donne also took some of his ambivalence about the body from his favorite New Testament author, St. Paul. Finally, I believe Donne's view of God's method of writing Scripture (as the "metaphorical God" who loves signs) undergirded his whole attempt to read the body as another book in which the metaphorical God writes his will.

Hellenistic Influences

Although Donne's representations of the body (and his methods of representation) were most directly rooted in Biblical material, they reflected the influence of Hellenistic philosophy. These influences were both direct and indirect. Indirectly, Donne's anthropology exhibited the Greek influences on Christian thought that permeated the Church from its early formation. Early Christianity, while holding creedally to the great doctrines of incarnation and resurrection, matured in a Gentile milieu peopled by followers of Greek mystery cults, Plato and Plotinus, Seneca and Epictatus, Pythagoras, Democritus, and the Gnostics. A pervasive message of many of these thought systems was "*soma sema*": the body is a tomb.[4] Philosophers and theologians in the West since Plato have tended to privilege mind over body.[5] This tendency was evident in the early church fathers and medieval theologians who imported concepts from Greek philosophy to build up a coherent theological anthropology. Of most significance for later Christian thought as a whole, and for Donne's picture of the human body, were Platonic and Aristotelian anthropologies and epistemologies, which I will examine in more detail in the next section. Within the spectrum of orthodoxy, Christians embraced both of these views of human nature.

Donne's early images of the human body had some direct ties to Greek philosophy, reflecting the renewal of interest in such philosophy among the English intellectuals of the time. Found mostly in Donne's poetry, they reflect general influences rather than specific arguments. Perhaps the most significant Hellenistic influence on Donne's early work was Neoplatonism, which enjoyed a revival in England during the sixteenth and seventeenth centuries. Donne stood at the center of a revival of English poetry that drew its inspiration from Italian Neoplatonic models.[6] In addition to Platonism, Donne used arguments and images related to naturalism, Pyrrhonic skepticism, Epicurean atomism, and Pythagorean ideas on the transmigration of souls in his early images of the human person.[7] While some themes associated with these philosophies also surfaced in his later sermons, Donne seemed careful to subordinate them to more orthodox Christian sources for theological anthropology. For instance, Donne's fascination with bodily fragmentation into dust and atoms probably owed something to his exposure to a renewed interest in atomism among the budding scientists of his day.[8] However, in his sermons he grounded his references firmly in biblical and patristic sources. Although he occasionally used Neoplatonic images of the body in his sermons, he most often filtered them through earlier Christian theologians.

Patristic and Medieval Sources

Donne's representations of the body drew heavily from patristic and medieval concepts of the human person transmitted formally through the church fathers, medieval scholastics, and monastic writers. They also owed much to the web of less formal images, attitudes, and practices that his age inherited. Much of this "background" of attitudes that informed Donne's thinking reflected Hellenistic ideas. Let me take up, in brief compass, three of these ideas that particularly influenced Donne's images of the human body. These are (1) the idea that the soul and the body are separate entities (although both are essential to the human person); (2) the image of soul and body as a hierarchy, with soul seen as superior to and ruling over body; and (3) the use of Aristotelian philosophy by Thomas Aquinas and his followers to reassert the unity of the human person.[9] I have already discussed the related and influential image of the human composite as a microcosm of the larger material and spiritual macrocosm in chapter 1 and will not rehearse that history again here.

Separation of Soul and Body

Early Christianity grew toward philosophical maturity in the Greco-Roman world among competing philosophies and cults, many of which shared similar ideas of the makeup of the human person. One such idea was that, contrary to Jewish tradition, the soul and body were separate entities or substances. Plato, Plotinus, and their followers saw the realm of ideas or the spirit as the "really real," while the material was only a shadow. Forms of Christian Gnosticism grew up in the early centuries of the Church, reflecting in part the Hellenistic philosophies and cults of the surrounding culture. These Christian gnosticisms tended to share the image of the soul as a divine, pure, and immortal substance living in a mortal and evil body. While this denigration of the material sat uneasily with both Jewish tradition and orthodox Christian doctrine, it has had both philosophic and visceral appeal through the centuries. In the milieu of paganism, persecution, and worldliness that early Christians confronted, hatred of the "world" combined with the Platonic idea of the material as unreal, if not outright inimical to the spiritual. This combination proved irresistible to many of the early church fathers, even to those who struggled against Gnostic and other heterodox influences to defend the doctrines of God's creation of the material world and Christ's bodily incarnation and resurrection. Even orthodoxy's defenders tended to accept and foster a distinction between soul and body, representing the body as inherently weaker than and lower than the soul. This division between soul and body supported the ascetic ideal which has been a constant part of Christianity from its early centuries. Whether one reads the ascetics as despising the body, or simply as using it to attain spiritual ends, the distinction between soul and body undergirded the idealization of the ascetic life.

Hierarchy of Soul over Body

Patristic and medieval thinkers also tended to understand body and soul as part of a larger physical and spiritual hierarchy. As the author of the *Cloud of Unknowing* claimed, "By its nature every physical thing is farther from God than any spiritual."[10] In this scheme, the human person "is the soul, not the body."[11] Within the dominant devotional traditions that grew out of the monastic life, the body was a source of temptation or, at best, an inconvenience and a tie to the world. Thomas á Kempis expresses this convention in his influential *Imitation of Christ*:

> The more spiritual a man desires to become, the more bitter does this present life grow for him, for he sees and realizes more clearly the defects and corruptions of human nature. For to eat and drink, to wake and sleep, to rest and

labor, and to be subject to all the necessities of nature is a great trouble and affliction to the devout man, who would rather be released and get free from all sin. The inner life of man is greatly hindered by the needs of the body.[12]

Most patristic and medieval thinkers also supported the valuation of soul over body by reading the biblical creation story as evidence that God placed his image specifically in the soul, not in the body or the whole human composite. In one sermon, Donne quoted Tertullian to the effect that the image of God was not located in the body, "not even in the image of the body which Christ was to assume."[13] Theologians often located the image of God not simply in the soul but only in its highest part, the rational capacity (*mens* or *nous*). This understanding of the image of God in the human person fostered a tendency to identify true humanity with the mind alone. Even orthodox theologians such as Aquinas and Bonaventure, who stressed that the "real" human person was a composite of body and soul, located the image of God in the higher capacities of the soul. This identification of the image of God with human rationality supported the valuation of soul over body and spiritual over material.

While he often adopted this hierarchy of body and soul, Donne joined earlier theologians in uniting it with biblical nuances of stewardship and responsibility. The soul was to govern the body humanely. He opposed "indiscreet fastings . . . inhuman flagellations . . . unnatural macerations, and such disciplines, as God doth not command, nor authorize, so wither, and shrink, and contract the body, as though the soul were sent into it, as into a prison."[14] To support this position, he quoted Tertullian to the effect that the body was a benefit bestowed by God, and "he that does not use a benefit reproaches the benefactor."[15]

Reassertion of the Unity of the Human Person

In spite of the attractions of Platonic, Gnostic, and Manichaean philosophies, many of the early Fathers engaged in a battle to assert the doctrines of creation, incarnation, and resurrection (all of which affirmed the goodness and significance of material creation in general and the human body in particular) against the trends to devalue the body found in much of the pagan thought that surrounded them. Irenaeus in *Adversus Omnes Haereses (Against the Heresies)* opposed gnostic dualism, providing an influential anthropology. He portrayed the human body as essentially good, as a basic component of the human person, as only a secondary source of sin (after the will has already fallen), and as finding its perfection in union with the risen Christ at the final resurrection.[16] Donne often quoted the church fathers who tended to argue for a unified view of the human person: Irenaeus, Clement, Gregory Nazianzen, Basil, Gregory of Nyssa, and

Tertullian.[17] Even though they had tried to move away from the Platonic idea of the body as the prison of the soul, these theologians still tended to view the body as problematic and to espouse a Platonic epistemology in which "the senses played only the role of awakening the soul to turn inward to an interior truth."[18] Two of the theologians Donne quoted most often, St. Augustine and St. Bernard, shared this Platonic theology.

The most significant break with Platonic dualism in Christian anthropology came with Thomas Aquinas's use of Aristotelian philosophy to assert that the soul was not a separate substance, but the form of the body.[19] Aquinas used this idea to argue for the essential unity of the human person and the dignity of the body. Donne often referred to the soul as the form of the body, and used this concept of the soul for the same purpose as did Aquinas.[20] He also embraced Aquinas's epistemology, which downplayed Platonic inner illumination and instead stressed knowledge through the bodily senses as a crucial first step on the road to God. Paradoxically, while Donne's actual theological anthropology seemed to be taken mostly from Aquinas, his representation of the body as a sign and sacrament was closer to the Platonism of Augustine and Bernard of Clairvaux.

Reading the Body

Donne tended to "read" the body for spiritual significance. This disposition has several antecedents in the Christian past—the general traditions and practices of the Church, a specifically Augustinian way of looking at images, and later Protestant emphasis on Scripture as Word. In spite of the bias in some of the spiritual traditions within Christianity toward fear or denigration the body, both the body itself and the *representation* of the body often had great religious significance. Orthodox Christians believed that the body, although occupying a lower position in the hierarchy of being than the soul, was an integral part of the human person, connected to the soul for better or worse. The state of the body could influence the soul, just as the soul could inform the state of the body. Christians, for example, traditionally saw physical suffering (either through martyrdom, illness, or voluntary ascetic practice) as a trial for the purging and purification of the soul.

To the extent that body, soul, and God were interconnected throughout the history of Christian spirituality, the body often represented the soul or other spiritual realities. Biblical writings and subsequent interpretations of them are rife with bodily metaphors (illness, health, eating, drinking, sexual love) that point to spiritual realities. In the early centuries of the Church, the bodies of the virgins and martyrs (and then of the desert fathers and the early ascetic monks) had great symbolic and eschatological significance.[21] The understanding of the body as a sign of the spiritual or the holy reached its apogee in the Middle Ages.[22] In a largely illiterate culture, anyone could "read" the body for traces of the holy. The calm face of a madonna, the terrible wounds of Christ on an altarpiece, the stigmata of Francis, the mark of the cross on the viscera of a dead saint: all had spiritual significance and embodied spiritual reality. In two late medieval traditions, which continued in popularity into Donne's time, even the body of the ordinary sinner could exemplify a spiritual lesson. These were the *danse macabre* (the dance of death) and the *ars moriendi* (the "art" of dying).[23] Both these traditions depended on the imaginative, often visual representation of the dead or dying body as a reminder to the Christian of his or her own mortality and need for repentance and salvation.

Donne's "reading" of the body was similar to his methods of reading Scripture and God's related revelations in his other "books." He embraced an expansive and somewhat medieval approach to scriptural interpretation. Believing that God himself was a "metaphorical" God who loved to cram multiple meanings into Scripture, Donne refused to restrict himself to the preferred Protestant techniques of literal (historical) and typological interpretation. He believed God had much more meaning to bestow. Donne also refused to restrict God's meaning to Scripture alone. He believed that God "signified" through many material things. Donne's view of the material as a sign of spiritual reality had much in common with Augustine's theology of signs in *De Doctrina Christiana* and the medieval traditions of exegesis that grew from it. For Augustine, images, both in the mind and in literature, were a function of the spiritual interpretation of corporeal nature by which the physical objects of the world become signs of God's purpose and creative power.[24] Donne certainly shared this dependence on image as a way to God. Much of Donne's discussions of the way God signified through Scripture owed a great deal to Augustine.

Donne and the Transition to the Modern Body

Donne lived in a time that offered competing models of the human person. Both the representation and, arguably, the lived experience of human embodiment underwent a major transition from medieval to modern: from open and public to closed and private, from sacred to secular, from site of God's action to locus of society's manipulations, from icon to object.[25] Donne drew from several of these competing models of the body. He reached back to the images of the Middle Ages, around him into the Renaissance stew of Neoplatonism, alchemy, skepticism, and reformation, and forward into the emerging sciences for images and ideas. In this last section, I will focus on three sets of influences on Donne's representations of the body: certain views of the Renaissance, of the Reformers, and finally, of the "new" sciences.

Renaissance Bodies

The currents of new ideas and practices that wafted through Europe in the fifteenth and sixteenth centuries brought new ideas and new representations of the human body. Of these new ways of looking at the body, one of the most influential was a brand of Neoplatonism that was, as one scholar puts it, "marked by a more positive view of the body as a result of a new enthusiasm for Greek art and literature."[26] Taking their cue from Petrarch, Augustine, and Plato, artists and writers celebrated beautiful flesh as a reflection of spiritual beauty and truth.[27] While he was part of a revival of love poetry in England in the 1590s that employed these Neoplatonic conventions to speak of feminine loveliness, Donne seemed suspicious of the Petrarchan cult of beauty. As I discussed in chapter 2, Donne took these paeans to feminine beauty with a grain of salt in his secular poetry and was just as apt to satirize the Neoplatonic conceits as to use them. As discussed in chapters 3 through 5, his only straightforward representations of the body as reflecting the beauty of the soul came in his sacred poetry and applied only to certain Christian women. He was, for one thing, too realistic and too earthy to be carried away by Platonic flights. Neither Donne nor his God are truly Renaissance gentlemen. Both wanted to get their hands dirty in the clay of creation, the blood of the cross, and the decay of the grave. Both loved matter as it really was, not as it was idealized. While one scholar has said the Renaissance portrayed the body as a "quasi-sacrament" of spiritual truth,[28] Donne in his later sacred work construed the body as truly sacramental, and that sacrament involved pain and death.

Donne's representations of the body also bore the marks of a renewed interest in the occult sciences (including alchemy and astrology) in sixteenth- and seventeenth-century Europe.[29] Alchemy especially fascinated Donne. Some of his most powerful images of the body relied on the doctrine of correspondences, one of the foundations of Renaissance alchemy. The alchemists believed that there were correspondences between parts of the body and the larger physical world and that there were direct ties between the material and the spiritual. The two-level model employed by the alchemists ("as above, so below") appealed to Donne both as a poet and as a Christian who believed that these correspondences depended on God's original creative act.[30] While Donne often used alchemical imagery, however, some of the central dynamics of alchemy were foreign to his sensibility. The object of the Renaissance magus was power over matter through his own spiritual power and gnosis.[31] Donne emphasized instead God's power as constitutive of the human body and human identity.

The most direct influence from this occult revival on Donne's depictions of the body derived from Paracelsus.[32] Donne shared Paracelsus's fascination with the human body and was in sympathy with his core image of the human body as a microcosm of the world. Donne often used his imagery in speaking of the body, most directly in the *Devotions*. While Donne often borrowed Paracelsus's images, his depictions of the body differed from those of Paracelsus in some profound ways. While Paracelsus essentially unified the human body and soul (along with the spiritual and the corporeal universes),[33] Donne carefully preserved their distinction. Paracelsus saw matter as active, while Donne represented it as passive. The human body as Donne envisioned it was made of matter that naturally fell into decay and disorder unless preserved by the human spirit or the direct action of God. Even when he used Paracelsus's images in which body "enacted" spirit, for Donne these were not natural parallels. They were results of the direct action of God. Donne's identification of matter with spirit was not literal, as it was for Paracelsus, but a matter of analogy, metaphor, and (most directly) sign and sacrament.

Another influential Renaissance model of the human person, the new spirit of individuation and self-determination, had a backhanded influence on Donne's representations of the body. He rebelled against it. The philosophy of Pico della Mirandola, widely disseminated in England, exemplified this attitude of independence.[34] In his *Oration on the Dignity of Man*, Pico said that the true basis for the dignity of man was not his place in the great chain of being as mediator between higher and lower creations, but the fact that humanity was the only creature with "unlimited power of self-determination."[35] Pico has his God tell Adam,

> A limited nature in other creatures has been confined by Us within fixed laws. In conformity with your free will, in whose hands I have placed you, you are enclosed by no boundaries; and you will fix limits of nature for yourself. . . . You . . . are the mother and maker of yourself; you may sculpt yourself into whatever shape you prefer.[36]

This trend toward individualization and independence of the human person in the Renaissance involved cutting the body off from nature, from community, and from cosmos, leaving it "an ontologically empty form, depreciated and accidental."[37]

These attitudes toward the body were anathema to Donne. Even in his early secular poetry, he represented the body on one hand as an indication of humanity's limits and dependence on the Creator and, on the other, as a connection to God, community, and cosmos. In his sacred writings, he continually employed images of the body to call attention to humanity's place in the great chain and to its utter dependence on God as creator and resurrector. Far from believing that the human person could or should "sculpt" himself or herself, Donne often uses the image of God "sculpting" the body, not only as the potter who sculpted the original clay of the creation, but in present illness and future glory. Donne thought the body was full of meaning, connected both actually and rhetorically to a great web of material signs that were in turn connected to spiritual reality. Donne's was not the closed and independent body of polite modern society that was emerging in the Renaissance. In many ways, his represented body remained the open and communal body of his medieval heritage.[38]

Bodies in the Reforming Movements

Donne's representations of the human body also had antecedents in the various movements for religious reform of the sixteenth and seventeenth centuries. Most of the theologians, Reformers, and devotional writers of this period shared an essentially medieval theological anthropology and some basic sentiments about the body. While it was originally good, in practice it was an unfortunate encumbrance, the lower part of man that had to be overcome and disciplined in the service of the spirit.[39] Few of the Reformers of the sixteenth and seventeenth centuries (either Catholic or Protestant) shared the zest for all things bodily that Martin Luther displayed or his focus on the theological implications of bodiliness. While there was general agreement on a traditional theological anthropology, there was a range of attitudes toward the status of the material itself that has implications for understanding the body. Catholicism during this period asserted the importance of the material and of the body in devotional and liturgical life. Radical Protestantism, at the other end of the spectrum, rejected many of the doctrines and practices that linked spirituality with material signs: transubstantiation and the practices associated with the veneration of the eucharistic host, vestments, anointment, use of images to aid devotion, and even such bodily gestures as kneeling and making the sign of the cross on the body.

The Church of England during this period attempted to hold the middle ground in relation to the body and embodied practice. While it was careful to avoid the doctrine of transubstantiation as too "Roman," corporate Anglicanism emphatically rejected the spiritualized religion of Zwingli and the more radical Reformers with regard to liturgy, sacraments, vestments, and church polity. Richard Hooker, in his formative *Of the Laws of Ecclesiastical Polity*, argued for an Aquinian approach to religious life that recognized a continuity between nature and grace, making room for "embodied" practices in the church. While Donne never refers to Hooker's work directly, they shared some positions on the body and embodied practices. They agreed on the Aristotelian idea that the soul is the "form" of the body. They also shared an Aristotelian epistemology in which one learns by the reflection of the intellect on sense impressions. Neoplatonism also played a formative role in Anglican theology, in part through the early influence of Catholics such as Erasmus and John Colet and in part through continental Reformers such as Zwingli and Calvin. This Neoplatonic strain in English thought placed great emphasis on the spiritual and ethical and downplayed the role of the body, or embodied practices, in religious life. During Donne's time, while almost all theologians and devotional writers in England agreed on the orthodox doctrines of the importance of the body to the human composite and its essential goodness, in actual practice these same writers tended to denigrate the body or ignore it in their devotional work and sermons.[40] Despite sharing their orthodox anthropology, Donne accorded the body unusual prominence, and his use of the body as a locus of meaning is distinctive.

Among the Reformers, John Calvin probably had the most influence on the English Church and on Donne himself. Despite this influence, Donne's Christian anthropology owed little to Calvin's. Calvin's view of the human person drew heavily on Platonic Christian theology, whereas Donne tended toward Aristotelianism. Calvin understood body and soul as two separate substances. He depicted the soul as an immortal yet created essence.[41] In typical Platonic parlance, Calvin spoke of the body as a prison.[42] Although sometimes invoking such Platonic language, Donne, by contrast, referred to the soul as the form of the body. He expresses his doubts as to whether it was, by nature, either separable or immortal. Calvin tended to downplay the role of the body in religious life, although not to the extent of more radical Reformers. Donne emphasized it. One telling instance of Donne's and Calvin's varying treatment of the human body came in their statements about the nature of the "spectacles" through which people can correctly read the nature of the world and of God. Calvin said in the *Institutes* that it is Scripture that forms the "spectacles" through which a fallen humanity can "read" the signs of God within the mind and in the world that are otherwise unclear and diffuse.[43] Donne, by contrast, said that it is finally *adversity* and *suffering*, profoundly involving the life of the body, that are the "spectacles" that clear humanity's vision so they may see God in creation and in his action in their own lives. Donne even claimed that the faithful could read as Scripture the signs God wrote on their bodies. Despite these differences, Donne's representations of the body bear the marks of Calvin's theology in an indirect way.[44] His deployment of the body as an exemplar of God's sovereignty and humanity's utter dependence on God may relate to Calvin's emphasis on this theme. Protestant, especially Calvinistic, doctrines of Word and sacraments also played an indirect role in Donne's representations of the human body.

Donne, the New Sciences, and Modernity

Donne's statement in *The First Anniversary* that "new philosophy" had called "all in doubt" has served as a handy slogan for the whole crisis of faith and knowledge in the seventeenth century, a marker of the death of the medieval cosmos and the birth of the modern world of science. Where are Donne's representations of the body located within this crisis of knowledge? Did they reflect the "new philosophy," or were they relics of the waning Middle Ages? While Donne's portrayal of the human body reflected the perturbations of the coming of different ways of seeing the world, it lay suspended between the old and the new, partaking of fragments of both. Donne, like other well-read men of his time, was familiar with Aristotelian, Platonic, Galenic, Paracelsian, and hermetic "sciences," as well as the "new" sciences of Bacon, Kepler, Galileo, Harvey, and the new Epicurean atomists. Many of these influences surface in his representations of the human body. The implications of the new sciences for the understanding of the human person were slow to develop, and the images and conventions of the old worldview were slow to fade.[45] Many scientists and philosophers during Donne's time, as well as most theologians, continued to speak of the human person as a composite of body and soul and to understand the body in a theological context.

Donne's portrayal of the body was not "modern" in the straightforward sense of a body viewed as a material object, governed by scientific laws, and placed firmly in a medical and scientific context. That understanding of the body was in its infancy in his day. Although he drew on the new sciences for some of his imagery, his basic understanding of the human person bore a greater resemblance to earlier models. Keenly interested in the medical sciences, including the emerging science of anatomy, he tended to use images of whichever medieval or proto-modern medical system suited him rhetorically.[46] He subordinated any scientific or quasi-scientific system to theological concerns and questions. The developing modern idea (rooted in Cartesian philosophy and the new empirical sciences) of a body consigned to a separate realm of the material and scientific, somehow separated from the continual actions of spirit and the realm of theological significance, was inimical to both his religious and poetic sensibilities. Donne's interest in the new discoveries in astronomy also influenced his metaphors of the body. As in medicine, he tended to mix images cheerfully from the medieval understanding of the cosmos with the new images from Tycho Brahe and Galileo.

Even considering modernity in a larger sense, Donne's body does not seem "modern." Some of the characteristics historians have associated with modernity are, first, the privileging of human consciousness; second, the separation of the realms of matter and spirit; and third, the related embrace of a law-governed cosmos.[47] These tendencies, emerging in Donne's time, had implications for the understanding of the body that took hold only later. Donne rejected all of these tendencies, and his representations of the body reflect that rejection.

Perhaps the quintessential move of modernity was the privileging of human subjectivity as the ground of knowledge, summed up in Descartes' statement *Cogito ergo sum*. Faced with his age's crisis of uncertainty that a century of religious wars, new scientific discoveries, and a revival of Greek skepticism had precipitated, Descartes sought certainty in what seemed to him the purity of consciousness. His conception divorced the mind from the changes, contradictions, and decay of the material world. Although this interior turn has many roots, including Platonic philosophy, the *devotio moderna,* and the spiritualities of Catholic and Protestant reforming movements, Descartes' work marked the definitive emergence of a distinctly modern way of privileging consciousness. He consigned the body to the separate realm of extension, apart from the realm of spirit where the "I" resided.[48] He anchored certitude in human thought, rather than in world or God. Although he tried to maintain that the human being was a basic unity of body and soul because God willed it so, Descartes' explanation of the workings of the union was never satisfactory. Whether he intended it or not, he bequeathed to the modern world a philosophy that divided the person into ethereal mind and mechanical body.

In the search for a new ground of certainty in the seventeenth century, Francis Bacon and the empiricists formed a rival school to Descartes and the rationalists. While Bacon and other scientists of the time turned outward to study the material world instead of inward as did the rationalists, they were alike in their trust of human reason. The linchpin of Bacon's project of understanding and then subduing material nature to the will of humankind was the reliability of human reason distinct from the material world it intended to dominate.

Living in the same time and intellectual milieu as Descartes and Bacon, Donne arrived at profoundly different conclusions. Influenced early in his intellectual life by the revival of Greek skepticism, Donne always felt that human reason had distinct limits. By itself, reason was not competent to understand the nature of reality, either through innate ideas or through sense impressions. Indeed, Donne believed that the (fallen) mind was just as fallible as the body, perhaps more so. Wary of both human objectivity and human subjectivity, he distrusted perception and reason apart from the intervention of God's grace. He also distrusted the interior turn toward private revelation, mysticism, and "enthusiasm" as sites of certainty. For Donne there was no certainty, just faith that God still spoke to humanity through sign and sacrament: through his Church, in Scripture and preaching, and through material signs and sacraments that included even the bodies of believers. Donne likewise rejected the idea of human beings as autonomous agents. He believed they were dependent creatures. They relied continually on God, first, for their very existence; second, on his grace to rectify their reason and perceptions; and third, on his gift of the outward means of salvation through the Church. They also relied on the charity and community of their fellow creatures. In Donne's work, the human body served as a perduring sign of this dependence.

The penchant for understanding the cosmos, society, and the human person as law-governed instead of God-governed is another feature of the dawning modern intellectual project. As with the turn to interiority alone as a ground of knowledge, this tendency evolved in part from a desire for intellectual certainty and control over life. The growth and practice of the new sciences depended on the predictability of an orderly physical realm operating by principals of universal law and on the reliability of human reason to understand and master those laws. Most of the new scientists and philosophers continued to speak of God as author of the laws of nature and society. They qualified this discourse by rejecting the interfering, unstable, and unpredictable God of the biblical narratives. Donne, by contrast, still understood the human body and the world it reflected as unstable and unpredictable, prone to decay and disaster if separated from God's constant care. Donne's exposure to the new sciences in their earliest stages, when they were struggling with competing systems, served to reinforce his skepticism of human reason as a guide to their cosmos or to human nature.[49] The "scientific" idea of stable, predictable, unchangeable processes working on matter was foreign not only to him, but to many of his contemporaries.

In the interest of the pursuit of certainty, both rationalists and empiricists found it useful to sever the spiritual from the material.[50] The ensuing chasm became a hallmark of modern intellectual life. It had profound implications for the understanding of the human composite, which the Middle Ages had seen precisely as the linchpin of two orders, material and spiritual, that were created and joined by God.[51] Any separation of body from soul, material from spiritual, or science from theology was anathema to Donne, who understood the human person as part of a web of interrelated correspondences and connections. For Donne, religious imagination was essential to the understanding of *anything,* especially the body. There could be no separation between the realms, for God encompassed them all. Donne passionately affirmed God's love of the material and his use of it as sign and sacrament that communicated both knowledge and grace to believers.[52] He had little interest in nature in itself, much as he talked of the "book of creatures." He was interested in it as a text that spoke about God and humanity. Donne had no concern with the body as a natural object, but as an instrument of experience and as a text that revealed God and soul.

Body as Book

In Donne's view, God "wrote" not only the books of nature and of Scripture, but also in the books of bodies.[53] God, wishing to be known, manifested himself "openly, intelligibly, manifestly, by the book."[54] He authored the books of nature and Scripture to reveal himself to human reason, aided by grace. Donne saw reading and writing as ways to enter into that realm of divine signification. He identified himself closely with his role as the reader and interpreter of God's Word to his congregations. Suspicious of traditional mystical experience and of the "private" revelations of the spiritualists of his day, Donne believed that God revealed himself openly, through clear and "material" means: nature, Scripture, sacraments, and preaching. He often spoke of these open revelations through the image of the book. This image grows out of the tradition in Christian thought, going back to the Fathers, of nature and Scripture as two books in which God reveals himself to humanity. Most of those who wrote in this tradition, including Augustine, Aquinas, and Bonaventure, believed that nature was inferior to Scripture as a source of knowledge of God but thought that it did reveal God to natural reason. Hooker expressed this traditional idea in his *Laws* when he stated, "Some things she [wisdom] openeth by the sacred books of Scripture; some things by the glorious works of Nature."[55]

Donne's God authored bodies just as he did the other books. This view was consistent with his notion that creation was not a thing of the past, but an ongoing reality. Donne's lively sense of the author, divine or human, as creator of the "work," and of books as the instruments through which authors could and did communicate their knowledge, thoughts, and intent to others, funded his metaphor of the body as a text. God means for all of his creations, whether bodies or books, to communicate his nature and intentions to humanity.

Donne emphasized the physicality of both books and bodies.[56] Books as material objects mesmerized Donne. He loved to talk of their spines, their chapters, their indices, and their leaves as material things. Donne saw books as physical products, likening them to the products of craftsmen or to the world God made. In Donne's spirituality, all physical things had a sacramental quality since God created them, continued to sustain them, and used them as vehicles of his presence and grace. Seeing all things as sacramental in a relative sense, Donne accorded a special place to books and bodies. All books have an affinity with the signifying Word as Scripture; all bodies have a connection to the signifying Word as Christ, who assumed and redeemed the human body.

Donne read the body not simply as one of the "books" of God, but specifically as a scriptural text. When Donne spoke of "texts," he had something very specific in mind. The text was the portion of Scripture chosen as the sermon topic for a particular day. The text was a "given" around which the preacher wove his eloquence and through which the Holy Spirit poured his riches on the congregation. Donne had a vivid sense of the texts from which he preached as gifts from God, as living realities. He believed passionately that any fragment contained the whole. The text was one verse from Scripture, but it implied the whole of Scripture. It was simply a way in to the whole. Thus, for Donne, "text" and "book" could be interchangeable, since the part participated in the whole. Donne expanded this root metaphor of the text as a Bible verse and applied it to many other things (the world, a book of rhetoric, a blade of grass, a dead body), because any physical object or circumstance was a word of God as well.

These images of the books of nature and Scripture were still current in Donne's time, although the connection and harmony between the books were being called increasingly into question from two fronts: anti-scholastic theology and the new sciences. Both these forces tended to separate revealed and natural knowledge into two orders of truth.[57] Faced with this separation, Donne evolved his own views on the relationship between the books of nature and Scripture. He did not use the "books" as a simple retreat to the traditional medieval position. Bishop Hall, one of Donne's Anglican contemporaries, used a standard medieval scholastic representation of the book of nature when he called the "the volumes of Natural history . . . but . . . so many commentaries upon the several creatures wherein we may read God."[58] Donne, on the other hand, sometimes took a more radical approach. In a sermon preached a year or two before he wrote the *Devotions*, he said, "There is an elder book in the World than Scriptures; it is not well said, in the World, for it is the World it self, the whole book of Creatures." To that point, he simply expressed the traditional view. But then he went on to say, "And indeed the Scriptures are but a paraphrase, but a comment, but an illustration of that book of Creatures."[59] In putting Scripture in the subordinate position of a paraphrase of the book of nature, Donne transgressed both medieval scholastic views and contemporary Protestant opinions, both of which saw Scripture as the superior revelation. Donne sometimes expressed the orthodox view that the Bible is a superior revelation and necessary to salvation, while at other times he subordinated it to the other books through which God reveals himself.

One example of Donne's tendency to "read" the human body to discern the will of God came in a sermon he preached on a text from Job 36:25, "Every man may see it; man may behold it afar off." Donne rhapsodized on the fecundity of God's manifestations to humankind. The heart of the sermon was an extended metaphor, linking God's created works to literary works. After speaking at length of the world as a "work" that revealed

God as creator, Donne said that even those who shied away from the Bible and the books of the church fathers perforce encountered the Creator God in all the books of "humane Authors."[60] The books of pagan orators, philosophers, and poets all spoke of God as creator. Then Donne made the transition from these literal books to the "book" of the world, saying that even if one did not have money or leisure for the "great volumes" of mathematics or politics, which also spoke of God, one could descend to the

> Georgiques, the consideration of the Earth, a farm, a garden, nay seven foot of earth, a grave, and that will be book enough. Go lower; every worm in the grave, lower, every weed upon the grave, is an abridgement of all; nay lock up all doors and windows, see nothing but thy self; nay let thy self be locked up in a close prison, that thou canst not see thy self, and doe but feel thy pulse; let thy pulse be intermitted, or stupefied, that thou feel not that, and doe but think, and a worm, a weed, thy self, thy pulse, thy thought, are all testimonies, that All, this All, and all the parts thereof, are *Opus*, a work made, and *opus ejus*, his work, made by God.[61]

In another sermon from 1625, Donne turned to the same "text" in the form of the dead bodies of the saints as one of a multitude of Scriptures open to his congregation. He noted how abundant God was in the texts he offered the saints.

> He writes his Law once in our hearts, and then repeats that Law, and declares that Law again in his written Word, in his Scriptures. . . . And as he is every way abundant, as he hath added Law to Nature . . . and by that Text which we have read to you here, and by that Text which we have left at home, our house and family, and by the Text which we have brought hither, our selves, and by that Text which we find here, where we stand, and sit, and kneel upon the bodies of some of our dead friends or neighbors, he gives to us, he repeats to us, a full, a various, a multiform, a manifold Catechism.[62]

The human body was one text Donne returned to again and again throughout the course of his life and ministry.

Conclusion

Donne and most of his contemporaries lived, sometimes gloriously and sometimes uneasily, in an uncertain world between two worlds of certainty. While theologians such as Hooker still might have eloquently asserted it, the medieval synthesis that reached its height with Aquinas was passing. The new world of the scientific synthesis was barely dawning. If Donne was aware of the new proposals for certitude of Descartes or Bacon, he did not avail himself of them. Donne avers no ground for certainty, but he does embrace the way of faith, faith that God has acted and is acting in the world. In the midst of uncertainties, Donne turned often to that which was closest to him, his own body and the bodies of his fellows. He saw those bodies as instruments through which God acted and as books upon which God wrote the large story of salvation history, as well as the smaller chapters of his actions in individual lives. Donne turned from the uncertainties of the macrocosm to the more readily accessible microcosm to "read" God.

Donne, with the power of his language and his images, fought a rearguard action against the desacralization of his world. He also attempted to move forward. He realized that the old literal cosmic order had been called into doubt by the new sciences and that the old sacramental order had been called into doubt by Protestant iconoclasm. Although he used many of the old categories in talking about the human person, he attempted to use the body in new ways and to speak in new terms and new categories that were responsive to new discoveries in both science and theology. His way of speaking about the body emphasized the personal and individual aspects of the new Protestant sensibility, while holding on to some of the old communal emphasis of Catholicism. His ways of speaking of the actions of God on the body, in illness and in resurrection, evoked the newer "Protestant" emphasis on God's grace, will, and providence instead of primarily speaking the old Catholic, Aristotelian language of cosmic hierarchy. His references to the body as a text both invoked and undermined Protestant reliance on the text of Scripture as the primary means of knowing the work and will of God. Donne asserted the body as *Scripture,* not simply as the "book of creatures," but as a manifestation of God's specific and ongoing word.

Notes

1. I will not attempt any comprehensive summary of the history of the body in Western thought, since to attempt more than a brief summary would be both a daunting task and a step beyond the scope of this study. The literature on the history of the body is extensive, but as yet there is no definite "history" of the body. The book that comes closest to such a history for the Christian West is Frank Bottomly's *Attitudes to the Body in Western Christendom* (London: Lepus Books, 1979). Another relevant and comprehensive study from a more strictly theological perspective is Benedict Ashley's *Theologies of the Body: Humanist and Christian* (St. Louis, Mo.: Pope John Center, 1985).

2. John Donne, *Devotions upon Emergent Occasions,* ed. Anthony Raspa (New York: Oxford University Press, 1987), 17, 60, 63.

3. Peter Brown points out that Paul frequently associates his own body with sin (as in the "law in his members" that wars against the spirit). Brown identifies Paul's distinction between spirit and flesh as the primary source for the dualism between soul and body in

later Christian thought, whether Paul intended it that way or not. *The Body and Society: Men, Women and Sexual Renunciation in Early Christianity* (New York: Columbia University Press, 1988), 48.

4. As many have observed, the identification of the denigration of the body with Platonism must be nuanced. Even Plato's own work contains statements that variously value or denigrate the body. While Plato insisted on the difficulties of the body and its lower place in the anthropological hierarchy, in his early philosophy he also represented the body as the necessary beginning of the human way to the realm of ideas. For instance, Arthur O. Lovejoy points out that Plato's picture of God as self-transcending fecundity in the *Timaeus* implies the necessity and goodness of material embodiment. *The Great Chain of Being: The Study of the History of an Idea* (Cambridge, Mass., and London: Harvard University Press, 1936; repr., 1964), 53.

5. For instance, in *The Languages of Psyche: Mind and Body in Enlightenment Thought* (Berkeley: University of California Press, 1990), G. S. Rousseau argues that splitting mind from body and assigning it a lower position in an anthropological hierarchy originated with Plato, continued with Aristotle and the Stoics, and permeated the thinking of the West (9). Jonathan Sawday, in *The Body Emblazoned: Dissection and the Human Body in Renaissance Culture* (London and New York: Routledge, 1995), contends that Plato's depiction of a "perpetual dualistic struggle between body and soul," transmitted via Neoplatonism, patristic authority, and medieval theology, served as the dominant model for understanding the relationship between body and soul within Western culture prior to the fifteenth century (17). In his history of the body in the Christian West, Frank Bottomly argues that the writers of the ancient world generally seem to either despise or fear the body and that the institutions of the ancient world tended to depersonalize it, using it as a site and instrument for the exercise of power (167). This model continued its sway largely undiminished into the early seventeenth century.

6. See, for instance, Charles Webster, ed., *The Intellectual Revolution of the Seventeenth Century* (London: Routledge and Kegan Paul, 1974), 104, and Donald L. Guss, *John Donne: Petrarchist: Italianate Conceits and Love Theory in "The Songs and Sonnets"* (Detroit: Wayne State University Press, 1966).

7. Only one of Donne's preordination writings, however, has a totally and identifiably non-Christian anthropological model. In the long, and unfinished, satirical poem entitled *Metempsychosis*, dating from 1601, Donne uses the doctrine of transmigration to follow an unidentified soul through a series of ironic adventures in various bodies (plant, bird, fish, land animal, and human), criticizing humanity and society along the way. Donne, in his introduction to the poem, reminds his readers that "the Pythagorean doctrine doth not only carry one soul from man to man, nor man to beast, but indifferently to plants also: and therefore you must not grudge to find the same soul in an emperor, in a post-horse, and in a mushroom." *John Donne: The Complete English Poems*, ed. A. J. Smith (London: Penguin Books, 1971; repr., London: Penguin Classics, 1986), 176.

8. David Hirsch discusses Donne's exposure to the circles that were trying to revive scientific atomism and his use of the theories in his imagery in "Donne's Atomies and Anatomies: Deconstructed Bodies and the Resurrection of Atomic Theory," *Studies in English Literature: 1500–1900* 31 (1991): 69–94.

9. It is difficult to trace specific sources for Donne's representations of the body. Even on the infrequent occasions when he discusses theological anthropology in a systematic way, he rarely quotes other authors directly or even refers to them specifically. Further, many of the anthropological ideas Donne draws on had simply become commonplaces in theological discourse.

10. *The Cloud of Unknowing and Other Works,* trans. Clifton Wolters (London: Penguin Books, 1978), 116.

11. Ibid., 136.

12. Thomas á Kempis, *The Imitation of Christ,* trans. Leo Sherley-Price (London: Penguin Books, 1952), 55.

13. John Donne, *The Sermons of John Donne,* 10 vols., ed. Charles Edmund Merrill Jr. (New York: Sturgis & Walton, 1910), 9:76–78. Donne implies elsewhere, however, that once Christ assumed the human body, it also became in some sense the image of God.

14. Ibid., 7:106.

15. Ibid.

16. Ashley, *Theologies of the Body,* 114.

17. From the number of times he referred to them in his sermons, Donne apparently approved of their work. However, he seldom quoted or alluded to them specifically on this subject.

18. Ashley, *Theologies of the Body,* 135.

19. *Summa theol.* I.q.76, a.4.c. For an analysis of Aquinas's views on the human soul and body, see Etienne Gilson, *The Philosophy of St. Thomas Aquinas,* ed. G. A. Elrington, trans. Edward Bullough, 2nd ed. (New York: Dorset Press, 1929), 204–20, and F. C. Copleston, *Aquinas* (London: Pelican Books, 1955; repr., London: Penguin Books, 1991), 156–98.

20. He also shares with Aquinas the difficulties of embracing a thoroughgoing Aristotelian doctrine of the soul as the form of the body in the face of the need to maintain the capacity of the soul for a separate existence in heaven until it is reunited with the body at the general resurrection.

21. See Peter Brown's *The Body and Society* for a discussion of the symbolic functions of the body of the virgin in the early Church.

22. Paul Binksi, in his work on death in the Middle Ages, points out that "one important fact about late-medieval devotion [was that] many of its preoccupations were with the spiritual significance and representation of the body, whether divine or not." *Medieval Death: Ritual and Representation* (Ithaca, N.Y.: Cornell University Press, 1996), 47. He refers to works like Grunewald's crucifixion in the Isenheim altarpiece as an example of this concern with the body (47). He also cites the common practice of the bodily division of royalty and saints, with separate body parts going to various places of honor and veneration (63). Caroline Walker Bynum, in many of her studies of this period, has detailed the somatic component of medieval spirituality. Two of her works, *The Resurrection of the Body in Western Christianity, 200–1336* (New York: Columbia University Press, 1995), and *Fragmentation and Redemption: Essays on Gender and the Human Body in Medieval Religion* (New York: Zone Books, 1992), are particularly relevant in this regard. Jonathan Sawday also discusses medieval "sacred anatomy" and the

"dispersal burial" of important persons (and contrasts these practices with the emerging practice of scientific anatomy in the seventeenth century) in *The Body Emblazoned*, esp. 98–100.

23. See Betty Anne Doebler's *"Rooted Sorrow": Dying in Early Modern England* (Rutherford: Fairleigh Dickenson University Press, 1994) for an account of the influence of these traditions on the English devotional tradition.

24. Augustine, *On Christian Doctrine*, trans. D. W. Robertson Jr. (New York: Macmillan, 1958). Patrick Grant's *Images and Ideas in Literature of the English Renaissance* (Amherst, Mass.: University of Massachusetts Press, 1979) explores the influence of Augustine's theology and ideas about language on the English Renaissance. He says that for Augustine "spiritual vision involves a mixture of mutability (derived from the corporeal) and immutability (derived from the intellectual), and the hallmark of spiritual vision is the image" (9). Although he does not have much to say about Donne's work, his point is that the medieval poetic vision was based on an essentially Augustinian tradition in which the continuity of matter, symbol, and idea was assumed and assured by the idea of correspondences. Donne is, in many ways, still part of this medieval, Augustinian way of looking at language and symbol.

25. Among those who have observed this transition are Michel Foucault, *Discipline and Punish: The Birth of the Prison*, trans. Alan Sheridan (New York: Vintage Books, 1979); Stephen Greenblatt, *Renaissance Self-Fashioning: From More to Shakespeare* (Chicago: University of Chicago Press, 1980); Mikhail Bakhtin, *Rabelais and His World* (Bloomington: Indiana University Press, 1984); Jacques Bosquet, *Mannerism: The Painting and Style of the Late Renaissance* (New York: Braziller, 1964); Lawrence Stone, *The Family, Sex and Marriage in England, 1500–1800* (New York: Harper & Row, 1977); Bryan S. Turner, *The Body and Society: Explorations in Social Theory* (Oxford: Basil Blackwell, 1984); Jonathan Sawday, *The Body Emblazoned*; and Frank Bottomly, *Attitudes to the Body*.

26. Ashley, *Theologies of the Body*, 165.

27. Anthony Synnott argues that the belief that physical beauty reflected spiritual goodness and harmony was characteristic of the Renaissance. He cites Shakespeare, Milton, and Browne as English exemplars of this Platonic notion that the outer (material) reflects the inner (spiritual). *The Body Social: Symbolism, Self and Society* (London and New York: Routledge, 1993), 87–88. Of course, other scholars have seen this Renaissance idealization of the body in secular art from a difference perspective. Bottomly, for instance, argues that the real divorce of body and soul in Christian culture began in the Renaissance. The body became the object of the artist and the viewer rather than an icon of the eternal and the spiritual. He says that the body "was divorced from spirit in art long before Descartes separated them in his philosophy" as art became increasingly secularized and commercial (*Attitudes to the Body*, 163). He also points to the Renaissance portrayal of the body as object as the beginning of the rise of pornography.

28. Bottomly, *Attitudes to the Body*, 137.

29. For good accounts of this revival, see Brian Vickers, "Analogy versus Identity: The Rejection of Occult Symbolism, 1580–1680," in *Occult and Scientific Mentalities in the Renaissance*, ed. Brian Vickers (Cambridge: Cambridge University Press, 1984); and Wayne Shumaker, *The Occult Sciences in the Renaissance: A Study in Intellectual*

Patterns (Berkeley: University of California Press, 1972). For an extended discussion of Donne's interest in alchemy and his use of its imagery, see Douglas Bush, "Science and Literature," in *Seventeenth Century Science and the Arts,* ed. Hedley Howell Rhys (Princeton: Princeton University Press, 1961).

30. Brian Vickers, in his article "Analogy versus Identity," argues that all the occult science of the Renaissance (alchemy, cosmology, psychology, astrology, and numerology) used a "continuous two-level model" in which "the changes in the external world moved in parallel with those in the soul" (129).

31. See, for example, Frances Yates, *Giordano Bruno and the Hermetic Tradition* (London: Routledge & Kegan Paul, 1964), 156.

32. Donne had certainly read some of Paracelsus's works. See Don Cameron Allen, "John Donne's Knowledge of Renaissance Medicine," in *Essential Articles: John Donne's Poetry,* ed. John R. Roberts (Hamden, Conn.: Archon Books, 1975), 93; Sidney Monas, "Literature, Medicine, and the Celebration of the Body in Rabelais, Tolstoi and Joyce," in *The Body and the Text: Comparative Essays in Literature and Medicine,* ed. Bruce Clarke and Wendell Aycock (Lubbock: Texas Tech University Press, 1990), 58; and W. A. Murray, "Donne and Paracelsus: An Essay in Interpretation," in *Essential Articles,* 122.

33. See Vickers, "Analogy versus Identity," 132, and Caroline Merchant, *The Death of Nature: Women, Ecology and the Scientific Revolution* (San Francisco: Harper & Row, 1980; Harper & Row, 1982), 105.

34. John S. Mebane, *Renaissance Magic and the Return of the Golden Age: The Occult Tradition and Marlowe, Johnson and Shakespeare* (Lincoln: University of Nebraska Press, 1989), 38.

35. Quoted in Mebane, *Renaissance Magic,* 38.

36. Ibid.

37. David Le Breton, "Dualism and Renaissance: Sources for a Modern Representation of the Body," *Diogenes* 142 (1988): 53.

38. Donne's body bears a great resemblance to the "grotesque" body that Mikhail Bakhtin describes in *Rabelais and His World*. Rabelais' body, like Donne's, was open, communal, connected to the cosmos, and essentially premodern.

39. Some scholars have argued that the Protestant Reformation continued the process started by the fourteenth-century nominalists who "desacralized" the human body and turned instead to a legalistic, voluntaristic conception of Christian life and ethics. See, for instance, Ashley in *Theologies of the Body,* 118, 182, and Bottomly in *Attitudes to the Body,* 145. While the Protestant Reformation may have contributed somewhat to a gradual and larger cultural change in attitudes toward the body, it seems to me that the true "desacralization" came from more secular sources: the "new sciences" and the new culture of self-possession. Reformers and devotional writers on both Catholic and Protestant "sides" tended still to share an orthodox Christian anthropology and a propensity to denigrate the body that arose not from any Protestant "desacralization," but from Platonic tendencies inherent in Christianity from very early in its story.

40. This largely negative role for the body is evident in many of the devotional works of seventeenth-century divines, both traditional Anglicans and Puritans. Such works include Joseph Hall, *The Arts of Divine Meditation* and *The Balm of Gilead* in *The Works of the Right Reverend Joseph Hall, D.D., Bishop of Exeter and Afterwards of*

Norwich, ed. Philip Wynter, 10 vols. (Oxford: Oxford University Press, 1863); Jeremy Taylor, *Holy Living* and *Holy Dying* in *The Whole Works of the Right Reverend Jeremy Taylor, D.D. with a Life of the Author*, 10 vols., ed. Reginald Heber and Charles Page Eden (London: Longman, Green, Longmans, Robert, & Green, 1847–52); George Herbert, *The Temple* in *George Herbert: The Country Parson, The Temple*, ed. John N. Wall Jr. (New York and Ramsey, Toronto: Paulist Press, 1981); William Perkins, *How to Live, and That Well: In All Estates and Times, Especially When Helps and Comforts Fail* (Cambridge: John Legat, printer to the University of Cambridge, 1601), and *Death's Knell: Or The Sicke Mans Passing-Bell*, 9th ed. (London: printed for M. Trundle, 1628); John Downame, *A Guide to Godlynesse* (London: F. Kingstone and W. Standsby, 1622); and Lewis Bayly, *The Practice of Piety*, 53rd ed. (Boston: Green for Eliot & Henchman, 1718). Although not strictly a devotional work, Thomas Browne's *Religio Medici* provides another interesting contrast to Donne. Browne, another erudite Anglican, was also a physician. While he shares some of Donne's images of the body, his cast of mind is more Platonic. His experiences of the human body did not inspire him to "read" it as Donne did or to give it much place in his work. In *Thomas Browne: The Major Works*, ed. C. A. Patrides (London: Penguin Books, 1977).

41. John Calvin, *Calvin: Institutes of the Christian Religion*, ed. John T. McNeill, trans. Ford L. Battles, vols. 20 and 21, *The Library of Christian Classics* (Philadelphia: Westminster Press, 1960), bk. 1, chap. 15, sec. 2; bk. 2, chap 16, sec. 1.

42. Ibid., 1.15.2; 2.11.22.

43. Ibid., 1.6.70.

44. In this area, as in many others, Donne seldom quotes or refers to his sources. Since the whole tenor and theology of the English Church owed much to Calvin, it is likely that Donne owes the same debt. Since both Calvin and Donne were assiduous readers of Augustine, however, it is also possible that some of the theology that influences his representations of the body comes directly from the more ancient source.

45. Stephen Toulmin argues that at the beginning of the seventeenth century, most Europeans still accepted "at least in its main outlines, the jigsaw picture of the earth and heavens that had been built up during the middle ages from the forcible union of parts of Greek science with Christian dogma" (4). He points out that ideas of physiology were even slower to change. Harvey had succeeded in clarifying the nature of the arterial system, but in general the workings of the body remained mysterious. Harvey and many others retained the main outlines of Galen's physiology, with its animal and vital spirits. Toulmin says, "Astronomy apart . . . the ideas expressed in seventeenth-century literature look back for the most part to earlier times . . . even John Donne (whose debt to the new astronomy was considerable) drew most of his scientific imagery and ideas about nature from much older sources." "Seventeenth Century Science and the Arts," in *Seventeenth Century Science and the Arts*, ed. Hedley Howell Rhys (Princeton: Princeton University Press, 1961), 19. See also Grant, *Images and Ideas*, 20; Bottomly, *Attitudes to the Body*, 164; Sawday, *The Body Emblazoned*, 230; and Rosalie Osmond, *Mutual Accusation: Seventeenth-Century Body and Soul Dialogues in Their Literary and Theological Context* (Toronto: University of Toronto Press, 1990), 21. Charles Monroe Coffin writes extensively about Donne and the reception of the new sciences in *John Donne and the New Philosophy* (Morningside Heights, N.Y.; Columbia University Press, 1937).

46. For a detailed account of the emergence of the science of anatomy, its theological significance, and the implications of Donne's interest in it, see Sawday's *The Body Emblazoned*. For a specific study of Donne's knowledge of Renaissance medicine generally, see Don Cameron Allen's article "John Donne's Knowledge of Renaissance Medicine," in *Essential Articles: John Donne's Poetry*, ed. John R. Roberts (Hamden, Conn.: Archon Books, 1975).

47. For the larger argument over the definition of modernity, see David Pacini, *The Cunning of Modern Religious Thought* (Philadelphia: Fortress Press, 1987); Timothy Reiss, *The Discourse of Modernism* (Ithaca and London: Cornell University Press, 1982); and Louis Dupre, *Passage to Modernity: An Essay in the Hermeneutics of Nature and Culture* (New Haven and London: Yale University Press, 1993).

48. For a discussion of the interior turn in the history of ideas, see Isaiah Berlin, *Against the Current: Essays in the History of Ideas*, ed. Henry Hardy (New York: Viking Press, 1980).

49. Donne's expression of the unease that resulted from the discoveries of the new astronomy is well known. Jonathan Sawday points out in *The Body Emblazoned* that during Donne's time the newly emerging science of anatomy caused a similar unease, revealing not certain truth but the sense of exploring a dark and undiscovered country among its practitioners.

50. While Bacon, Descartes, and their followers made definitive statements of this divide in the early seventeenth century, and its implications became more apparent during the latter part of that century, the seeds of the divide had been sown in the Middle Ages and continued to sprout in the Renaissance through nominalism, the development of the natural sciences, and progress in the mechanical arts. See Ashley's *Theologies of the Body* and Bottomly's *Attitudes to the Body*, 144.

51. David Le Breton has expressed the chasm in this way: "The modern definition of the body implies that man is cut off from the cosmos, cut off from others, cut off from himself. Theology is the residue, what is irreducibly left after these three separations." "Dualism and Renaissance: Sources for a Modern Representation of the Body," *Diogenes* 142 (1988): 53.

52. See also Vickers, "Analogy versus Identity." The essay draws a distinction between scientific and occult mentalities on their views of the relationship of language to reality. He says that the scientific tradition made a clear distinction between language and reality, while occult traditions treated words as equivalent to things (95). In my reading, Donne differed from both. His view, influenced by Augustine, is that language and things could be signs or sacraments of reality if so used by God.

53. In exploring Donne's reading of the body as a text, one should take care to distinguish Donne's sense of the meanings of both "reading" and "text" from those current in cultural studies. The "body as text" has been a popular theme in recent anthropology, social sciences, cultural studies, and literary criticism. Many of these approaches see the body as a cultural construct, a field of representation that can be "read." This is a reaction against modern views of the body as a (mere) physical object, relegated to the realms of science and medicine. One might say that the body did *not* serve as a text in most of modern thought. With Descartes as their preeminent teacher, moderns learned that the body existed apart from the realm of meaning, the realm of mind and ideas. With the

contemporary critique of modernity, the body has reentered the realm of meaning as a passive page inscribed by social forces. One could read the history of ideologies from such body-texts. This way of reading the body has its roots in modern anthropology, exemplified by the work of Mary Daley, and its use by historians and critical theorists, especially those following Michel Foucault. See Thomas J. Csordas, ed., *Embodiment and Experience: The Existential Ground of Culture and Self* (Cambridge: Cambridge University Press, 1994), 121, for a further discussion of this theme. Donne's understanding of what it might mean to read the body as text operates from profoundly different premises and methods.

54. Donne, *Devotions*, 49.

55. Richard Hooker, *Of the Laws of Ecclesiastical Polity*, 2 vols. (London, 1594–1597), II.i.iv. Quoted in Herschel Baker, *The Wars of Truth: Studies in the Decay of Christian Humanism in the Earlier Seventeenth Century* (Cambridge: Harvard University Press, 1952), 143.

56. For one view of Donne's materiality in reference to language, books, and the body, see Elaine Scarry, "Donne: 'But yet the body is his booke.' " Scarry analyzes with great insight the way in which Donne connects the material, especially human bodies, and language through the metaphor of the page. However, my reading differs considerably from hers in the area of the religious motivations and implications behind the metaphor.

57. For an extensive discussion of this separation, see Baker's *Wars of Truth*. Baker says, "To understand the temper of seventeenth-century thought, it is, I think, impossible to stress too strongly this segregation of the natural from the supernatural" (168).

58. Joseph Hall, *Works of the Right Reverend Joseph Hall*, 509.

59. Donne, *Sermons*, 3:264.

60. Ibid., 4:166.

61. Ibid., 167.

62. Ibid., 6:350–51.

WORKS CITED

Allen, Don Cameron. "John Donne's Knowledge of Renaissance Medicine." In *Essential Articles: John Donne's Poetry*. Edited by John R. Roberts. Hamden, Conn.: Archon Books, 1975.

Ashley, Benedict. *Theologies of the Body: Humanist and Christian*. St. Louis, Mo.: Pope John Center, 1985.

Augustine. *On Christian Doctrine*. Translated by D. W. Robertson Jr. New York: Macmillan, 1958.

———. *Concerning the City of God against the Pagans*. Translated by Henry Bettenson. London: Pelican Books, 1972. Repr., London: Penguin Classics, 1984.

———. "The Grace of Christ and Original Sin." In *Answer to the Pelagians I*. Part 1, vol. 23, or *The Complete Works of Augustine: a Translation for the 21st Century*. Edited by John E. Rotelle. Translated by Roland J. Teski. New York: New City Press, 1997.

Baker, Herschel. *The Wars of Truth: Studies in the Decay of Christian Humanism in the Earlier Seventeenth Century*. Cambridge: Harvard University Press, 1952.

Bakhtin, Mikhail. *Rabelais and His World*. Bloomington: Indiana University Press, 1984.

Bald, R. C. *John Donne: A Life*. New York: Oxford University Press, 1970.

Barkan, Leonard. *Nature's Work of Art: The Human Body as Image of the World*. New Haven and London: Yale University Press, 1975.

Baumlin, James S. *John Donne and the Rhetorics of Renaissance Discourse*. Columbia and London: University of Missouri Press, 1991.

Bayly, Lewis. *The Practice of Piety*. 53rd ed. Boston: Green for Eliot & Henchman, 1718.

Berlin, Isaiah. *Against the Current: Essays in the History of Ideas*. New York: Viking Press, 1980.

Binski, Paul. *Medieval Death: Ritual and Representation.* Ithaca, N.Y.: Cornell University Press, 1996.

Bosquet, Jacques. *Mannerism: The Painting and Style of the Late Renaissance.* New York: Braziller, 1964.

Bottomley, Frank. *Attitudes to the Body in Western Christendom.* London: Lepus Books, 1979.

Bredvold, Louis I. "The Religious Thought of Donne in Relation to Medieval and Later Traditions." In *Studies in Shakespeare, Milton and Donne.* New York and London: Macmillan, 1925.

Brown, Norman O. *Life against Death: The Psychoanalytical Meaning of History.* New York: Vintage Books, 1959.

Brown, Peter. *The Body and Society: Men, Women and Sexual Renunciation in Early Christianity.* New York: Columbia University Press, 1988.

Brown, Sir Thomas. *The Major Works.* Edited by C. A. Patrides. London: Penguin Books, 1977.

Bush, Douglas. "Science and Literature." In *Seventeenth Century Science and the Arts.* Edited by Hedley Howell Rhys. Princeton: Princeton University Press, 1961.

Bynum, Caroline Walker. "Material Continuity, Personal Survival and the Resurrection of the Body: A Scholastic Discussion in Its Medieval and Modern Contexts." In *Fragmentation and Redemption: Essays on Gender and the Human Body in Medieval Religion.* New York: Zone Books, 1992.

———. *The Resurrection of the Body in Western Christianity, 200–1336.* New York: Columbia University Press, 1995.

Calvin, John. *Calvin: Institutes of Christian Religion.* Edited by John T. McNeill. Translated by Ford L. Battles. 2 vols. Philadelphia: Westminster Press, 1960.

Carey, John. *John Donne: Life, Mind, and Art.* New York: Oxford University Press, 1981.

Carrithers, Gale H., Jr. *Donne at Sermons: A Christian Existential World.* Albany: State University of New York Press, 1972.

Chadwick, Owen, ed. *The Reformation.* Vol. 3 of *The Penguin History of the Church.* Edited by Owen Chadwick. London: Penguin Books, 1964. Reprint, 1984.

Chamberlin, John. *Increase and Multiply: Arts-of-Discourse Procedure in the Preaching of John Donne.* Chapel Hill: University of North Carolina Press, 1976.

Clarke, Bruce, and Wendall Aycock, eds. *The Body and the Text: Comparative Essays in Literature and Medicine.* Lubbock: Texas Tech University Press, 1990.

Clive, Mary. *Jack and the Doctor.* London, Melbourne, and Toronto: Macmillan; New York: St. Martin's Press, 1966.

Coffin, Charles Monroe. *John Donne and the New Philosophy*. Morningside Heights, N.Y.: Columbia University Press, 1937.

Coleridge, Samuel Taylor. *Coleridge on the Seventeenth Century*. Edited by Roberta E. Brinkley. Durham, N.C.: Duke University Press, 1955.

Conger, George. *Theories of Macrocosms and Microcosms in the History of Philosophy*. 1922. Reprint, New York: Russell & Russell, 1967.

Copleston, F. C. *Aquinas*. London: Pelican Books, 1955. Reprint, London: Penguin Books, 1991.

Cresswell, Catherine J. "Reading Subjectivity: The Body, the Text, the Author in John Donne." Ph.D. diss., State University of New York at Buffalo, 1993.

Csordas, Thomas J., ed. *Embodiment and Experience: The Existential Ground of Culture and Self*. Cambridge, N.Y.: Cambridge University Press, 1994.

Davies, Horton. *Worship and Theology in England from Andrewes to Baxter and Fox, 1603–1690*. Princeton: Princeton University Press, 1975.

Dickens, A. G. *The English Reformation*. New York: Schocken Books, 1964.

Docherty, Thomas. *John Donne, Undone*. London and New York: Methuen, 1986.

Doebler, Bettie Anne. *'Rooted Sorrow': Dying in Early Modern England*. Rutherford: Fairleigh Dickenson University Press, 1994.

Donne, John. *LXXX Sermons, Preached by That Learned and Reverend Divine, John Donne*. London: printed for Richard Royston and Richard Marriot, 1640.

———. *Poems on Several Occasions, Written by the Reverend John Donne, D.D., Late Dean of St. Paul's, with Elegies on the Author's Death*. London: printed for J. Tonson, 1719.

———. *Devotions by John Donne DD with Two Sermons*. London: William Pickering, 1840.

———. *Letters to Severall Persons of Honour*. Edited by Charles Edmund Merrill Jr. New York: Sturgis & Walton, 1910.

———. *The Sermons of John Donne*. 10 vols. Edited by Evelyn M. Simpson and George R. Potter. Berkeley and Los Angeles: University of California Press, 1953–62.

———. *Essays in Divinity*. Edited by Evelyn M. Simpson. Oxford: Clarendon Press, 1967.

———. *Ignatius His Conclave*. An edition of the Latin and English texts with an introduction and commentary by T. S. Healy. Oxford: Clarendon Press, 1969.

———. *John Donne: The Divine Poems*. Edited by Helen Gardner. 2nd ed. Oxford: Clarendon Press, 1978.

———. *Paradoxes and Problems*. Edited by Helen Peters. Oxford: Clarendon Press, 1980.

———. *Biathanatos*. Edited by Ernest W. Sullivan. Newark: University of Delaware Press, 1984.

———. *John Donne: The Complete English Poems*. Edited by A. J. Smith. London: Penguin Books, 1971. Reprint, London: Penguin Classics, 1986.

———. *Devotions upon Emergent Occasions*. Edited by Anthony Raspa. New York: Oxford University Press, 1987.

———. 1993. *Pseudo-Martyr*. Edited by Anthony Raspa. Montreal: McGill-Queens University Press, 1993.

———. *The Variorum Edition of the Poetry of John Donne*. Vol. 6, *The Anniversaries and the Epicedes and Obsequies*. Edited by Gary Stringer et al. Bloomington: Indiana University Press, 1995.

———. *The Variorum Edition of the Poetry of John Donne*. Vol. 2, *The Elegies*. Edited by Gary Stringer et al. Bloomington: Indiana University Press, 2000.

Downame, John. *A Guide to Godlynesse*. London: F. Kingstone & W. Standsby, 1622.

Dupre, Louis. *Passage to Modernity: An Essay in the Hermeneutics of Nature and Culture*. New Haven and London: Yale University Press, 1993.

Eliot, T. S. "Donne in Our Time." In *A Garland for John Donne: 1631–1931*. Edited by Theodore Spencer. Cambridge, Mass.: Cambridge University Press, 1931.

Esdaile, Katharine A. *English Church Monuments, 1510–1840*. London and Malvern Wells, Worcestershire: B. T. Batsford, 1946.

Fausset, Hugh I'Anson. *John Donne: A Study in Discord*. New York: Russell & Russell, 1924. Reprint, 1967.

Foucault, Michel. *Discipline and Punish: The Birth of the Prison*. Translated by Alan Sheridan. New York: Vintage Books, 1979.

Frontain, Raymond-Jean and Frances Malpezzi, eds. *John Donne's Religious Imagination: Essays in Honor of John T. Shawcross*. Conway, Ariz.: University of Central Arizona Press, 1995.

Gardner, Helen, ed. *John Donne: A Collection of Critical Essays*. Englewood Cliffs, N.J.: Prentice-Hall, 1962.

Gilson, Etienne. *The Philosophy of St. Thomas Aquinas*. Edited by G. A. Elrington. Translated by Edward Bullough. 2nd ed. New York: Dorset Press, 1929.

Glacken, Clarence J. *Traces on the Rhodian Shore: Nature and Culture in Western Thought from Ancient Times to the End of the Eighteenth Century*. Berkeley, Los Angeles, and London: University of California Press, 1967.

Grant, Patrick. *Images and Ideas in the Literature of the English Renaissance*. Amherst, Mass.: University of Massachusetts Press, 1979.

Greenblatt, Stephen J. *Renaissance Self-Fashioning: From More to Shakespeare*. Chicago: University of Chicago Press, 1980.

Guss, Donald L. *John Donne, Petrarchist: Italianate Conceits and Love Theory in "The Songs and Sonnets."* Detroit: Wayne State University, 1966.

Halewood, William H. *The Poetry of Grace: Reformation Themes and Structures in English Seventeenth-Century Poetry.* New Haven and London: Yale University Press, 1970.

Hall, Joseph. *The Works of the Right Reverend Joseph Hall, D.D., Bishop of Exeter and Afterwards of Norwich.* Edited by Philip Wynter. 10 vols. Oxford: Oxford University Press, 1863.

Harding, D. W. "The *Devotions* Now." In *John Donne: Essays in Celebration.* Edited by A. J. Smith. London: Methuen, 1972.

Herbert, George. *George Herbert: The Country Parson, The Temple.* Edited by John N. Wall Jr. New York and Ramsey, Toronto: Paulist Press, 1981.

Hirsch, David. "Donne's Atomies and Anatomies: Deconstructed Bodies and the Resurrection of Atomic Theory." *Studies in English Literature: 1500–1900* 31 (1991): 69–94.

Hooker, Richard. *Of the Laws of Ecclesiastical Polity.* 2 vols. London, 1594–97.

Hughes, Richard E. *The Progress of the Soul: The Interior Career of John Donne.* New York: William Morrow, 1968.

Husain, Itrat. *The Dogmatic and Mystical Theology of John Donne.* London: SPCK; New York: Macmillan for the Church Historical Society, 1938. Reprint, Westport, Conn.: Greenwood Press Publishers, 1970.

Johnson, Jeffrey. *The Theology of John Donne.* Cambridge, UK: D. S. Brewer, 1999.

Kempis, Thomas á. *The Imitation of Christ.* Translated by Leo Sherley-Price. London: Penguin Books, 1952.

Keynes, Sir Geoffrey. *A Bibliography of Dr. John Donne, Dean of Saint Paul's.* 4th ed. Oxford: Clarendon Press, 1973.

Kremen, Kathryn R. *The Imagination of the Resurrection: The Poetic Continuity of a Religious Motif in Donne, Blake, and Yeats.* Lewisburg, Pa.: Bucknell University Press, 1972.

Kristeva, Julia. *Powers of Horror: An Essay on Abjection.* Translated by Leon S. Roudiez. New York: Columbia University Press, 1982.

Larson, Deborah Aldrich. *John Donne and Twentieth-Century Criticism.* London and Toronto: Associated University Presses, 1989.

Le Breton, David. "Dualism and Renaissance: Sources for a Modern Representation of the Body." *Diogenes* 142 (1988): 47–69.

Le Comte, Edward. *Grace to a Witty Sinner: A Life of Donne.* New York: Walker, 1965.

Lewalski, Barbara K. *Donne's Anniversaries and the Poetry of Praise: The Creation of a Symbolic Mode.* Princeton: Princeton University Press, 1973.

Lovejoy, Arthur O. *The Great Chain of Being: The Study of the History of an Idea.* Cambridge, Mass., and London: Harvard University Press, 1936. Reprint, 1964.

Malpezzi, Frances M. "As I Ride: The Beast and His Burden in Donne's 'Goodfriday,' " *Religion and Literature* 24 (1992): 23–31.

———. "Donne's Transcendent Imagination: The Divine Poems as Hierophantic Experience." In *John Donne's Religious Imagination: Essays in Honor of John T. Shawcross*. Edited by Raymond-Jean Frontain and Frances Malpezzi. Conway, Ariz.: University of Central Arizona Press, 1995.

Mebane, John S. *Renaissance Magic and the Return of the Golden Age: the Occult Tradition and Marlowe, Jonson and Shakespeare*. Lincoln: University of Nebraska Press, 1989.

Merchant, Carolyn. *The Death of Nature: Women, Ecology and the Scientific Revolution*. San Francisco: Harper & Row, 1980. Reprint, 1982.

Mueller, Janel. "The Exegesis of Experience." *Journal of English and German Philology* 67 (1968): 1–19.

Mueller, William R. *John Donne, Preacher*. Princeton: Princeton University Press. 1962.

Murray, W. A. "Donne and Paracelsus: An Essay in Interpretation." In *Essential Articles: John Donne's Poetry*. Edited by John R. Roberts. Hamden, Conn.: Archon Books, 1975.

Neill, Stephen. *Anglicanism*. 4th ed. New York: Oxford University Press, 1977.

The New Oxford Annotated Bible with the Apocrypha, Expanded Edition, Revised Standard Version. Edited by Herbert G. May and Bruce M. Metzger. New York: Oxford University Press, 1977.

Oliver, P. M. *Donne's Religious Writing: A Discourse of Feigned Devotion*. London and New York: Longman, 1997.

Osmond, Rosalie. "Body and Soul Dialogues in the Seventeenth Century." *English Literary Renaissance* 4 (1974): 364–403.

———. *Mutual Accusation: Seventeenth-Century Body and Soul Dialogues in Their Literary and Theological Context*. Toronto: University of Toronto Press, 1990.

Pacini, David S. *The Cunning of Modern Religious Thought*. Philadelphia: Fortress Press, 1987.

———. "Excursus: Reading Holy Writ: The Locus of Modern Spirituality." In *Christian Spirituality: Post-Reformation and Modern*. Vol. 18 of *World Spirituality: An Encyclopedic History of the Religious Quest*. Edited by Louis Dupre and Don E. Saliers. New York: Crossroads, 1991.

Panofsky, Erwin. *Tomb Sculpture: Four Lectures on Its Changing Aspects from Ancient Egypt to Bernini*. New York: Harry N. Abrams, 1964.

Pelikan, Jaroslav. *The Christian Tradition: A History of the Development of Doctrine*. Vol. 4 of *Reformation of Church and Dogma (1300–1700)*. Chicago and London: University of Chicago Press, 1983. Reprint, 1985.

Perkins, William. *Death's Knell: Or The Sicke Mans Passing-Bell*. 9th ed. London: printed for M. Trundle, 1628.

---. *How to Live, and That Well: In All Estates and Times, Especially When Helps and Comforts Fail.* Cambridge: John Legat, printer to the University of Cambridge, 1601.

Ramsey, Mary Paton. *Les Doctrines Medievales Chez Donne, Le Poete Metaphysicien de l'Angleterre (1573–1631).* London: Oxford University Press, 1917.

Reiss, Timothy J. *The Discourse of Modernism.* Ithaca and London: Cornell University Press, 1982.

Rhys, Hedley Howell, ed. *Seventeenth Century Science and the Arts.* Princeton: Princeton University Press, 1961.

Roberts, John R. *John Donne: An Annotated Bibliography of Modern Criticism, 1912–1967.* Columbia: University of Missouri Press, 1973.

---. *Essential Articles: John Donne's Poetry.* Hamden, Conn.: Archon Books, 1975.

---. *John Donne: An Annotated Bibliography of Modern Criticism, 1968–1978.* Columbia: University of Missouri Press, 1982.

Rousseau, G. S. *The Languages of Psyche: Mind and Body in Enlightenment Thought.* Berkeley: University of California Press, 1990.

Saintsbury, George. *Prefaces and Essays,* Essay Index Reprint Series. Freeport, N.Y.: Books for Libraries Press, 1933. Reprint, 1969.

Sawday, Jonathan. *The Body Emblazoned: Dissection and the Human Body in Renaissance Culture.* London and New York: Routledge, 1995.

Scarry, Elaine. "Donne: 'But yet the body is his booke.'" In *Literature and the Body: Essays on Populations and Persons.* Edited by Elaine Scarry. Baltimore and London: Johns Hopkins University Press, 1988.

Schleiner, Winfried. *The Imagery in John Donne's Sermons.* Providence: Brown University Press, 1970.

Sencourt, Robert. *Outflying Philosophy: A Literary Study of the Religious Element in the Poems and Letters of John Donne and in the Works of Sir Thomas Browne and of Henry Vaughan the Silurist.* London: Simpkin, Marshall, Hamilton, Kent, 1925.

Shami, Jeanne. "Donne's Sermons and the Absolutist Politics of Quotation." In *John Donne's Religious Imagination: Essays in Honor of John T. Shawcross.* Edited by Raymond-Jean Frontain and Frances Malpezzi. Conway, Ariz.: University of Central Arizona Press, 1995.

Sherwood, Terry G. *Fulfilling the Circle: A Study of John Donne's Thought.* Toronto: University of Toronto Press, 1984.

Shumaker, Wayne. *The Occult Sciences in the Renaissance: A Study in Intellectual Patterns.* Berkeley: University of California Press, 1972.

Simpson, Evelyn M. *A Study of the Prose Works of John Donne.* 2nd ed. Oxford: Clarendon Press, 1948.

---. "The Literary Value of Donne's Sermons." In *John Donne: A Collection of Critical Essays.* Edited by Helen Gardner. Englewood Cliffs, N.J.: Prentice-Hall, 1962.

Smith, A. J., ed. *John Donne, Essays in Celebration*. London: Methuen, 1972.

Stone, Lawrence. *The Family, Sex and Marriage in England, 1500–1800*. New York: Harper & Row, 1977.

Synnott, Anthony. *The Body Social: Symbolism, Self and Society*. London and New York: Routledge, 1993.

Taylor, Jeremy. *The Whole Works of the Right Reverend Jeremy Taylor, D.D., with a Life of the Author*. 10 vols. Edited by Reginald Heber and Charles Page Eden. London: Longman, Green, Longmans, Robert & Green, 1847–52.

Toulmin, Stephen. "Seventeenth Century Science and the Arts." In *Seventeenth Century Science and the Arts*. Edited by Hedley Howell Rhys. Princeton: Princeton University Press, 1961.

Turner, Bryan S. *The Body and Society: Explorations in Social Theory*. Oxford: Basil Blackwell, 1984.

Vickers, Brian. "Analogy versus Identity: The Rejection of *Occult Symbolism, 1580–1680*." In *Occult and Scientific Mentalities in the Renaissance*. Edited by Brian Vickers. Cambridge: Cambridge University Press, 1984.

Walton, Izaak. *The Lives of Dr. John Donne, Sir Henry Wotton, Mr. Richard Hooker, Mr. George Herbert and Dr. Robert Sanderson*. London: John Major, 1825.

Warnke, Frank J. *John Donne*. Boston: Twayne Publishers, 1987.

Watson, Robert N. *The Rest Is Silence: Death as Annihilation in the English Renaissance*. Berkeley: University of California Press, 1994.

Webster, Charles, ed. *The Intellectual Revolution of the Seventeenth Century*. London: Routledge & Kegan Paul, 1974.

Wolters, Clifton, ed. *The Cloud of Unknowing and Other Works*. Translated by Clifton Wolters. London: Penguin Books, 1978.

Yates, Frances A. *Giordano Bruno and the Hermetic Tradition*. Routledge & Kegan Paul, 1964.

INDEX

Adam, x, 17, 31, 36, 42, 44, 48, 64, 75, 91, 144
Adversus Omnes Haereses (Against the Heresies) (Irenaeus), 140
Against the Current (Berlin). *See* Berlin, Isaiah
"Air and Angels" (Donne), 8, 29, 58, 129
Alchemy, 88, 93, 94, 101n.43, 143, 157n.29
Allen, Don Cameron, 157n.32, 159n.46
Ambrose, Saint, xvn.5
"Anagram, The" (Donne), 37, 54n.32
"Analogy versus Identity" (Vickers). *See* Vickers, Brian
Anamnesis, 73
Anatomy, 40, 54n.27, 55n.47, 106, 108, 124n.38, 147, 156.n22, 159n.46 and n.49.
Anatomy of the World, An (The First Anniversary) (Donne). *See Anniversaries, The*
Andrewes, Lancelot, 59
Anglicanism, 59, 124n.37, 128, 145, 146, 157n.40, 158n.44. *See also* Donne, John: influences, Renaissance and Reforming Movements
Anniversaries, The (Donne), 9, 105–10
"Anniversary, The" (Donne), 29
"Annunciation" (Donne), 54n.27 and n.28, 59, 78n.10, 78n.11
Aquinas, Thomas. *See* Thomas Aquinas, Saint.

Aristotle and Aristotelianism, 7, 106, 109, 137, 138, 141, 145, 146, 154n.5, 155n.20
Ars moriendi (the art of dying), 142
Arts of Divine Meditation, The (Hall). *See* Hall, Joseph (Bishop)
"As due by many titles" (Donne), 55n.51, 79n.23
"As I Ride: The Beast and His Burden in Donne's 'Goodfriday'" (Malpezzi). *See* Malpezzi, Frances
"Ascension" (Donne), 66, 79n.23
Asceticism, 13, 15, 66–68, 73–74, 90, 139, 140, 141
Ashley, Benedict, 23n.4, 153n.1, 157n.39, 159n.30
Astronomy, 64–65, 108, 115, 147, 158n.45, 159n.49
Astrology, 143, 157n.30
"At the round earth's imagined corners" (Donne), 79n.23, 88
Atomism, 138, 147, 154n.8
Atonement, 64, 66, 73. *See also* Jesus Christ: sacrifice, suffering and death of
Attitudes to the Body in Western Christendom (Bottomly). *See* Bottomly, Frank
Augustine of Hippo, Saint
  and baptism, 67
  and desire, 18
  Donne compared to, xiii, xivn.5
  and the fall and original sin, 28, 41–44, 46, 48

169

influence on Donne, 18, 28, 41, 141–42, 158n.44
and language and Scripture, 142, 150, 156n.24, 159n.52
and Platonism, 141, 143, 156n.24
and the senses, 16
works by: *The City of God*, 42; *De Doctrina Christiana (On Christian Doctrine)*, 142, 156n.24; *The Grace of Christ and Original Sin*, 42
"Autumnal, The" (Donne), 37

Bacon, Francis, 148, 153, 159n.50
Baker, Herschel, 131n. 6, 160n.57
Bakhtin, Mikhail, 156n.25, 157n.38
Bald, R.C., 102n.50 and n.53
Balm of Gilead, The (Hall). *See* Hall, Joseph (Bishop)
Baptism, 67, 68, 74, 117, 119. *See also* sacraments
Basil (the Great), Saint, 140
"Batter my heart" (Donne), 66
Baumlin, James S., xvn.8, 131n.6
Bayly, Lewis, 158n.40
Berlin, Isaiah, 159n.48
Bernard of Clairvaux, Saint, 2, 46, 141
Biathanatos (Donne), 53n.12, 66
Bible. *See* Scripture, Holy
Bibliography of Dr. John Donne (Keynes). *See* Keynes, Sir Geoffrey
Binski, Paul, 100.n7, 102n.51, 155n.22
"Blossom, The" (Donne), 38
Body and Society, The (Brown), 137, 155n.21
Body and Society: Explorations in Social Theory, The (Turner), 156n.25
"Body and Soul Dialogues in the Seventeenth Century" (Osmond). *See* Osmond, Rosalie
Body Emblazoned, The (Sawday). *See* Sawday, Jonathan
Body, human
  as book, ix–x, 7, 9–11, 70–71, 109–22, 149–52, 159n.53
  and the book of creatures, ix, x, xiv, 1, 9–11, 22, 71, 113–15
  and creation, x, 1–22, 98, 107, 113
  and critical evaluations of Donne's work, 129–30
  dissection of. *See* Anatomy
  and the fall, xi, 5–7, 16–17, 27–52, 107, 115
  fragmentation and decay of, 38–40, 49–52, 54n.47, 55n.49, 85, 88–90, 97–98, 106–08. *See also* Anatomy
  influences on Donne's understanding of. *See* Donne, John: influences
  as paradise, 2, 5–6, 107
  redemption of, 109, 118–22
  resurrection of, 6, 7, 12, 85–87, 96–99, 122, 135, 155n.20
  as sacrament, x, 57, 69, 73–77, 111, 117
  as scripture, 115–18, 124n.40, 125n.67, 150–52
  and the senses, 7, 16–19, 58, 135
  as sign, ix–xi, 1, 57, 60, 69–77, 115–22, 141–42, 145
  and sin, xi, 2, 5, 27, 31, 45–52, 66
  and soul, relationship between, 1, 4–8, 11–16, 21–22, 30–37, 86–87, 139–41, 146, 155n.20
  and suffering, 66–69, 112, 119–20, 141, 146
  See also Microcosm, human being as
Body Social, The (Synott), 156n.27
Boehme, Jacob, 2
Bonaventure, Saint, 140, 150
Book of creatures, 7, 10, 22, 24, 70–71, 109, 149, 151. *See also* Body, human: and the book of creatures
Book of nature. *See* Body, human: and the book of creatures *and* Book of creatures
Bosquet, Jacques, 156n.25
Bottomly, Frank, 153n.1, 154n.4, 156n.25 and n.27, 157n.39, 158n.45
Brahe, Tycho, 114, 147
Bredvold, Louis I., 131n.6
Brown, Norman O., 100n.11
Brown, Peter, 137, 153n.3, 155n.21
Browne, Thomas, 156n.27, 158n.40
Bruno, Giordano, 2
Bush, Douglas, 157n.29
Bynum, Caroline Walker, 100n.6, 100n.15, 155n.22

Calvin, John, and Calvinism, 7, 76, 81n.93, 146, 158
  influence on Donne, 146, 158n.44
  and Platonism, 146
Campanella, Tommaso, 2
Carey, John, 25n.61, 99n.5, 103n.68, 130, 131n.6

Carr, Robert. *See* Karre, Sir Robert
Carrithers, Gale H., 131n.6
Cartesianism, 134, 146. *See also* Descartes, Renee
Catholicism, 7, 72, 73, 124n.37, 145, 146, 153
Chadwick, Owen, 132n.12
Chirurgia magna (Paracelsus), 3
Christ. *See* Jesus Christ
Christmas. *See* Jesus Christ: incarnation of
Church (Christian), the, 19, 20, 25n.62, 60, 63, 65, 67, 76
Church of England, the. *See* Anglicanism
Clement of Alexandria, Saint, 140
Clive, Mary, xvn.8
Cloud of Unknowing, The, 139
Coffin, Charles M., 23n.6, 130, 158n.45
Coleridge, Samuel Taylor, 128, 132n.15
Colet, John, 146
"Comparison, The" (Donne), 37
Conger, George, 23n.2 and n.3
Corona, La (Donne), 35, 59, 62, 79n.23, 93. *See also* titles of particular poems
Cotton, John, xivn.5
Creswell, Catherine J., 48, 101n.48, 124n.38, 130
"Cross, The" (Donne), 66, 72, 73
"Crucifying" (Donne), 79n.23
Csordas, Thomas J., 160n.53
Cunning of Modern Religious Thought, The (Pacini). *See* Pacini, David S.
Cusanus. *See* Nicholas of Cusa

Daley, Mary, 160n.53
"Damp, The" (Donne), 39
Dance of death *(danse macabre)*, 85, 142
Davies, Horton, 132n.12
Death, xi, 5, 15–16, 30, 38–41, 46–52, 81, 83–99, 114, 142, 152. *See also* Anatomy *and* Body, human: fragmentation and decay of
"Death be not proud" (Donne), 101n.37
Death of Nature, The (Merchant), 157n.33
Death's Knell (Perkins). *See* Perkins, William
Descartes, Renee, 148, 153, 156n.27, 159n. 50 and n.53. *See also* Cartesianism
Desire, 1, 12, 16, 18, 19, 21, 22, 39–40, 83
Devotio moderna, 148

Devotional literature and tradition, Christian, 111, 116, 124n.37 and n.38, 139, 146, 148, 156n.23, 157n.39 and n.40
Devotions by John Donne DD (Donne), xvn.5
Devotions upon Emergent Occasions (Donne), 3, 9, 111–22
Dickens, A. G., 132n.12
Discipline and Punish (Foucault), 156n.25
Discourse of Modernism, The (Reiss). *See* Reiss, Timothy
Disease. *See* Illness.
"Dissolution, The" (Donne), 38
"Divine Meditations" (Donne), 33, 36, 40, 72, 79n.23, 88. *See also* titles of particular poems
Divine Poems, 110. *See also* titles of particular poems
Docherty, Thomas, xvn.8
Doctrines Medievales Chez Donne, Les (Ramsey). *See* Ramsey, Mary Paton
Doebler, Betty Anne, 156n.23
Dogmatic and Mystical Theology of John Donne, The (Husain). *See* Husain, Itrat
"Donne and Paracelsus" (Murray). *See* Murray, W. A.
"Donne: 'but yet the body is his book'" (Scarry). *See* Scarry, Elaine
Donne, John
  critical interpretations of, xi–xiii, 127–30
  effigy in St. Paul's, 95, 96, 101n.48, 102n.50, 102n.52 and n.55
  and Holy Orders, xvn.5, 9, 24n.30, 110
  and illness. *See* Illness
  influences: Hellenistic, 137–38; medieval, 139–42, 155n.22, 157n.39; patristic, 139–41; Renaissance and Reforming Movements, 143–46, 157n.39; Scriptural, 135–37, 142; *See also* particular authors and movements
  and interpretation of Scripture, 9–10, 112, 115–18, 125n.67, 135–37, 142, 151–52
  and modernity, 147–49
  and orthodoxy, x, xi, xvn.8, 11, 29, 59, 115, 129, 134, 138, 151
  and patronage, xiii–xiv, xvin.10
  and preaching, xii, 19, 69, 110, 117, 124n.35, 128, 148, 150

INDEX 171

and skepticism, xvn.8, 7, 138, 148, 149
as theologian, ix–xi, 2, 16–20, 41, 69, 73, 119, 128–30, 146
works by. *See* individual titles
Donne, John (the younger), xivn.5, 24n.30, 102n.55, 128
"Donne's Atomies and Anatomies" (Hirsh). *See* Hirsh, David
Donne's Religion Writing (Oliver). *See* Oliver, P. M.
Downame, John, 158n.40
Drury, Elizabeth, 72, 105–10
"Dualism and Renaissance" (Le Breton). *See* Le Breton, David
Dupre, Louis, 159n.47

Easter. *See* Jesus Christ, resurrection of *and* Body, human: resurrection of
Eating, images of, 18, 19, 21, 141
"Ecstasy, The" (Donne), 8, 70, 129
Eden. *See* Body, human: as paradise
Effigy. *See* Donne, John: effigy in St. Paul's *and* Tombs and effigies
LXXX Sermons (Donne), xivn.5
Election, 10, 69, 75–76, 115, 118, 124n.40
Elegies (Donne), 37, 54n.32. *See also* titles of particular poems
"Elegy on Mrs. Bulstrode" (Donne), 91, 94
"Elegy on the Lady Markham, An" (Donne), 5, 94–95, 101n.37
Eliot, T. S., 128, 132n.14
Embodiment and Experience (Csordas). *See* Csordas, Thomas J.
Enthusiasm, 148
Epiphany, 60–61, 74
"Epitaph on Himself: To the Countess of Bedford" (Donne), 93
"Epithalamion made at Lincoln's Inn" (Donne), 66
Erasmus, Desiderius, xvin.9, 146
Erotic love. *See* Marriage and erotic love, images of
Eschatology, x, xi, 6, 10, 55n.49, 60, 63–64, 83, 86–97, 118–22, 137
Esdaile, Katherine A., 102n.53
Essays in Divinity (Donne), 9–11
Eucharist, 19, 63, 65, 69, 73, 76–7, 79n.16, 119, 121. *See also* Sacraments

Fall, the. *See* Body, human: and the fall
Family, Sex and Marriage in England, The (Stone). *See* Stone, Lawrence

Fausset, Hugh, xiii, xvn.7, xvn.8
"Fever, The" (Donne), 54n.39
Food. *See* Eating, images of
Foucault, Michel, 156n.25, 160n.53
Fragmentation and Redemption (Bynum). *See* Bynum, Caroline Walker
Frontain, Raymond-Jean, 131n.6
Fulfilling the Circle (Sherwood). *See* Sherwood, Terry
"Funeral, The" (Donne), 99n.1
"Funeral Elegy, A" (Donne), 105, 106

Galen and Galenic medicine, 158n.45
Galilei, Galileo, 147
Gardner, Helen, 53n.16
Glacken, Clarence J., 24n.28
Gluttony, 46, 47
God, 115–18
  as creator, x, 1, 15, 144–45, 150, 152
  dependence on, xi
  and his love of the human body and material creation, x, 1, 11–13, 15, 85–86
  as "metaphorical," ix, 47, 115, 117–18, 137, 142
  as object of desire, 18–19
"Goodfriday, 1613. Riding Westward" (Donne), 58
"Good Morrow, The" (Donne), 3
Goodyer, Sir Henry, 4, 5, 35, 59, 71
Grace, 7, 57–58, 148
Grace to a Witty Sinner (Le Comte). *See* Le Comte, Edward
Grant, Patrick, 156n.24, 158n.45
Great Chain of Being, The (Lovejoy). *See* Lovejoy, Arthur O.
Greenblatt, Stephen, 156n.25
Gregory the Great, Saint (Pope), 2
Gregory Nazianzen, Saint, 2, 3, 23n.3, 140
Gregory of Nyssa, Saint, 2, 3, 140
Guide to Godlynesse, A (Downame). *See* Downame, John
Guss, Donald L., 154n.6

Halewood, William H., 131n.6
Hall, Joseph (Bishop), 151, 157n.40
Harding, D. W., 131n.6
Harvey, William, 158n.45
Heaven, 86, 115, 155n.20. *See also* Eschatology *and* Visio Dei
Herbert, George, 158n.40

Hirsh, David, 130, 154n.8
Holy Dying (Taylor). *See* Taylor, Jeremy
Holy Ghost. *See* Holy Spirit
Holy Living (Taylor). *See* Taylor, Jeremy
Holy Spirit, 36, 75
Hooker, Richard, 145, 150
How to Live, and That Well (Perkins). *See* Perkins, William
Hughes, Richard E., 131n.6
Huntington, Countess of, 4
Husain, Itrat, 129

"I am a little world" (Donne), 33
"If poisonous minerals" (Donne), 80n.23
Ignatius His Conclave (Donne), 3
Illness, 46–47, 66, 111–22
Imagery in John Donne's Sermons, The (Schleiner). *See* Schleiner, Winfried
Images and Ideas in Literature of the English Renaissance (Grant). *See* Grant, Patrick
Imagination of the Resurrection (Kremens). *See* Kremens, Kathryn
Incarnation. *See* Jesus Christ: incarnation of
Inns of Court, xvin.9, 43, 44, 48, 52, 79, 87
Intellectual Revolution of the Seventeenth Century, The (Webster). *See* Webster, Charles
Irenaeus, Saint, 77, 87, 140

Jack and the Doctor (Clive). *See* Clive, Mary
James I (King of England), 19
Jesus Christ, 35, 48, 57, 75, 87
    attitude toward the human body, 136
    blood of, 61–63, 72, 118
    incarnation of, 35, 57–62, 69, 78n.13, 79n.15, 91
    resurrection of, 91, 92
    sacrifice, suffering and death of, 61–64, 66, 75, 89, 112, 119–21
John Donne: Life, Mind and Art (Carey). *See* Carey, John
John Donne and the New Philosophy (Coffin). *See* Coffin, Charles M.
John Donne: Petrarchist (Guss). *See* Guss, Donald L.
John Donne and the Rhetorics of Renaissance Discourse (Baumlin). *See* Baumlin, James S.

John Donne: A Study in Discord (Fausset). *See* Fausset, Hugh
John Donne, Undone (Docherty). *See* Docherty, Thomas
"John Donne's Knowledge of Renaissance Medicine" (Allen). *See* Allen, Don Cameron
Johnson, Jeffrey, 129
Jonson, Ben, 106
Justification, 74

Karre, Sir Robert, xii
Kepler, Johannes, 114
Keynes, Sir Geoffrey, xivn.4, 23n.5, 127
King, Henry, xivn.5
Kremens, Kathryn, 130
Kristeva, Julia, 102n.56

Languages of Psyche (Rousseau). *See* Rousseau, G. S.
Larson, Deborah, 100n.5, 128
Le Breton, David, 157n.37, 159n.51
Le Comte, Edward, xvn.8
"Legacy, The" (Donne), 39
"Letter to the Lady Carey and Mrs. Essex Rich, A" (Donne), 72
Letters to Severall Persons of Honour (Donne), 4, 5, 8, 35, 54n.39, 59, 98
Lewalski, Barbara K., 131n.6
Lincoln's Inn. *See* Inns of Court
"Litany, A" (Donne), 36, 41, 58, 66, 72, 80n.23, 110
Lives of Dr. John Donne, [etc.], The (Walton). *See* Walton, Sir Izaak
Lovejoy, Arthur O., 154n.4
"Love's Exchange" (Donne), 40
Lust, 37, 38, 39, 46, 47, 53n.12
Luther, Martin, and Lutheranism, 76, 145

Malpezzi, Frances, 129, 131n.6
Mannerism (Bosquet). *See* Bosquet, Jacques
Marriage and erotic love, images of, 3, 6, 8, 18–22, 39, 66, 86, 134, 141
Martyrs and martyrdom, 66, 141
Mary, the Virgin, 35–36, 58–59, 66, 71, 78n.6, 79n.14, 82n.101
Maximus the Confessor, Saint, 2, 3
Mebane, John S., 157n.34
Medicine, 25, 62, 157n.32, 159n.46 and n.53. *See also* Galen and Galenic medicine; Harvey, William; *and* Illness

INDEX 173

Medieval Death (Binski). *See* Binski, Paul
Memento mori, 81n.83, 93–95
Merchant, Caroline, 157n.33
"Message, The," 39
Metempsychosis (The Progress of the Soul) (Donne), 31–32, 123n.1, 154n.7
Microcosm, human being as, 1–4, 6, 12–17, 37, 48, 65, 70, 86, 106–10, 112–15, 134. *See also* Body, human: and the book of creatures
Modernity. *See* Donne, John: and modernity
Monas, Sidney, 157n.32
Moriae encomium (Erasmus). *See* Erasmus, Desiderius
Muller, Janel, 125n.40
Murray, W. A., 157n.32
Mutual Accusation (Osmond). *See* Osmond, Rosalie
Mysticism, 16, 115, 148, 150

Narcissism, 84, 99
"Nativity" (Donne), 54n.27 and n.29
Nature, 17, 31, 43–45, 53n.12, 57, 114, 149. *See also* Book of creatures *and* Body, human: and the book of creatures
"Negative Love" (Donne), 29
Neill, Stephen, 132n.12
Neoplatonism, 7, 14, 129, 134, 138, 143, 146, 154n.5. *See also* Platonism
New Jerusalem, 60, 92. *See also* Eschatology
New philosophy (new sciences). *See* Sciences, the new. *See also* Astronomy *and* Donne, John: and modernity
Nicholas of Cusa, 2, 3
"Nocturnal upon St. Lucy's Day, A" (Donne), 5, 38
Nominalism, 157n.39, 159n.50

"Obsequies upon the Lord Harrington" (Donne), 92, 97, 100n.23
Occult (occult sciences), 134, 143, 156n.29, 157n.30, 159n.52. *See also* Alchemy *and* Astrology
Occult Sciences in the Renaissance, The (Shumaker). *See* Shumaker, Wayne
Of the Laws of Ecclesiastical Polity (Hooker), 145

Of the Progress of the Soul (The Second Anniversary) (Donne). *See* Anniversaries, The
Oliver, P.M., xiv.n3, 124n.37
"O my black soul" (Donne), 79n.23
Oration on the Dignity of Man (Pico della Mirandola). *See* Pico della Mirandola
Origen, Saint, 136
Original sin. *See* Sin, original
Osmond, Rosalie, 130, 158n.45

Pacini, David S., 124n.39, 159n.47
Panofsky, Erwin, 102n.51, 102n.52
Paracelsus (Theophrastus von Hohenheim), xivn.1, 2, 3, 143–44, 157n.32
Paradoxes and Problems (Donne), xvn.9, 7, 53n.12
Passage to Modernity (Dupre). *See* Dupre, Louis
Paul, Saint, 28, 48, 55n.73, 68, 89, 136, 137, 153n.2
Pelikan, Jarislov, 81n.73
Perkins, William, 158n.40
Peters, Helen, xvn.9
Petrarch and Petrarchanism, 37, 143
Philo of Alexandria, 2
Pico della Mirandola, 144
Plato, 2, 29, 53n.1, 137, 139, 143, 154n.4, 154n.5. *See also* Neoplatonism *and* Platonism
"Platonic Love" (Donne). *See* "The Undertaking"
Platonism, 7–8, 12, 22n.1, 28–37, 53n.1, 100n.11, 130, 137, 141. *See also* Neoplatonism and Plato
Plenitude, 11, 15
Poems on Several Occasions (Donne), xvn.5
Potter, George R., xivn.1, 79n.15, 128, 131n.6
Practice of Piety, The (Bayly). *See* Bayly, Lewis
Progress of the Soul, The (Donne). *See* Metempsychosis
Protestantism, 73, 74, 76, 79n.14, 79n.16, 111, 124n.37, 125.n67, 130, 145–46, 153
and interpretation of Scripture, x, 125n.67, 141–42, 151, 153
Providence, 115, 118, 153
Pseudo-Martyr (Donne), 33

Pythagorus and Pythagoreanism, 22n.1, 29, 31, 53n.11, 137, 138, 154n.7

Rabelais and His World (Bakhtin). *See* Bakhtin, Mikhail
Ramsey, Mary Paton, 130, 131n.6
Raspa, Anthony, 124n. 37, 124n.40, 125n.60
Raymond of Sabunde. *See* Sebonde, Raymond
"Reading Subjectivity" (Creswell). *See* Creswell, Catherine J.
Reformation. *See* Donne, John: influences, Renaissance and Reforming Movements. *See also* particular authors
Reiss, Timothy, 159n.47
"The Relic" (Donne), 99n.1
Religio Medici (Brown). *See* Browne, Thomas
Renaissance Magic (Mebane). *See* Mebane, John S.
Renaissance Self-Fashioning (Greenblatt). *See* Greenblatt, Stephen
Resurrection. *See* Body, human: resurrection of *and* Jesus Christ, resurrection of
"Resurrection" (Donne), 62, 79n.23, 93
"Resurrection Imperfect" (Donne), 92, 94, 95
Resurrection of the Body in Western Christianity, The (Bynum). *See* Bynum, Caroline Walker
Roberts, John, 127
Rochester, Viscount of, 98
"Rooted Sorrow" (Doebler). *See* Doebler, Betty Anne
Rousseau, G. S., 154n.4

Sacraments, 17, 57, 62–3, 67–68, 74–77, 80n.62, 118, 150. *See also* Baptism *and* Eucharist
Saintsbury, George, xii, xvn.6
Salvation, 13, 22, 36, 48, 57–68, 74–75, 117–19
Sanctification, 65, 69
"Sappho to Philaenis" (Donne), 23n.16
Satan, 45, 49, 50, 75, 88, 89, 90, 92, 97
"Satire 5" (Donne), 4
Sawday, Jonathan, 55n.47, 124n.38, 130, 154n.5, 155n.22, 156n.25, 158n.45, 159n.46 and 49

Scarry, Elaine, 124n.38, 130, 160n.56
Scepticism. *See* Donne, John: and skepticism
Schleiner, Winfried, xivn.1, 24n.28
"Science and Literature" (Bush). *See* Bush, Douglas
Sciences, the new, 108, 115, 134, 142, 147–49, 153, 157n.39, 158n.45, 159n.52. *See also* Anatomy; Astronomy; Donne, John: and modernity; *and* Medicine
Scripture, Holy
Acts
9:4   89
Colossians
1:19–20   62
1 Corinthians
15:26   50
2 Corinthians
5:6   47
Genesis   136
1   x
1:1   9, 10
3:14   49
Ezekial
2:8–10   123n.28
Isaiah
7:14   60
Job
19:26   52
36:25   151
Psalms
32:9   45
38:3   44
89:48   50
Revelation
5:1   123n.28
21   x
Romans
6:23   48
7:5   55n.73
Scripture, interpretation of. *See* Donne: and interpretation of Scripture
Sebonde, Raymond, 10, 24n.33
Sencourt, Robert, 128
Separatists, English, 78n.3
Sermons of John Donne, The (Donne)
the created body in the, 11–22
death in the, 85–87, 89–91, 100n.37
the fallen body in the, 41–52
incarnation in the, 59–63

redemption and sanctification in the, 65–69, 73–74, 77–78
resurrection in the, 97–98
suffering and death of Christ in the, 61–66, 74–76
"Seventeenth Century Science and the Arts" (Toulmin). *See* Toulmin, Stephen
Severianus, Saint (Bishop), 101n.24
Shami, Jean, 128
Sherwood, Terry, 23n.6, 130, 131n.6
Shumaker, Wayne, 156n.25
Sickness. *See Devotions upon Emergent Occasions* and Illness
Simpson, Evelyn M., xivn.1, 24n.29, 99n.5, 128, 131n.6
Sin, xi, 2, 5, 7, 27, 28, 31–33, 36, 40–52, 89–90, 118
Original sin, 31, 42–43, 46, 75, 77, 88, 114
Skepticism. *See* Donne, John: and skepticism
Songs and Sonnets (Donne), 84. *See also* titles of particular poems
Soul, 5, 7, 8, 11, 14, 103n.69
as form of the body, 146
transmigration of, 31–32, 138, 154n.7
See also Body, human: and soul, relationship *and* Microcosm, human person as
"Spit in my face" (Donne), 54n.30, 66, 72, 73
Stone, Lawrence, 156n.25
Summa theologica (Thomas Aquinas), 155n.19
"Sun Rising, The" (Donne), 3
Synnott, Anthony, 156n.27

Taylor, Jeremy, 158n.40
Temple, The (Herbert). *See* Herbert, George
Tertullian, 14, 15, 48, 75, 77, 98, 140, 141
Theologies of the Body (Ashley). *See* Ashley, Benedict
Theology of John Donne, The (Johnson). *See* Johnson, Jeffrey
"This is my play's last scene" (Donne), 88
Thomas á Kempis, Saint, 139
Thomas Aquinas, Saint, 2, 3, 7, 138, 140, 141, 150, 155n.19 and n.20
"To the Countess of Bedford ('Honor is so sublime')" (Donne), 71–72

"To the Countess of Bedford ('To have written then')" (Donne), 34, 54n.21
"To the Countess of Huntingdon ('That unripe side of earth')" (Donne), 4
"To the Countess of Salisbury" (Donne), 70, 109
"To His Mistress Going to Bed" (Donne), 6, 8
"To Mr. B.B." (Donne), 78n.7
"To Sir Henry Goodyer" (Donne), 35, 71
Tombs and effigies, 85, 95–96, 102n.50–53, 102n.55. *See also* Donne, John: effigy in St. Paul's
Toulmin, Stephen, 158n.45
Transfiguration, 118–19, 121
Transubstantiation, 63, 76, 82n.96, 145. *See also* Eucharist
Trinity, the, 112, 129
Turner, Bryan S., 156n.25

Ubiquity. *See* Eucharist
"Undertaking, The" (Donne), 29
"Upon the Annunciation and Passion" (Donne), 62, 80n.23

"Valediction Forbidding Mourning, A" (Donne), 30
"Valediction of My Name in the Window, A" (Donne), 40, 99n.1
Vickers, Brian, 156n.29, 157n.30, 159n.52
Visio Dei, 67, 87, 97, 98

Walton, Sir Izaac, xivn.5, 95, 102n.55, 124n.35
Warnke, Frank, 99n.5
Wars of Truth, The (Baker). *See* Baker, Hershel
Watson, Robert N., 103n.68
Webster, Charles, 154n.6
"What if this present" (Donne), 72, 80n.23
Women, images of, 3, 6–7, 35–38, 66, 70–72, 93–95, 143
and patronage, xvi
See also Drury, Elizabeth *and* Mary, the Virgin
Wotton, Sir Henry, 7–8
Wrangham, Francis, 102n.55

Zwingli, Ulrich, 76, 145, 146